LOVE, LONGING, INTIMACY AND CONTENTMENT

Kitāb al-maḥabba wa'l-shawq wa'l-uns wa'l-riḍā

BOOK XXXVI of
THE REVIVAL OF THE RELIGIOUS SCIENCES
Iḥyā' ʿulūm al-dīn.

OTHER TITLES IN THE ISLAMIC TEXTS SOCIETY
AL-GHAZĀLĪ SERIES

FROM THE *Iḥyā' ʿulūm al-dīn*

Al-Ghazālī on Invocations & Supplications

Al-Ghazālī on the Manners Relating to Eating

Al-Ghazālī on Disciplining the Soul & Breaking the Two Desires

Al-Ghazālī on Patience & Thankfulness

Al-Ghazālī on the Remembrance of Death & the Afterlife

OTHER WORKS

Al-Ghazālī on the Ninety-Nine Beautiful Names of God
(*al-Maqṣad al-asnā fī sharḥ asmā' Allāh al-ḥusnā*)

Al-Ghazālī Letter to a Disciple
(*Ayyuhā'l-walad*)

AL-GHAZĀLĪ

LOVE, LONGING INTIMACY AND CONTENTMENT

Kitāb al-maḥabba wa'l-shawq wa'l-uns wa'l-riḍā

BOOK XXXVI of THE REVIVAL OF THE RELGIOUS SCIENCES

Iḥyā' ʿulūm al-dīn · translated with an INTRODUCTION & NOTES by ERIC ORMSBY

This first edition published 2011 by
THE ISLAMIC TEXTS SOCIETY
MILLER'S HOUSE
KINGS MILL LANE
GREAT SHELFORD
CAMBRIDGE CB22 5EN, U.K.

British Library Cataloguing-in-Publication Data.
A catalogue record for this book is
available from the British Library.

ISBN: 978 1903682 265 cloth
ISBN: 978 1903682 272 paper

CONTENTS

THE BOOK OF LOVE, LONGING, INTIMACY AND CONTENTMENT

ABBREVIATIONS

Abū Nuʿaym	:	Abū Nuʿaym al-Iṣfahānī, *Ḥilyat al-awliyāʾ*
B	:	Beirut 1417/1996 ed. of *Iḥyāʾ ʿulūm al-dīn*
Bouyges	:	Bouyges, *Essai de chronologie…*
*EI*²	:	*The Encyclopaedia of Islam* (second edition)
Fihrist	:	Ibn al-Nadīm, *K. al-Fihrist*
GAL	:	Brockelmann, *Geschichte der arabischen Litteratur*
GAS	:	Sezgin, *Geschichte des arabischen Schrifttums*
Gramlich	:	Gramlich, *Muḥammad al-Ġazzālīs Lehre…*
Hourani	:	"A Revised Chronology of Ghazālī's Writings"
Iḥyāʾ	:	Ghazālī, *Iḥyāʾ ʿulūm al-dīn*
JAOS	:	*Journal of the American Oriental Society*
Lane	:	Lane, *An Arabic-English Lexicon*
Lumaʿ	:	Sarrāj, *K. al-Lumaʿ*
M	:	Text of *Iḥyāʾ* printed on margin of Zabīdī, *Itḥāf*
Makkī	:	Makkī, *Qūt al-qulūb*
Munqidh	:	Ghazālī, *al-Munqidh min al-ḍalāl*
Q.	:	*Qurʾān*
Qushayrī	:	Qushayrī, *Risāla*
Sulamī	:	Sulamī, *Ṭabaqāt al-ṣūfiyya*
WKAS	:	*Wörterbuch der klassischen arabischen Sprache*
Z	:	Text of *Iḥyāʾ* embedded in text of Zabīdī, *Itḥāf*
Zabīdī	:	Zabīdī, *Itḥāf al-sādat al-muttaqīn*

PREFACE

The thirty-sixth book of Ghazālī's *Iḥyā' ʿulūm al-dīn* deals with a difficult and sometimes problematic subject: the love of God for man and of man for God. It may sound odd to hear the subject of divine love described as problematic. After all, nothing is more characteristic of Sufi literature in Arabic, Persian, Turkish and other languages, than the rapturous evocation of God's love; indeed, such love could rightly be called the principle theme of most mystical poetry in Islam, though expressions of love for the Prophet Muḥammad come close in frequency and in fervour. (As Ghazālī emphasizes, love of the Prophet is often emblematic of, and equivalent to, love of God.) Nevertheless, as the Introduction shows, many early Sufis as well as dogmatic theologians objected to the notion that there might be between God and man any sort of relation of love, as love is commonly understood. It was one aspect of Ghazālī's achievement to have answered these objections. In so doing, he made possible the eventual efflorescence of a conception of divine love which would have profound implications, for Sufism in particular and for Islam in general. If he was not alone in this endeavour—his younger brother Aḥmad al-Ghazālī played a crucial part—he was nevertheless the first Muslim theologian and mystic to elaborate a doctrine of divine love rigorously and systematically, employing carefully structured arguments and proofs based on both tradition and reason. Addressing himself to an audience of cultured readers, rather than to a coterie of fellow Sufis, he made the love of God a topic for respectable discourse. Later elaborations of the topic rest on the foundations which he laid.

This is the first complete translation of the *Kitāb al-maḥabba wa'l-shawq wa'l-uns wa'l-riḍā* into English. My initial translation has been based on the text of the *Iḥyāʾ ʿulūm al-dīn* published, in four volumes, in Cairo in 1334/1916. I have supplemented and sometimes revised this text with reference to three others. First, the text embedded in the ninth volume of *Itḥāf al-sādat al-muttaqīn*, the magnificent and indispensable commentary of the great lexicographer and *ḥadīth* expert, Murtaḍā al-Zabīdī (d.1205/1791); in the endnotes, this is referred to as Z. I have also consulted the text printed on the margin of the same volume of the *Itḥāf* since the two texts occasionally differ; this is referred to in the endnotes as M. Finally, I have used the more recent edition of the *Iḥyāʾ*, in five volumes, published in Beirut in 1417/1996. I refer to this text as B. It is also, with a few exceptions as indicated, the text referred to in the notes as "*Iḥyāʾ*". I have followed this course because the Beirut edition, though the least reliable of the four texts, is probably the most readily available to those who wish to consult the original Arabic.

The annotated German translation by the late Richard Gramlich of Books 31 to 36 of the *Iḥyāʾ* has been of inestimable help, and (as my notes throughout attest) I am deeply indebted to his meticulous and pioneering precedent. As a translator, I have aimed to convey the sense of the original Arabic as closely as possible while, at the same time, striving to convey, however imperfectly, some sense of the eloquence, subtlety and sheer stylistic beauty of Ghazālī's remarkable prose.

I wish particularly to thank Ms. Fatima Azzam, Director of the Islamic Texts Society, for inviting me to undertake this project many years ago. I am deeply grateful for her unfailing encouragement and support, as well as for her uncommon patience. She has not only edited the text line by line throughout with great care but has improved it considerably by felicitous rephrasing as well as by the addition of a number of scholarly annotations.

INTRODUCTION

1. The Love of God as a Paradox

The doctrine of the love of God has a long and somewhat fractious history in the early centuries of Islam. Certainly theologians, Sunnī and Shīʿī, gave it short shrift, consistently disdaining even to include or mention it in their magisterial treatises. But among Sufis too there was both unease and frequent disagreement over the notion; many early masters considered it unsuitable to characterise the relationship between God and man as one of love, and even those who accepted the notion defined such love strictly as "obedience". The suggestion of a reciprocal relationship of love between God and man struck them as unseemly—if not downright blasphemous—as well as profoundly illogical.[1]

Thus, in his commentary on Q. III.31—"Say, if you love God, then follow me, so that God will love you and forgive your sins"—the great exegete Abū al-Qāsim al-Zamakhsharī (d. 538/1144) indulges in a remarkable outburst. He says, "When you see someone speaking of love of God who claps his hands, exclaims, moans and passes out, have no doubt that such a person does not know what God is, nor what love of Him is. His clapping, outbursts of exaltation, groans and swoons, are based on the fact that inside his filthy soul he pictures a pleasing and lovable figure which in his folly and corruption he calls God."[2] For Zamakhsharī, the love of God has only one meaning and that is "obedience" (*ṭāʿa*); as he remarks with reference to Q. V.59, "Man's love for God lies in obedience to Him, in striving for His approval and in not doing whatever necessarily brings His wrath and punishment. God's love for His servants lies in that He lets them enjoy the finest reward for their obedience."[3] Zamakhsharī's condemnation is directed against Sufis, whom he calls "that lying faction which takes its name from 'wool' (*ṣūf*)." He goes so far as to say that the very term Sufi is synonymous with "liar" (*kadhdhāb*).[4] And he is particularly incensed by the fact that Sufis "connect God's love with His essence and teach that love of God must be accompanied by 'the pangs of love'."[5] In such statements, it is clear, Zamakhsharī intends to demolish the notion, dear to certain Sufi masters, that a reciprocal love between God and humankind is conceivable: God does love us—He especially "loves the just" (Q. v.42)—and we are obliged to love Him, but there can be no question of a relationship of love between God and His creatures.

In the Qur'ān, of course, God is described as "loving" (*wadūd*), as in Q. xi.90 and elsewhere,[6] but in general, divine love is presented there under the form of compassion or mercy (*raḥma*). Certainly Ghazālī accepts this understanding too. In his treatise on the divine names, written shortly after the *Iḥyā'*, he comments on the name *al-Wadūd* ("the Loving") and describes it as characterising "one who wishes all creatures well and accordingly favours them and praises them."[7] In contradistinction to "mercy", this form of God's love is sovereign and disinterested; it does not presuppose a recipient in need of mercy nor is it the result of any "empathy" on God's part. This is an aspect of the generalised benevolence which centuries before the Muʿtazilite author Jāḥiẓ (d. 255/868) had urged upon his readers when he wrote, "Compassion (*raḥma*) has a single form. He who is uncompassionate to the dog has no compassion for the gazelle; he who has no compassion for the gazelle, has none for the kid; he who has no compassion for the sparrow has none for the young boy: the least of things leads to the greatest."[8] Whatever his other differences with a Muʿtazilite such as Jāḥiẓ, Ghazālī would have agreed with this precept; in the present book, and indeed, throughout the *Iḥyā'*, he shows an affection and a striking tenderness of concern for the least of creatures—the gnat, the bee, the fly. But this is a far cry from the love of God in its all-consuming ardour which he expounds and defends as the ultimate goal of every human endeavour in the *Kitāb al-maḥabba*.

The intensity of Zamakhsharī's condemnation of the Sufi doctrine of love may have arisen from factors other than the strictly theological. For orthodox Muslims of all schools and traditions, religious devotion and the rituals of worship involved a certain decorum. Piety too has its protocols. The expressions of love uttered by some Sufis threatened to subvert the rules of devotional etiquette; they may have represented an assault on divine transcendence but at the same time, and perhaps even more annoyingly, they were bad religious manners. One would not indulge in such intimate declarations of love to a monarch; how much the more offensive and presumptuous must they be when directed to the Lord of the Worlds? Unseemly outpourings of affection were not merely examples of *lèse-majesté* on a cosmic scale but breaches of pious tact. The great lexicographer Ibn Manẓūr (d. 710/1311) suggests the force of this sense of decorum when he states, in another context, that "In praising God, excellent things are connected with Him, and not evil things… In prayer it is recommended that one say, 'O Lord of heavens and earth!' and not, 'O Lord of dogs and swine!' although He is their Lord."[9] The tenth-century Sufi author Sarrāj makes a similar point when he admonishes those who boast of "intimacy" (*uns*) with God to recover "proper manners" (*ādāb*) and to observe established "limits" (*ḥudūd*).[10] Ghazālī too stresses such decorum throughout Book XXXVI, but most especially in his chapters on intimacy with God, itself the ultimate goal of his teaching on love.[11]

Still, even for less vehement commentators than Zamakhsharī, the notion of the love of God involved a fundamental paradox. Certainly God loves His creatures, but are there any grounds for claiming that a relationship of love can exist between God and humankind? How reconcile a God who is transcendent and utterly dissimilar to creatures, a God who "neither slumbers nor sleeps" and who is described as "the light of the heavens and earth"—and indeed, as "light upon light"—with the human creature, a perishable, frail, insubstantial being, formed "from a drop of dirty water"—or, as Ghazālī himself puts it, "a dung heap covered with skin?" Is any affinity, let alone relationship, possible between two such disparate entities? Moreover, to demonstrate the full force of the disparity, Allāh alone possesses being in the only genuine sense. According to Ghazālī himself, divine existence is "real" (*ḥaqīqī*), while human existence is at best "figurative" (*majāzī*).[12] (The great Iranian philosopher Mullā Sadrā (d. 1050/1641) would sum this up succinctly, centuries later, by saying, "In the habitation of existence there is no inhabitant other than He."[13]) Nevertheless, Ghazālī will also argue that the human love of God cannot be considered merely figurative. In Chapter Ten of the present work, he makes this clear when he says, "Man's love for God actually exists; it is no mere metaphor."[14] But he elucidates this apparent contradiction by quoting Abū Saᶜīd al-Mīhanī who commented, with reference to Q. v.54 (*He loves them and they love Him*), "In truth, He loves them for He loves only Himself." For, indeed, "God is all and...there is nothing in existence other than God."[15] This introduces an important qualification, which modifies our conventional notions of "reciprocity", and I will return to its implications later.

Zamakhsharī's position was not isolated, nor was it in fact particularly surprising. As a Muᶜtazilite, an adherent of that theological school which placed great emphasis on God's utter transcendence, he was consistent in rejecting any notion of affinity between God and His creatures. The "official" position—and not only among Muᶜtazilites—was perhaps best summarised by the Shāfiᶜite jurist Ibn Surayj (d. 306/918) who held that it is an "obligation" (*farḍ*) for humans to love God; however, such love could only be understood as "obedience" to Him.[16] In fact, Zamakhsharī represented an old and long-standing view which goes back at least to Jahm ibn Safwān (d. 129/746) and his followers, the Jahmīyah, in the "formative period" of Islamic theology.[17] As the later theologian ᶜAlī al-Qāri' al-Harawī (d. 1014/1605) summarised it, "The Jahmīya deny the reality of love on both sides; by this they mean that love presupposes an adequate relation (*munāsaba*) between the lover and the object of love."[18] (This is an objection which, as we shall see, lies at the heart of Ghazālī's treatment and indeed, impels it throughout.) Moreover, for certain early thinkers, not only love but "friendship" with God was unthinkable, and some of them paid the price. When Jaʿd ibn Dirham (d. 125/743), another independent thinker of the period, denied that Abraham could be called "the friend of God" (*khalīl Allāh*), he was executed for his offense by the *amīr* of Iraq, Khālid ibn ʿAbd Allāh al-Qasrī, who personally "came down from the *minbar* and slaughtered Jaʿd in accord with the *fatwā*s of the legal scholars of the time."[19] But it was not necessary to be either a Jahmite or a Muʿtazilite to find the notion of a loving relationship with God troublesome. Many Sufis were uncomfortable with the notion too.

II. A Question of Terminology: *maḥabba* or *ʿishq*?

Some of their discomfort arose from a question of terminology. Should love of God be expressed by the word *maḥabba* (equivalent to Greek *philia* and which might be rendered, following Mohamed Arkoun, as "measured affection") or should the stronger—and non-Qur'ānic—term *ʿishq* (with its passionate and even erotic connotations) be employed? Arkoun defines *ʿishq* as "the irresistible desire to obtain possession of a loved object or being; it betokens a want or lack."[20] It is also the term used not only in love poetry but in philosophical discourse—both suspect sources for more scrupulous Sufis. Its use divided Sufis among themselves and, as it were, within themselves. For example, the prominent Sufi Ibn al-Khafīf, born around 268/882 in Shiraz, underwent a decisive change of heart on this matter. He had written two treatises on the love of God in which he rejected the notion that such love could be described as *ʿishq*. Like many Sufis before and after him—including Ghazālī himself—Ibn al-Khafīf preferred to use the word *maḥabba*. But after reading a treatise by Abū al-Qāsim al-Junayd (d.c. 298/910), the influential Sufi master of Baghdad, he came to accept the stronger, and more controversial, term. Junayd had himself been influenced by Muḥāsibī in this regard.[21]

One bold early Sufi who had no such terminological qualms was Abū al-Ḥusayn al-Nūrī (d. 295/907).[22] In certain of his pronouncements, he went so far as to draw on the conventions of erotic poetry, using the charged term *ʿishq* with its passionate connotations; he was accused of stating, "I am in love with God, and He with me."[23] According to a later source, he even declared, "I am God's lover."[24] This was one of the reasons why he, and some seventy-five other like-minded mystics, were brought up on charges of blasphemy by the zealous Ghulām al-Khalīl (d. 275/888), an ascetic Sufi of the old school, and put on trial for their lives.[25] Such was Nūrī's eloquence that the judges themselves wept at his trial;[26] after he offered to be executed first in place of his co-defendants, he was acquitted, but had to exile himself from Baghdad for fourteen years.

In the present work, Ghazālī refers to this episode and denounces Ghulām al-Khalīl's view as "the doctrine of a flawed and limited person who knows nothing but mere husks...and so fancies that nothing but husks exists."[27] Indeed, it might be said that the entire thirty-sixth book of the *Iḥyāʾ* represents a strenuous and reasoned attempt to answer such early critics definitively; and not only that, but to answer in such a way that no doubt could remain as to the possibility—indeed, the overwhelming reality—of God's love for man and man's for God. In this Ghazālī succeeded to an extent he could neither have foreseen nor imagined.

Nevertheless, the terminological question continued to trouble certain Sufis even up to Ghazālī's time. He himself is notably circumspect, usually preferring to use *maḥabba* throughout his discussions in Book XXXVI.[28] Still, it is probably not a coincidence that Ghazālī has frequent recourse to examples drawn from sexual life to illustrate his thesis; these occur often enough to suggest that beneath his circumspection, a certain delicate play of oblique allusion—what the Sufis term *ishāra*—may be at work.[29] Nevertheless, his choice of words was probably not dictated entirely by caution.

Maḥabba is not only a safer word but a more capacious one; it encompasses a wider range of nuance, allowing for friendship and affection as well as intense love,[30] whereas *ʿishq* is by its nature fiercely exclusive. His preference may owe something too to the teaching of his own masters. Thus, Abū ʿAlī al-Daqqāq (d. 405 or 6/1015 or 16) held that "*ʿishq* is an overstepping of the limit in love but God cannot be described as overstepping the limit and so He cannot be characterized by *ʿishq*."[31] He went on to say that use of the term was "to be rejected since there is no way to apply it to God;" indeed, "it applies neither on the part of God towards humans, nor on the part of humans towards God."[32]

Daqqāq's censure is significant. He headed a madrasa in Nishapur where the young Qushayrī studied and in fact, Qushayrī was not only his student but, in keeping with good Sufi custom, became his son-in-law.[33] There is probably no Sufi *shaykh* more frequently cited in Qushayrī's *Risāla* than Daqqāq. Qushayrī had been, of course, the teacher of Ghazālī's revered early master al-Farmadhī—as well as one of his principal sources in the *Iḥyā'*—and it is not unreasonable to assume that his view influenced his pupil. Aside from the unseemliness of the word *ʿishq*, drawn as it was from the florid lexicon of erotic poetry, it had other, less savoury connotations as well: its use raised the notorious spectre of Ḥallāj, a disciple of Nūrī and like him, notorious for giving *ʿishq*, the passionate love of God, a paramount place in his doctrine.[34]

III. Suspect Sources

Though the Sufis who objected to the term *ʿishq* do not say so, the word had other suspect associations. Philosophers had adopted it in their discussions of love. It is the word of choice for the Ikhwān al-Ṣafā'—the early Ismāʿīlī "Brethren of Purity" of tenth century Basra—in their encyclopaedic *Rasā'il*—the first such philosophical treatment of the topic in Arabic—which influenced Ibn Sīnā; both of these sources in turn exerted a major influence on

Ghazālī.[35] Thus, according to a later account by his younger contemporary Abū ʿAbd Allāh al-Māzarī (d. 536/1141), a critic of his work, we learn that Ghazālī "was addicted to reading the *Rasāʾil Ikhwān al-Ṣafāʾ*" and from the same source we learn that, as Māzarī wryly put it, "Abū Ḥāmid was made sick by *The Healing*" (i.e., the *Shifāʾ* of Ibn Sīnā).[36]

Nevertheless, however indebted he may have been to such predecessors, Ghazālī's treatment in the present book is distinctively different from theirs. The impulse governing the discussion of love by the Ikhwān al-Ṣafāʾ is resolutely philosophical (as is that of Ibn Sīnā). Their purpose is to determine the very "quiddity of passionate love" and, more generally, of the love innate in human souls; they aim to discover its "true nature" (*ḥaqīqa*) as well as its origin and its causes.[37] Though Ghazālī devotes a significant part of his treatment to the "causes" (*asbāb*) of love—and his discussion owes much to his philosophical predecessors—his perspective is hortatory rather than explicative. He wants to persuade his readers not only that love of God is possible but in fact, irresistible, and he wants to show them the way to it. Again, for the Ikhwān, love is something innate in human nature; passionate love may be marked by extravagance and by excess and yet, as they write, "no one is devoid of it, and there exists no one who does not love and feel drawn to one thing rather than to something else."[38] For Ghazālī, neither the "quiddity" nor the origins of love is of particular interest; he does begin by discussing "the essential character of love in itself," but his comments on this are more dutiful than searching. Moreover, the notion that love might be something intrinsic and unceasing in human nature was questionable; indeed, he rejected the whole concept of "natures" (*ṭabāʾiʿ*). From his Ashʿarite (and therefore, occasionalist) position, the philosophers' insistence on "natures", allied to their unwavering belief in natural causality, was repugnant; it challenged and undermined divine agency. "Nature" was not something inbuilt; it was the direct result of God's will, atom by atom and moment by moment.[39]

But on the other hand, he had much in common with the philosophical endeavour of the Ikhwān and their successors. For one thing, and on the most fundamental level, he held, like them, that love, and specifically, love between God and man, could not only be rationally discussed but analysed and proved. For another, this was to be no rarefied mystical disquisition, but one aimed at all who aspired to the love of God. The Ikhwān had noted that while love might be considered by some—physicians as well as philosophers—to be a "sickness" akin to melancholy, they were determined to speak about love "as it is known to most people," rather than merely to specialists.[40] This broad objective was one which Ghazālī shared, and it is apparent throughout the discussion, not least in his appeal to self-love, that form of passionate attachment which we all know so well. Moreover, certain of his examples and methods of argument bear a close resemblance to those of the philosophers. The key notion of the importance of loving something for its own sake, which he stresses in the present book, may owe much to the teaching of Ibn Sīnā, for whom the notion is fundamental; after all, God loves His own essence and accordingly, He is not only to be "loved for Himself" but is also the true source of both pleasure and beauty.[41] Pleasure and beauty are invoked repeatedly in Ghazālī's argument, in ways reminiscent of Ibn Sīnā's earlier treatment of them.[42] Furthermore, Ghazālī's insistence on God as the only true beloved, beyond all appearances, rests in part on Ibn Sīnā's characterisation of God as the "first good that is loved" (*al-khayr al-maʿshūq al-awwal*), though of course the terms Ghazālī uses are usually drawn from the lexicon of Sufism.[43] In this respect, it is significant that in his *Tahāfut al-falāsifa*, his harsh critique of philosophy, Ghazālī summarises the philosophers' teaching on God as the ultimate beloved not only dispassionately but with apparent approval.[44]

I do not wish to overstate this indebtedness. Ghazālī clearly drew on certain aspects of philosophical doctrine, even while rejecting much of it, and yet his method is not always easy to delineate. It is both opportunistic and eclectic. What the philosophers taught him, it seems safe to say, was a method of systematising a large and diffuse body of teachings, as well as a way of marshalling his arguments in a coherent and compelling manner. Persuasion was his aim. For that, logic was required, and logic, accompanied by certain forceful examples and modes of argumentation, he took from the philosophers.

IV. The Proponents of Divine Love

There were Sufis who boldly asserted their love for God, and His for them. Their assertions often took riddling and paradoxical forms but the thrust was unmistakable. They include some of the most famous—and sometimes the most notorious—names in the history of Sufism, beginning with the celebrated Rābiʿa al-ʿAdawīya (d. 185/801) and culminating in the tormented and ecstatic figure of Ḥusayn ibn Manṣūr al-Ḥallāj, cruelly executed for blasphemy in 309/922. Although these, and other exponents of divine love, appear as isolated masters, that is an illusion, prompted as much by the fragmentary nature of the record as by the efforts of their opponents (the two factors are, of course, connected). In fact, they form a persistent spiritual lineage. At the same time, almost all were wildly individualistic, frequently to the point of eccentricity—as the tales recounted of them, both by Ghazālī in the present work, and by many others—make dramatically clear. It is one of Ghazālī's signal accomplishments in his *Kitāb al-maḥabba* to have revealed the surprising consistency which that wildness concealed.

The closer we look, the more connections we find among these seemingly diverse mystics. Thus, Ibn al-Khafīf, whom we met earlier, was not only influential but well-placed. He was personally acquainted with such masters as Abū Bakr al-Shiblī[45] (to whom the characteristically extravagant remark was attributed, "Creation loves You because of Your blessings to it but I love You because of the afflictions You dispense"[46]). Ibn al-Khafīf had visited Ḥallāj in prison before his execution.[47] But at another extreme, he reportedly met the theologian Ashʿarī in Basra and later made the acquaintance of Bāqillānī, the second great theologian of the Ashᶜarite *madhhab*.[48] (This wide span of contacts might be said to prefigure, if only symbolically, the peculiar amalgam of Sufism and Ashᶜarism which Ghazālī would advance some two centuries later.) More importantly for our purposes, Ibn al-Khafīf represents an important link in a chain of individual mystics who expounded a doctrine of divine love on which both his student Abū al-Ḥasan al-Daylamī[49]—the first Sufi author whose attempt at a systematic treatment of the subject survives—and later, Ghazālī himself, would draw.[50] Reportedly, several early Sufis, including Ibn al-Khafīf, composed treatises on the subject, but only their titles have survived.[51] In the classic compendia by such later writers as Abū Ṭālib al-Makkī and Qushayrī, there are chapters devoted to the subject of love—and Ghazālī depended on these heavily, sometimes to the point of outright, almost verbatim appropriation. But even these are little more than compilations of sayings and maxims.

v. Ghazālī's *Kitāb al-maḥabba*

Though love of God was to become a dominant theme in Sufi literature,[52] pervading the couplets of Rūmī and the *ghazals* of Ḥāfiẓ, its first manifestations tended to be fragmentary; they are pithy, sometimes quite piercing, and often outrageous, utterances, aphoristic in form and in impact; many would be later grouped in the category of the so-called *shaṭḥīyāt*—shocking and paradoxical statements verging on blasphemy (such as Bisṭāmī's notorious *subḥānī* ("Glory be to me!") or Ḥallāj's exclamation *anā al-Ḥaqq* ("I am the Truth," i.e., God) which led, among other charges, to his death on the scaffold).[53] For this reason, it is probably incorrect to use the term "doctrine" in describing this ragged tradition. Though the earliest mystics occasionally wrote treatises on the subject, their surviving views tend to be restricted to scattered utterances, lovingly collected and assembled by later writers; they do not constitute a coherent and consistent set of precepts.

In fact, it was Abū Ḥāmid al-Ghazālī who first gave compelling shape to these sporadic aperçus and isolated insights in the present work, one of the culminating chapters of his *Iḥyā' ʿulūm al-dīn*. His treatment, unlike that of his principal sources, does not rely simply on collections of sayings or compilations of edifying anecdotes. Certainly, these elements are present, and in abundance; but in the *Book of Love*, he weaves these threads into the very fabric of his argument. Because they are often vivid, they spice the work, and because they are often profound, they deepen and strengthen his case.

Love forms the subject of the entire thirty-sixth book of the *Iḥyā'*. It represents one of the most remarkable and influential analyses of the topic in the Islamic tradition.[54] Closely reasoned, marshalling not only scriptural but historical and even physiological facts and examples, at one moment veering into ecstatic expressions of rapture and wonder and at another into humorous and rather scabrous anecdotes, the book represents the most sustained attempt both to convince his readers that love of God is not only possible but essential, and indeed, obligatory, as well as to describe the various stages and gradations of love in painstaking detail and with surprising psychological acumen.

A mere generation or so before Zamakhsharī, Ghazālī had confidently asserted not only that love of God was conceivable, but that there existed a reciprocal loving relationship between God and man.[55] In the second 'quarter' of the *Iḥyā',* in the "Book of Intimate Friendship (*ulfa*)", he declared that "man loves God only because God loves him."[56] And in his fuller, more systematic treatment of the subject here, Ghazali not only re-asserts this claim but sets out to prove its validity, basing his arguments both on scripture and tradition as well as on logical proof.[57]

Zamakhsharī was, in any case, fighting a rear-guard action. Within a century of Ghazālī's death, the great theologian and exegete Fakhr al-Dīn al-Rāzī (d.606/1209) would note, in commenting on the same Qur'ānic verse III.31, that such objections of theologians represented little more than "a feeble doctrine."[58]

Admittedly, Rāzī was an adherent of Ghazālī's own Ashʿarite "school" of theology and might therefore be expected to follow in his predecessor's footsteps; and yet, this is but one of the indications, within theology as well as Sufi teaching, that the arguments marshalled by the "Proof of Islam" in support of a doctrine of reciprocal divine love had had a decisive impact.

VI. Ghazālī's Strategy

Ghazālī's strategy of argument deserves mention for it is calculated to address the subject in its most problematic aspects. His approach is methodical. He begins, as is his invariable procedure throughout the *Iḥyā'*, with proof-texts drawn from the Qur'ān and the Sacred Traditions, together with pertinent statements by earlier Sufi masters; these are then followed by "rational proof-texts" (*shawāhid ʿaqlīya*) and highly structured argument. Nothing could be more characteristic of Ghazālī's method than this fourfold structure of argumentation.[59] The number four and its multiples figure persistently throughout his work, both in its formal shape and in its inner dynamic; he thought, as it were, in fours.[60] I suspect that this approach represents more than a convenient method of intellectual organisation; it may have deeper underpinnings. Almost two centuries before, Nūrī had distinguished four levels of the heart: the breast (*ṣadr*) which is the locus of "submission;" the mind (*qalb*), which is the seat of faith; the "discerning heart" (*fu'ād*) where privileged knowledge resides; and finally, the "deep heart" (*lubb*) where awareness of God's oneness is lodged; and the same subdivisions appear in a contemporary treatise by the Sufi master al-Ḥakīm al-Tirmidhī.[61] As Nwyia has noted, Nūrī's fourfold division may owe something to the (lost) *Tafsīr* of Jaʿfar al-Ṣādiq (d. 148/765), the sixth Shīʿite imam, who employed a similar quadripartite schema.[62] Ghazālī's beloved fours thus had old and distinguished antecedents.

He next provides a methodical analysis of the nature and causes of love. This discussion leads into his central theme: God alone merits love. And here his earlier disquisitions on pleasure reveal their significance; for the highest of all pleasures, he argues, is to be found in the knowledge of God, insofar as He is knowable to man. Love and knowledge are intertwined throughout his discourse; for if the highest pleasure consists in knowledge of God, the culmination of that knowledge will occur in the actual vision of God in the hereafter. The dry Ashʿarite article of faith on the *ru'yat Allāh*, affirmed in opposition to the Muʿtazilite denial of the beatific vision, is here transformed by Ghazālī into something rich and strange: "Just as you know God in this world with a knowledge both real and entire, without either fantasy or mental representation or surmise of form and shape, so too will you behold Him in the world to come."[63]

Ever practical, despite his sublimer flights, he next considers those specific factors which strengthen love of God in the human heart; his argument turns throughout on the tension created by this-worldly observations and other-worldly expectations. A dynamic governs his thought. For while the lover of God may come to "behold Him in the world to come", God remains fundamentally unknowable to the human intellect. That unknowability sustains longing for God and leads Ghazālī, in his tenth chapter, to consider God's love for man; that chapter mirrors his earlier discussion, in chapter two, of man's love for God. The book is artfully constructed. In his concluding chapters on the signs or "marks" of love, he draws abundantly on the rich Sufi literature of his predecessors, moving boldly into considerations of the intimacy, lack of inhibition, and contentment, which identify the genuine lover of God. He concludes the treatise with an anthology of sayings and anecdotes illustrative of his theme.

As we have seen, theologians and jurists, as well as many Sufis, denied categorically that any relationship of love between God and His creatures, at least as we understand love, could be conceived. Though the classical works of dialectical theology, or *kalām*, deal with all those aspects or attributes of God for which there is Qur'ānic attestation—that is, with His power, will, knowledge, speech, life, etc.—no discussion of God's love is included. Attributes presuppose a subject—in this case, God—and an object—the focus of His power or will or speech. Love, by contrast, implies the congruence of two subjects; to be the object of God's power or will or knowledge, needless to say, does not involve reciprocity. It took ingenuity of argument to demonstrate that such reciprocity was possible. Ghazālī had to adopt an approach which was not merely compelling but incontrovertible. He used certain quite characteristic themes to make his case.

Self-Love

Ghazālī's starting-point is at once surprising and subtle: love as we know it begins in self-love. Human love is always self-interested; in everything we do, however altruistic it may appear, we act out of self-love and self-interest. Our love of ourselves therefore is the foundation upon which he slowly and systematically constructs his argument for a selfless and transcendent love. Why does he begin in this way? Clearly, because self-love is the one undeniable form of love which we all acknowledge. (The Biblical injunction to "love thy neighbour as thyself" rests on the same acknowledgement.) Towards the beginning of the book, Ghazālī puts it this way:

> For every living being the first object of love is its own self. Love of oneself signifies that in one's very nature there exists an inclination to prolong one's being and to avoid non-being and annihilation. There is a natural correspondence between him who loves and the object of his love. But what could be more perfectly in harmony [with him] than his own self and the prolongation of his own existence, and what could be more powerfully at variance with him than his own non-existence and destruction?[64]

Underlying this, of course, is an ancient doctrine: love depends upon a certain agreeable correspondence between the self and what best suits it whereas hate is based upon an aversion for what does not suit the self; first of all are pleasure and pain—we love what gives us pleasure and hate what gives us pain—but so simple a correspondence also betokens a kind of congruence that surpasses the senses.

There is something relentless in Ghazālī's analysis of self-love that on occasion makes readers squirm. This appears most sharply in his discussion of parental love. The love of a father for his son, he argues, is in effect a love for the father's own perpetuated existence; as he puts it, "he bears troubles for his child's sake because he will succeed him in existence after his own death."[65] Nevertheless, were the father forced to choose between his own death and that of his child, he would choose that his child die (assuming, as he says rather chillingly, that the father has a "sound well-balanced nature"); for actual is preferable to virtual survival.

Here it seems clear that Ghazālī is deliberately being somewhat brutal in his argument. He wants to hammer home the premise upon which his whole argument will rest: that we act, when we act on our own power, purely and exclusively out of self-love. To persuade us of another possible form of love—a disinterested love which belongs to God alone—he needs us to grant this initial, irrefutable proposition. Indeed, all the various causes of human love which he lists—love of those who do us good, love of those who do good to others, love based on beauty, and love based on mutual affinity—may be traced back to self-love. Even so, not all these loves are on the same level. And what Ghazālī wishes to persuade us of is that a love is possible, in however tenuous or fleeting a form, that is for something in itself. By beginning with the most obvious and undeniable form of love—our love for our own selves and our greed to go on living—he will progress to higher and higher manifestations of love which, however tinged with self-interest, yet bear witness to the possibility of a pure and disinterested love.

In the normal course of affairs, he contends, we do not love other people or things for themselves. We love someone who treats us with kindness not for himself but for the kindness he bestows. Even this is an illusion. The beggar who loves his benefactor, and the benefactor who takes pride in his generosity, are both equally deluded. The benefactor is merely an instrument of benevolence; and the benevolence which prompts him or her has been willed by God Himself. The beggar should thank God, not the benefactor; so, too, the benefactor should realize that the beggar was not an object of his compassion, but an instrument—in itself no more worthy of praise than the hand that extended the coin or the hand that received it—an instrument by which God's compassion is made manifest. We are shadows through whom the true actor plays out His part.

The Love of Beauty

The strongly aesthetic bent of Ghazālī's Sufism (and indeed, of Sufism in general) comes through most clearly in his discussion of beauty. For beauty is one thing which we are capable of loving for itself; indeed, beauty is intrinsically and immediately lovable. That we also derive pleasure from contemplation of beauty does not lessen its inherent lovability. This is, of course, a profound element in Islam generally and Ghazālī is quite fond of citing the well-known *ḥadīth*, which says: "God is beautiful and loves beauty."

With the subject of beauty, Ghazālī reaches a subtle turning point in his argument. We connect beauty chiefly with what we perceive, and particularly, with what we see. But there are other beauties: the beauty of music, accessible to hearing, or the beauty of women, perceptible most often, as he puts it, by the sense of touch. A scent may be beautiful. And he adduces the tradition of the Prophet who said, "Three things in this world of yours are precious to me: perfume, women and prayer, but prayer most of all." But is love based only on that which is agreeable to the senses? It would seem not, for we can feel love for someone distant whom we know only by report; furthermore, we feel love for eminent people who are dead and gone. Our senses cannot perceive the great jurist Shāfiʿī for the man himself is now nothing but dust; and yet, an adherent of his school of law may experience a passionate love for that long-dead jurist. So, too, of course, with the Prophet himself, as well as with other saints and masters. Therefore, it is entirely possible to love someone whom our senses do not perceive and of whom we know nothing except by report.

Love as Affinity

This leads us to the final and most profound cause of love: affinity between lover and beloved.[66] We most fully love that for which we feel a keen inner sympathy, a sense of likeness. For Ghazālī, it is the key to love of God in its truest sense, though it is also a key veiled in mystery.

How is a human creature to discover the secret affinity that links him or her with the most high God? The affinity, he says, is "explicable neither as resemblance of form nor similarity in outward shape. On the contrary, such affinity is due to secret precepts; some of these may be mentioned in books, others may not be written about but rather, are to be left behind the veil of bafflement..." As so often, whenever our author is on the verge of explaining a profound truth, he shrouds it in riddles. After all, his mission in the *Iḥyā'* is to elucidate the "mystical transactions" (*muʿāmalāt*), not the "hidden illuminations" (*mukāshafāt*).

In the simplest sense, the affinity between God and man is to be sought in that willed imitation of God which both scripture and tradition enjoin. "Mould your character to God's virtues," runs a famous maxim. Essentially, this entails modelling oneself upon the divine attributes, and especially those of knowledge, righteousness, kindness, mercy and good counsel. In *al-Maqṣad al-asnā,* his treatise on the Divine Names, Ghazālī offers a practical guide to meditation on God's attributes by which the aspirant can become ever more godlike. Thus, in such attributes as "creator" or "giver of form", a human being still may imitate God by imagining the process of conferring form on things, even if the actual conferral of form remains God's prerogative alone.[67]

In a Sacred Tradition ascribed to the Prophet, which Ghazālī cites, it is written: "God created Adam in His form." This cannot denote bodily form; therefore, there must be some sense in which a spiritual form, hidden from the eyes of sense, exists. To realise this, it is necessary to be stubborn in the practice of virtues, not only those that are prescribed by the Law, but supererogatory virtues as well. In another Sacred Tradition—this one a so-called *ḥadīth qudsī*, i.e., a tradition in which God speaks in the first person—we read: "Let man not cease coming close to Me by supererogatory works, so that I may love him; for when I love him, I become the hearing by which he hears, the sight by which he sees, and the tongue with which he speaks."

Here Ghazālī feels that he must "rein in his pen". And indeed, whenever he broaches the subject of identification with God, he becomes suddenly quite prudent. We must guard against, as he puts it, "overstepping the boundary of mere affinity into full-scale union; those who uphold this profess 'incarnationism' (*ḥulūl*) to the extent that one of them could say, 'I am God.'" He is referring here, of course, to Ḥallāj. But "incarnationism" is also uncomfortably close to Christian belief in the doctrine of the Incarnation, which Ghazālī had already condemned elsewhere; he obviously wishes to avoid its taint here.[68]

Sight vs. Insight

In the end, knowledge of God, which assumes knowledge of the affinity that may exist between Him and mankind, depends upon an occult or secret faculty—an "inner eye" which corresponds to, and surpasses, the eye of flesh.[69] Ghazālī is fond of playing on the concepts which he calls "eyesight" (*baṣar*) and "insight" (*baṣīra*), often in conjunction with analogy between the physician and the prophet: the physician sees our outward nature with his sight whereas the prophet sees the hidden reality by means of insight. Love is dependent upon knowledge; just as love occurs in stages, so too does knowledge. Just as love of God alone is the highest form of love, so too is knowledge of God the highest form of knowledge.

Knowledge brings pleasure with it necessarily; there is a natural human exuberance in knowledge which we all acknowledge. For example, as Ghazālī notes, "knowing how to play chess, despite its utter insignificance, means that a man cannot keep his mouth shut about it or refrain from offering instruction in it until he unlooses his tongue to display everything he may know about chess."[70] The point about knowledge is that, as with love, those who possess it at one stage tend to doubt its existence at higher stages. Thus, "to assert to young boys that the pleasures of sexual intercourse are superior to those of playing with a polo stick is impossible, just as it is to assert to the impotent that sexual pleasure is superior to the pleasure of sniffing violets." Here no "proof" is possible, for "he who has tasted knows."

The highest and most pleasurable form of human pleasure occurs through governing and yet, someone addicted to the pleasures of the table cannot even conceive of this, for the perception depends upon insight rather than sight. "If a man were to choose between the pleasure of a plump chicken and an almond pastry, on the one side, and the pleasure of ruling and conquering enemies and the attainment of political mastery, on the other, and he were a man of coarse aspirations, dead of heart and ruled by bestial tendencies, he would choose the meat and the pastry; however, if he were lofty in aspiration and perfected in his intelligence, he would choose governing, and hunger, even if endured for days, would seem a trifle." Nevertheless, there is a supreme pleasure, beyond chickens and almond pastries as well as governance itself, and that is contemplation and knowledge of God.[71]

Ghazālī's encomia on the pleasures of knowledge of God constitute some of the most beautiful passages of this book of the *Iḥyā'*, as when he writes:

> The breadth of the knowledge of God is only comparable with the heavens and the earth; it leads the gaze beyond all

> measurable quantities for its extent is infinite. The initiate ceaselessly acquires such knowledge in paradise, the breadth of which is that of the heavens and the earth; in those gardens he revels and picks their fruit, he sips from their cisterns. He is safe from any cessation since the fruits of this garden are neither finite nor forbidden. This pleasure is everlasting, death does not sever it, since death does not destroy the substrate of the knowledge of God. Its locus is the spirit which is a divine and heavenly thing; death alters only its circumstances...death frees it from its captivity but as for annihilating it? Certainly not![72]

The object of all our striving is to realise a love that is utterly unself-interested. Through knowledge, through incessant practice of the virtues, we may arrive at this realisation. But the way is complicated not only by our own faults, hesitations and defects. The way is dangerously entangled by the very nature of love. In the most daring chapters of his book, Ghazālī describes the lover's courtship of the beloved, who is God Himself, in erotic and amatory terms. As in human dalliance, love of God entails fierce longing, interludes of despair, wheedling and coquetry, complaint and heartbreak and self-deception, until finally, at rare instants, some intimacy may be achieved.

VII. The Paradox of Reciprocity

If the notion of a reciprocal love between God and man involves a paradoxical way of thinking, which Ghazālī sets out to resolve in Book XXXVI, it might be said that he complicates the issue even as he strives to clarify it. At several points in his discussion—and elsewhere in the *Iḥyā'*—he hints, or explicitly states, that the further the aspirant advances in knowledge and insight, the more plainly he sees that behind all his actions, it is God, and God alone, who acts. This seems a curiously circular conception of reciprocity.

Nevertheless, the love of God, as presented here, is a love the ultimate purpose of which is an ever deepening knowledge of the divine; and in fact, for all Ghazālī's recourse to the well-established terms and figures of amatory discourse, these betoken knowledge of God as much as love of Him. When he speaks of "intimacy" with God, this denotes not "union" but something more akin to an unending exploration of the mystery of God, an infinite foray into the unknowable. The reciprocity lies in the search itself, in the divine summons to the search. If there is "jubilance and gladness" in this intimacy, that is not only because of "nearness to God", but because that intimacy involves an incessant unveiling, a progression of epiphanies, rather than some final absorption into the godhead. If knowledge and love seem virtually indistinguishable at this ultimate stage, that is perhaps because they are mutually transfiguring. Love, in the end, is a matter of passionate cognition.

If this reading is correct, it modifies the notion of "reciprocity" with which we began. The love of God for man is that of the knower to the known; the love of man for God is that of the knower to the unknown. A human lover feels impelled to know the beloved in every sense, carnal as well as spiritual; this provides us with a crude if apposite analogy for the all-consuming ardour which the love of God inspires. By drawing on such analogies, Ghazālī wishes to convey something of the sheer urgency of this highest of all passions. The analogy is only approximate: all human loves are impermanent; they end in satiety or in loss. The love of God is different: it originates in God, it is prompted by God, He is its ultimate object, and it is everlasting. The Ghazālīan love of God is an eternal courtship in which the Beloved continually responds to the lover's suit with inexhaustible favours of insight.

Notes to Introduction

1 For Aristotle, as I. Goldziher noted almost a century ago, the distance between God and man was too great for friendship; see *Nicomachean Ethics*, 1159a (Loeb ed., 479) where Aristotle remarks that "when one [friend] becomes very remote from the other, as God is remote from man, it [friendship] can continue no longer;" cited in "Die Gottesliebe in der islamischen Theologie," *Der Islam* IX (1919), 158, n.3 (reprinted in *Gesammelte Schriften*, ed. Joseph DeSomogyi (Hildesheim, 1970), V. 432); cf. also G.-C. Anawati and L. Gardet, *Mystique musulmane* (Paris, 1976), 161. For Muslim theologians, it was not merely distance but a fundamental disparity between the human and the divine which made such "friendship" contradictory; see the remarks in Abrahamov, *Divine Love*, 15–16.

2 Zamakhsharī, *al-Kashshāf* (Cairo, 1972), I.424; cited in Goldziher, "Die Gottesliebe," 158 (432). With reference to Q. III.31, Zamakhsharī also remarks that the notion of human love of God is merely a "figure of speech" (*majāz*) which conveys a desire to worship God exclusively as well as to long for Him, and he further states that anyone who thinks otherwise "is a liar and God's book gives him the lie" (*ibid.*, I.423). For an earlier description of such Sufi ecstasies, see the *K. al-lumaᶜ* of Abū Naṣr al-Sarrāj (d. 378/988), 300–15, esp. 302–3.

3 Zamakhshari, *op.cit.*, I.621; Goldziher, 157 (431).

4 The term may be an allusion to the famous early Sufi master and advocate of human love of God, Sumnūn al-Muḥibb (d. 300/913)—"Sumnūn the Lover"—who liked to style himself "Sumnūn the Liar" (*al-kadhdhāb*); for this, see Sulamī, *Ṭabaqāt*, 186. Ghazālī cites several of his remarks about love in the present work (see below, pp. 164 and 190); also Abrahamov, *Divine Love*, 147.

5 Zamakhsharī, I.621.

6 "Merciful and loving is my Lord" (tr. Dawood, 231).

7 *Al-Maqṣad al-asnā*, 132; tr. Burrell, 118. For this work, see Bouyges, no. 33; Hourani, 298.

8 Jāḥiẓ, *K. al-ḥayawān*, IV.428.

9 *Lisān al-ᶜarab*, VI.67; cit. in my *Theodicy*, 247, n. 109.

10 Sarrāj considers such claims delusional; cf. *Lumaᶜ*, 432–3.

11 See below, esp. Chapter Eleven.

12 See, for example, his Persian correspondence where he makes this distinction and notes further that the existence or the non-existence of a thing comes not from itself, but "from the divine nature;" *Makātīb-i fārsi-yi Ghazālī* (ed. Iqbāl; Tehran, 1333), 20.

13 Mullā Ṣadrā, *al-Asfār al-arbaʿa*, I/2.292: *laysa fī dār al-wujūd ghayrahu dayyār*.

14 *Iḥyā'* IV.345; cf. below, p. 100.

15 *Ibid.* See also Wensinck, *La pensée de Ghazzālī*, (Paris, 1940), 20–21.

16 Goldziher, *op.cit.* p. 144 (418); as Louis Gardet and M.-M. Anawati note in their *Introduction à la théologie musulmane: essai de théologie comparée* (Paris, 1948), 316: "Ce n'est pas à promovoir la volonté à l'amour de Dieu qu'est destinée la 'science du kalâm'."

17 On Jahm, and his emphasis on the utter unknowability of God, see Josef van Ess, *Theologie u. Gesellschaft* (Berlin, 1992), II.500f. On Jaʿd, whose views remain obscure, see "Ibn Dirham" (G. Vajda) in *EI*² III.747–8, and J. van Ess, *Anfänge muslimischer Theologie* (Beirut, 1997), 233, for his denial of the divine attributes.

18 Goldziher, "Gottesliebe," 156 (430).

19 *Ibid.* On Khālid al-Qasrī, the successor to al-Ḥajjāj ibn Yūsuf, see also Goldziher, *Muslim Studies* (London, 1971), II.53, 82, 89.

20 *EI*² IV.118–19 (s.v. *ʿishk*). See also the useful discussion in L. Giffen, *Theory of Profane Love among the Arabs* (N. Y., 1971), esp. 3–4, 94–6, 127–29. Whereas *maḥabba* in its various permutations is used frequently in the Qur'ān, as is the synonymous term *mawadda*, *ʿishq* is non-Qur'ānic; for full references to the first two terms, see H. E. Kassis, *A Concordance of the Qur'an* (Berkeley, 1983), 509–11 and 1255–6, respectively. More generally, see also Joseph E. B. Lumbard, "From *Ḥubb* to *ʿIshq*: The Development of Love in Early Sufism," *Journal of Islamic Studies* 18:3 (2007), pp. 345–385, a useful article which came to my attention after the present work was completed.

21 His full name is Aḥmad ʿAbd Allāh Muḥammad ibn Khafīf ibn Iskafshādh (?) al-Shīrāzī (d.c. 371/981); cf. Sulamī, 485, and *GAS* I. 663–664 (both of whom give the name as Usfukshādh). His two treatises—now lost—were entitled *Kitāb al-maḥabba* and *Kitāb al-wudd wa'l-ulfa*; see Abū al-Ḥasan al-Daylamī, *A Treatise on Mystical Love*, tr. by Joseph Norment Bell and Hassan Mahmood Abdul Latif Al Shafie (Edinburgh, 2005), xxviii ff. For Muḥāsibī and his *Kitāb al-ḥubb*, see J. van Ess, *Die Gedankenwelt des Ḥārit al-Muḥāsibī* (Bonn, 1961), esp. 218–224.

22 Abū Nuʿaym, X.212–217. For Nūrī, see *GAS* I.650 and *EI*², VIII.139 (where it is stated, however, by A. Schimmel that he ranked *maḥabba* higher than *ʿishq*); also, L. Massignon, *Passion* I.121; trans. Mason, I.81: "Nūrī is the first to have preached the notion of pure

love (*mahabba*), the passionate fervor that the faithful must bring (without hope of recompense) to the practice of worship." For a fuller exposition of his teachings, based on a rediscovered manuscript of his writings, see P. Nwyia, *Exégèse coranique et langage mystique* (Beirut, 1970), 316–48.

23 "I am in love..." (*aʿshuqu*), in Nwyia, *Exégèse*, 317.

24 "*Man bi-khudāyi ʿāshiqam*," in Rūzbihān Baqlī, *Sharḥ shaṭḥīyāt* , ed. H. Corbin (Tehran, 1966), 165; cited in Keeler, *Sufi Hermeneutics*, 109. For this, Baqlī remarks, Nūrī was branded as a *zindīq* or "heretic" (in fact, a "dualist"); cf. also Abū Nuʿaym, x.213; and for the theological context, van Ess, *Theologie u. Gesellschaft*, IV.282 (who notes that the charge of *zandaqa* was raised only by Ghulām al-Khalīl and played no part in the legal proceedings) and his *The Flowering of Muslim Theology* (Cambridge, MA, 2006), 26–28. Jāḥiẓ, the Muʿtazilite polymath, had made a connection earlier between Sufis and *zanādiqa*, though on different grounds; cf. his *Kitāb al-Ḥayawān*, IV.428.

25 J. van Ess, *Theologie u. Gesellschaft*, IV.281–85; Massignon, *Passion,* III.118, n.3 (Mason trans. III.106), where he is quoted as saying, "Beware of sitting near someone who preaches affection and love (of God);" also, A. Knysh, *Islamic Mysticism* (Leiden, 2000), 61. For Ghulām Khalīl—i.e., Aḥmad b. Muḥammad ibn Ghālib al-Bāhilī—see van Ess, *Theologie u. Gesellschaft,* IV.281; also, van Ess, *Die Gedankenwelt*, 221; and *EI²,* VIII.139b.

26 Nwyia, *Exégèse*, 317.

27 See below, Chapter 12, p. 136; cf. also Wensinck, *La pensée de Ghazzālī*, 36.

28 Certainly he uses the word *ʿishq* in several passages of the present book, and without any obvious disapproval; thus, in *Iḥyāʾ* IV.314, he defines it merely as that intensified inclination we feel for anything pleasurable and later, at IV.333, he uses it to describe the exclusive, all-consuming love of God certain Sufis experience (cf. below, p. 100).

29 See below, e.g., pp. 46 and 54. The practice of *ishāra* could involve gesture as well as words: when Junayd was asked a question, he merely "indicated the heavens with his eyes;" cf. *Lumaʿ*, 223.

30 See, among other possible sources, Aḥmad ibn Muḥammad Miskawayhī's *Tahdhīb al-akhlāq*, ed. Zurayk (Beirut, 1967), esp. 137–8, where he discusses degrees of affection: thus, under *maḥabba* are grouped both *ṣadāqa* ("friendship"), characterised by *mawadda* ("affection"), and *ʿishq*, and the latter when pushed to extremes can become *walah* ("amorous frenzy"), which Miskawayhī identifies with "divine love" (*al-maḥabba al-ilāhīya*). For another discussion, this time on the distinction between *ḥubb* and *wudd*, see *Lumaʿ*, 228–9, where *wudd* is accorded a higher status since, unlike *ḥubb*, it is not dependent on

the fluctuations of "distance" and "proximity".

31 Qushayrī, *Risāla*, 615. For both the Sufi Daqqāq and the philosopher Miskawayhī, *ʿishq* denotes immoderation, but for the former it represents an "overstepping" (*mujāwaza*), which is reprehensible, while for the latter it is an "excess" (*ifrāṭ*), which culminates in love of God.

32 Qushayrī, *loc.cit.* For a partial, and somewhat different, translation, see Keeler, *Sufi Hermeneutics*, 122, n. 74.

33 H. Ritter, *The Ocean of the Soul*, 705; Knysh, *Islamic Mysticism*, 130.

34 See Daylamī, *op.cit.*, 71, for verses ascribed to Ḥallāj where "eros" (i.e., *ʿishq*) is presented as one of "the attributes of essence" of God; also, Massignon, *Passion*, I.120–123 (trans. Mason, I.79–82) and III.118 (trans., III.106–7). Massignon tends to translate the term as "desire" throughout, but he also—somewhat confusingly—considers it a "prudent term", at least as invoked by al-Ḥasan al-Baṣrī, used to "avoid the appearance of loving the divine essence" (*ibid.*, n.3); in that context, he renders it as "affection".

35 Their discussion occurs in Part 3, chapter 6, of the *Rasāʾil* (Beirut, 1957), III.269ff ; see also Susanne Diwald, *Arabische Philosophie und Wissenschaft in der Enzyklopädie* (Wiesbaden, 1975), 257–296, for a translation and commentary. For Ibn Sīnā, see in particular his *Risāla fī'l-ʿishq* in *Rasāʾil* (Qum, 1400), 373–397; also, L. Gardet, *La pensée religieuse d'Avicenne* (Paris, 1951), 167–74. For his influence on Ghazālī, see Richard M. Frank, *Creation and the Cosmic System: Al-Ghazālī and Avicenna* (Heidelberg, 1992).

36 Ibn Taymīya, cited in Yahya Jean Michot, "Misled and Misleading... Yet Central in their Influence: Ibn Taymiyya's Views on the Ikhwān al-Ṣafāʾ," in Nader El-Bizri (ed.), *The Ikhwān al-Ṣafāʾ and their Rasāʾil: an Introduction* (London, 2008), 176–7. For Māzarī, see further my *Theodicy*, 98–9.

37 They wish to ascertain *māhiyat al-ʿishq wa-maḥabbat al-nufūs* (*Rasāʾil*, III.269).

38 *Ibid.*, III.271.

39 See, among others, Toby Mayer, "Theology and Sufism" in T. Winter (ed.), *The Cambridge Companion to Classical Islamic Theology* (Cambridge, 2008), 273: "[T]he Greek concept of 'nature' (*physis=ṭabīʿa*) is condemned outright by Ashʿarism. God thus becomes the sole and absolute cause (*mukhtariʿ*) of the universe in its totality throughout its history."

40 *Ibid.*

41 Ibn Sīnā, *Shifāʾ*, I.4; ed./tr. Marmura, *The Metaphysics of* The Healing (Provo, 2005), 21. For God as "the lover of His own essence" (*ʿāshiq dhātihi*), see *Shifāʾ*, VIII.7.

42 Wensinck, for one, views the emphasis on the beauty of God as deriving ultimately from neo-Platonic influences, and from

Plotinus in particular; cf. *La pensée de Ghazzālī*, 24–27.

43 *Shifā'*, IX.2 (Marmura, 317). See, also, his great predecessor Fārābī (d. 339/950), for whom God, "the First", is "the first object of love and the first object of affection" (*al-maḥbūb al-awwal wa'l-maʿshūq al-awwal*), in his *Mabādi' ārā' ahl al-madīna al-fāḍila*, ed./tr. R. Walzer as *Al-Farabi on the Perfect State* (Oxford, 1985), 88–9.

44 Ghazālī, *Tahāfut al-falāsifa*, part V.34; ed./tr. Marmura, *The Incoherence of the Philosophers*, 95. Here he even defends Ibn Sīnā's application of the term "pleasure" (*ladhdha*) to God; in his later discussions in the *Tahāfut*, he introduces examples (sexual intercourse, playing chess) which he will return to in the present work (see pp. 44 and 54 below).

45 For Shiblī, who died in 334/945, see Sulamī, 340ff.

46 Sulamī, 348.

47 Bell and Al Shafie, *op.cit.*, LII, who also claim that while Ibn al-Khafīf had mixed feelings about Ḥallāj, he considered him "a true monotheist".

48 *Ibid.*, XXV. This seems a bit improbable, since Ashʿarī died around 324/935 and Bāqillānī around 403/1013, but given the 99-year lifespan accorded to Ibn al-Khafīf, it isn't impossible.

49 His birth and death-dates are unknown; cf. *GAS* I.664.

50 Daylamī's treatise, entitled *Kitāb ʿaṭf al-alif al-ma'lūf ʿalā al-lām al-maʿṭūf*, was first edited by J. C. Vadet (Cairo, 1962) and has now been translated by Bell and Al Shafie in the work cited above; they are preparing a new critical edition of the text as well.

51 Keeler, *Sufi Hermeneutics*, 109.

52 For some preliminary sense of the extent of the literature, see H. Ritter, "Arabische und persische Schriften über profane und mystische Liebe," *Philologika* VII, *Der Islam* 21 (1933), 84–109.

53 These were collected by the 6/12th century Persian writer Rūzbihān Baqlī in his *Sharḥ shaṭḥīyāt*, ed. H. Corbin (Tehran, 1966). For an earlier discussion, see *Lumaʿ*, 370ff.

54 Cf. Anawati and Gardet, *Mystique musulmane*, 162: "Disons sommairement qu'à partir de Ghazzālī l'amour de Dieu aura droit de cité dans le vocabulaire de l'Islām official."

55 The notion of a reciprocal love between God and man goes back at least as far as Muḥāsibī (243/857), an important influence on numerous Sufis, including Ghazālī; see van Ess, *Die Gedankenwelt*, 220. Massignon, for one, glosses *maḥabba* as "reciprocal love of God and the faithful;" see his discussion of the term and its history in *Passion*, III.117–18 (tr. Mason, III.106).

56 *Iḥyā'*, II.180. This may echo a statement by the 3/9th century Sufi master Abū al-Ḥasan al-Ḥawārī who said, "If God loves one of His servants, he loves Him. Man cannot love God unless God has begun by loving him;" cf. Sulamī, p. 90.

57 The entire discussion is given in condensed form in his Persian epitome of the *Iḥyāʾ* entitled *Kīmīyāʾ-yi saʿādat* (Bouyges, 45 and 222: Hourani, 300) in which love of God forms the subject of the penultimate chapter.

58 Rāzī, *al-Tafsīr al-Kabīr* (Tehran, n.d.), VIII.18.

59 For a discussion of his four-fold method, see my *Ghazali*, 113–15.

60 Examples abound throughout his work; thus, to mention only a few, in the *Munqidh*, the seekers after knowledge fall into four categories (theologians, philosophers, Ismāʿīlīs, and Sufis) and that work concludes with a "magic square" based on a four-square grid; at the beginning of the *Iḥyāʾ*, the science of the law is divided into four categories while the knowledge which leads to salvation is divided into two categories (*mukāshafa* and *muʿāmala*) which are set in contrast to the two excluded sciences, *kalām* and *falsafa*, etc.; cf. *Iḥyāʾ*, I.27ff.

61 Analysed in Nwyia, *Exégèse*, 321. For another such schematisation, see *A Treatise on the Heart* (*Bayān al-farq bayn al-ṣadr wa-al-qalb wa-al-fuʾād wa-al-lubb*), attributed to al-Ḥakīm al-Tirmidhī (d.c. 300/912), tr. Nicholas Heer in *Three Early Sufi Texts* (Louisville, 2003), 4–6 and *passim*; Heer translates *lubb* as "intellect," which is "the innermost sphere of the heart".

62 *Ibid*. On Jaʿfar, see F. Daftary, *Ismaili Literature* (London, 2004), 5–10; *GAS* I.571–2.

63 See below, p. 59.

64 See below, p. 13.

65 See below, p. 14.

66 Already listed as the main cause of love by the Ikhwān al-Ṣafāʾ who use the term *ittifāqāt* ("points of agreement" or perhaps better, "sympathetic correspondences") which they consider to be analogous to the correspondence between the organs of sense and their objects (*Rasāʾil*, III.276).

67 Cf. *Maqṣad*, 82; for a brief discussion, see my *Ghazali*, 62–3.

68 His *Al-Radd al-jamīl ʿalā ṣarīḥ al-Injīl* (Bouyges, 194), though its ascription to Ghazālī is disputed (Hourani, 296). Zaehner, however, argues that later in life, he did accept "incarnationism" as a consequence of his extreme monism, and that this constitutes his oft-mentioned "secret doctrine". Zaehner's argument strikes me as inconclusive; cf. *Hindu and Muslim Mysticism*, esp. 164–5. For an earlier critique of *ḥulūl*, which seems to me closer to Ghazālī's own position, see *Lumaʿ*, 426–7.

69 The concept of "insight" is perhaps most extensively developed in his late treatise *Mishkāt al-anwār* (Bouyges, 52; Hourani, 299–300); cf. *The Niche of Lights*, tr. David Buchman (Provo, 1998), esp. 23: "The masters of insight [*arbāb al-baṣāʾir*] never see a thing without seeing God along with it."

70 See below, p. 44.

71 According to Ibn Sīnā, the very definition of wisdom (*ḥikma*)

is "the best knowledge of the best thing known, for it is the best knowledge, that is, certainty (*yaqīn*) of the best thing known (that is, God, exalted be He)," *al-Shifā'*, I.2; tr. Marmura, 11–12.

72 *Iḥyā'*, IV.327; see below, p. 48.

THE BOOK OF LOVE, LONGING, INTIMACY AND CONTENTMENT

Being the Sixth Book of the Quarter of the Saving Virtues

[PROLOGUE]

In the Name of God, Most Compassionate and Merciful

PRAISED BE GOD, Who has exalted the hearts of His saints above all concern for the vanities and the glamour of this world, Who has purified their inmost beings from regard for anything but His presence, Who has singled out their hearts for devotion on the prayer rug of His grandeur and disclosed to them His names and His attributes so that they shone with the very fire of knowing Him, Who then revealed to them the splendours of His face until they burned in the fire of His love, and Who then concealed from them the essence of His majesty so that they wandered astray in the desert of His glory and His might! Then, whenever they trembled at a glimpse of His essential majesty, He darkened it with such astonishment as dusts the surface of both reason and perception. At last, when they were about to give up in despair, they heard a summons from the pavilions of beauty: "Patience! O you who despair of gaining the truth because of your ignorance and your haste!" And so their hearts remained suspended between rejection and acceptance, between denial and attainment, at once drowned in the sea of knowing Him and scorched in the fire of loving Him.

And abundant blessing and prayers upon Muḥammad, the Seal of the Prophets in the perfection of his prophethood, and upon his Family and his Companions, lords of creation, imams and leaders in truth and its reins!

Love of God is the utmost goal among the stages and the supreme summit of the steps. There is no stage beyond the grasp of love that is not one of its fruits and one of its consequences, such as longing (*shawq*), intimacy (*uns*), contentment (*riḍā*), and the like; nor is there prior to love any stage that is not preparatory to it, such as repentance (*tawba*), patience (*ṣabr*), and renunciation (*zuhd*), and the like. Attainment of the other stages is rare and yet, they are possible and hearts are not wholly without hope of them; but even the belief in love of God the Exalted is so scarce that one scholar even denies that it is possible. He states that love "has no meaning apart from persistent obedience to God the Exalted and that genuine love is inconceivable except between the same genus and species."[A] When such as he deny love, they also deny intimacy and longing and the pleasure of secret colloquies (*munājāt*) and all the other concomitants and effects of love. For this reason it becomes necessary to lay the whole matter bare.

In this book we shall [1] cite explanatory proof-texts from Revelation on the subject of love. We shall then [2] explicate its true nature and its causes. We shall also explain [3] that there is no one who truly deserves love except for God the Exalted. We shall explain as well [4] that the greatest of all pleasures resides in gazing upon the Face of God, and that [5] there is an even greater pleasure of gazing on His face in the life to come as compared to mere knowledge in this life. The exposition that follows this [6]

[A] Ghazālī does not identify the source of this objection but it was commonplace, especially among theologians; on such objections, see my Introduction above (p. xiv). Later, Fakhr al-Dīn al-Rāzī will note that for the *mutakallimūn*, "love belongs to the genus of the will (*irāda*) which, however, stands in no nexus with transient events and favours" and he dismisses their position as "feeble" (*ḍaʿīf*); cf. his *Tafsīr*, viii.18.

will deal with the means to strengthen love of God the Exalted, and that in turn will be followed [7] by an account of the disparity among people in the matter of love. A discussion [8] of the inability of the human mind to know God will come next, followed by a consideration [9] of the meaning of longing. After that we shall discuss God's love for His creature [10]. Then, a discourse [11] on the signs of human love for God will ensue, followed by an explanation [12] of the meaning of intimacy with God. We shall give an account [13] of what gladness in intimacy means, and discuss the meaning of contentment [14] and its particular virtue together with an explanation of its real nature. Next will come an exposition [15] of the fact that supplication and an aversion to sin do not deny it [contentment]; nor indeed does fleeing from sin. Finally, there will be a presentation [16] of the tales and sayings ascribed to various lovers.

These then are the matters to be discussed in this book.

CHAPTER ONE

An Exposition of the Proof-texts from Revelation Concerning Man's Love for God

KNOW THAT OUR community (*umma*) holds a consensus to the effect that love of God and His Messenger (may God bless him and grant him peace) is an obligation (*farḍ*); and yet, how could something that does not exist be made an obligation? And how might "love" be glossed as "obedience," seeing that obedience is one of the results and effects of love?[A] Love must necessarily come first and only then, in its aftermath, does he who loves obey. God's statement *He loves them and they love Him*[1] indicates that love for God does exist, as does His statement *and those who believe are the most fervent in love of God.*[2] This is a sign that love does exist as well as that there exist gradations within it.

In many Sacred Traditions[B], God's Messenger (may God bless him and grant him peace) makes love of God a condition of faith (*īmān*). Thus, Abū Rāzin al-ʿUqaylī asked, "O Messenger of God, what is faith?" He replied, "That God and His Messenger be dearer to you than anything else."[3] In another Sacred Tradition [it is said], "Not one of you believes unless God and His Messenger are more loved by him than anything else."[4] And in yet another

[A] As noted in the Introduction, this is the traditional orthodox definition of love of God; see, for example, the early eleventh-century Sufi theorist Daylamī on the six groups of "those who hold that love is obedience," in *A Treatise on Mystical Love*, p. 77f.

[B] We have chosen to use Sacred Tradition to translate *Ḥadīth*; Tradition refers to the sayings and anecdotes of other prophets and saintly persons.

Sacred Tradition, "A man does not believe unless I am more beloved by him than his family, his property, and anyone else."[5] (In another recension it reads "than himself.") How could it not be so, seeing that God (exalted is He!) says, *Say, if your fathers, your sons, your brothers…*[A6] That appears only in the form of an admonition and a rejection. The Messenger of God (may God bless him and grant him peace) commanded love, for he said, "Love God because of those favours with which He has nourished you but love me because of God's love for me." It is reported that a man said, "O Messenger of God, I love you" and that he (may God bless him and give him peace) replied, "Prepare for destitution." The man then said, "I love God (exalted is He!)," and he in turn rejoined, "Prepare for misery."[B7]

On the authority of ʿUmar (may God be pleased with him) it is related that the Prophet (may God bless him and grant him peace) saw Muṣʿab ibn ʿUmayr approaching; he had girded himself in a ram's hide.[C] The Prophet (may God bless him and grant him peace) said, "Look at this man whose heart God has illumined. I used to see him with his parents who fed him the choicest morsels and refreshments. Love of God summoned him to the state you now see."[8]

In another well-known Tradition [it is related] that Abraham[D] (upon whom be peace) said to the Angel of Death when he

[A] *your wives, your tribes, the wealth you have acquired, the trade that you fear you will lose, and the homes you love are more dear to you than God and His Messenger and striving in His cause, then await the punishment that God will bring upon you.*

[B] Meaning, that God tries the faith and love of those whom He wishes to bring closer to Him. See Chapter Ten below for similar *ḥadīth* and Ghazālī's explanation.

[C] Muṣʿab ibn ʿUmayr was a Companion known originally for his elegant dress and sumptuous way of life which he abandoned after hearing the Prophet preach; cf. *EI*[2] VIII. 649.

[D] Abraham (Ibrāhīm) is known as "the friend of God" (*khalīl Allāh*) in Islamic tradition, hence the force of the anecdote. In Midrashic tradition, Abraham dies by a kiss from the Angel of Death.

came to seize his soul, "Have you ever seen a friend who kills his friend?" But then God (exalted is He!) spoke to him secretly and said, "Have you ever seen a lover who was loathe to meet his beloved?" At that Abraham exclaimed, "O angel of death, seize me at once!"[9] Only he who loves God with all his heart discovers this; since he knows that death is a means of meeting, his heart is wild with longing for it and he has no lover other than death to whom he might turn.

In one of his prayers our Prophet (may God bless him and grant him peace) said, "O my God, grant me love of You and love of those who love You and love of whatever brings me closer to You. Make love of You dearer to me than cool water!"[10]

A desert Arab came to the Prophet (may God bless him and grant him peace) and asked, "O Messenger of God, when is the Hour?" He answered, "What have you prepared for it?" He said, "I have not prepared for it either much prayer or much fasting but I do love God and His Messenger." The Messenger of God (may God bless him and grant him peace) declared, "A man will be with those whom he loves."[11] Anas [ibn Mālik] said, "I have not seen Muslims happier over anything than that, apart from the coming of Islam itself."[12]

Abū Bakr al-Ṣiddīq (may God be pleased with him) said, "Whoever has tasted the pristine love of God is preoccupied from any worldly pursuit and becomes estranged from all mankind."

Al-Ḥasan [al-Baṣri] said, "Whoever knows his Lord loves Him. Whoever knows the world renounces it. The believer does not indulge in mindless frivolity for whenever he reflects, he grieves."

Abū Sulaymān al-Dārānī remarked, "Among those whom God created are some whom paradise itself with all its delights cannot distract from Him; how then could they possibly be distracted from Him by this world?"

It is reported that Jesus (peace be upon him) passed three men whose bodies were wasted and whose countenances were stark with pallor. He asked them, "What has happened to you that I see?" They answered, "Fear of hell." He said, "It behoves God to give safety to him who fears." Then he passed on to another three even more emaciated and pallid; he asked them, "What has come upon you that I see?" They replied, "Longing for paradise." He said, "It behoves God to give you what you hope for." He passed on to yet another three and indeed, these were surpassingly gaunt and utterly altered, as though their faces had become mirrors of light. He said, "What has come upon you that I see?" They replied, "We love God." At this he exclaimed, "You are those brought near to God! You are those brought near to God! You are those brought near to God!"[13]

ʿAbd al-Wāḥid ibn Zayd said, "I passed by a man standing in the snow. I said to him, 'Don't you find it cold?' and he replied, 'One whom love of God possesses feels no cold.'"[14]

It is reported that Sarī al-Saqaṭī said, "The nations will be summoned on the Day of Judgment by their prophets. Then there will be heard 'O community of Moses!' and 'O community of Jesus!' and 'O community of Muḥammad!' but not those who love God: they will be summoned by 'O friends of God, up! Come to God' and their hearts will be close to bursting with joy.

Harim ibn Ḥayyān said, "When the believer knows his Lord he loves Him and when he loves Him, he approaches Him and when he discovers the sweetness of the approach to Him, he no longer looks on this world with an avid eye, nor does he gaze on the hereafter with an indifferent eye, for what pains him in this world refreshes him in the next."

Yaḥyā ibn Muʿādh said, "His forgiveness (*ʿafw*) consumes sins; what then of His contentment (*riḍwān*)? His contentment consumes hopes; what then of His love? His love astonishes understanding; what then of His affection (*wudd*)? His affection causes oblivion of all but itself; what then of His grace (*luṭf*)?"

It stands written, "My servant, by your rights on Me, I love you and by My rights on you, love Me."

Yaḥyā ibn Muʿādh said, "The weight of a mustard seed of love is dearer to me than seventy years of worship without love."[15]

And he also said, "God, I am standing in Your courtyard and am riven with praise of You. You took me to You when I was young. You clothed me in the knowledge of You. You gave me strength through Your favour. You turned me this way, and then that, in my actions through veiling and repentance, renunciation and longing, contentment and love. You gave me to drink from Your cisterns. You let me wander untended in Your gardens. I clung to Your commandments and remained in love with Your word even after my moustache sprouted and the bird of my destiny appeared. Now that I am grown, how may I go away from You? I became accustomed to this on Your part when I was young. Now there remains for me in Your presence nothing but droning, and in entreating You nothing but groaning, for I am a lover and every lover is rapt in his beloved and uninterested in all but what he loves."

On the love of God (exalted is He!) anecdotes and tales might be adduced beyond measure. This aspect of the matter is clear; the more abstruse aspects appear only when we try to ascertain its true meaning. Let us therefore proceed to this.

CHAPTER TWO

An Exposition of the True Nature and Causes of Love, with an Explanation of the Meaning of Human Love for God

KNOW THAT THE object of this chapter may not be revealed except through knowledge of the true nature of love in itself and after that, by knowledge of its conditions and causes and only then, at the last, by scrutiny of the true nature of its meaning with respect to God.[A]

The first matter to be determined is whether love is inconceivable except after knowledge and perception (since man loves only what he knows). A mineral cannot conceivably be characterised by love. Rather, love is the essential characteristic of a living sentient being. Furthermore, perceptible things are divisible into that which corresponds to the nature of the perceiver—that which suits him and gives him pleasure—and into that which is at variance with him—what is averse to him and causes him pain—and into that which produces neither pain nor pleasure in him. The perception of what causes pleasure and ease is loved by the perceiver; the perception of what causes pain is hated by the perceiver; what is devoid of the imposition of either pain or pleasure cannot be described as something either to be loved or to be avoided. Hence, every pleasure is loved by the one who receives

[A] The approach here may owe something to the discussion in the *Rasā'il* of the Ikhwān al-Ṣafā', as noted in the Introduction; they too begin their discussion of love with a consideration of its "quiddity" (*māhiyat al-ʿishq*) though, significantly, Ghazālī uses the phrase *ḥaqīqat al-maḥabba*; cf. *Rasā'il*, III.269.

it. The meaning of its being loved is that there is some natural inclination towards it; the meaning of its being hated is that there is a natural aversion to it. Love, therefore, is an expression for the natural inclination to what is pleasurable. Whenever that inclination is reinforced or becomes intense, it is termed "passionate love" (*ʿishq*). Hatred is an expression for the natural aversion to something painful and troublesome; when it intensifies, it is called "detestation" (*maqt*). This is a constituent principle in the true nature of love that must be recognised.[A]

Since love is a consequence of perception and knowledge, it is necessarily divisible in accord with the way in which the senses themselves and their perceptible objects are divided. For every sense a perception accrues according to the species of perceptible; to each sense furthermore there pertains a pleasure in certain perceptibles. Thus, a given nature, if healthy, will incline to a particular perceptible and love it. And so the eye's pleasure resides in sights and in the perception of beautiful objects and attractive forms that are both lovely and agreeable. The ear's pleasure lies in beautiful and measured melodies. Sweet fragrances exist for the pleasure of smell. The pleasure of taste lies in foods. The pleasure of touch resides in whatever is soft and smooth. Whenever these sense perceptions are pleasurable, they are loved, i.e., a healthy nature inclines to them. For this reason the Messenger of God (may God bless him and grant him peace) said, "Three things of this world of yours have been made loveable to me: perfume and women and prayer has been made the apple of my eye."[1] He called perfume a thing to be loved. Neither the eye nor the ear has any share in this, as is well known; on the contrary, it applies

[A] Ghazālī's use of "passionate love" (*ʿishq*) betrays the influence here, and throughout, not only of the Ikhwān al-Ṣafāʾ, as already noted, but of Ibn Sīnā (d. 429/1037)—as well as, ultimately, of Aristotle—far more than of typical Sufi writings on the subject. For the philosopher, love represents a universal animating principle present not only in human souls but in all nature, including inanimate objects, such as minerals. See, among other sources, Ibn Sīnā's treatise entitled "Risāla fi'l-ʿishq" in *Rasāʾil*, 1.474ff.

solely to the sense of smell. And he termed women loveable even though only sight and touch partake of them, but not smell, taste or hearing. He termed prayer "the apple of his eye" and declared it most worthy of love, even though, as is obvious, the five senses play no part in prayer; on the contrary, it involves a sixth sense whose seat is the heart and he alone perceives it *who possesses such a heart.*[2]

Beasts partake along with man in the pleasures of the five senses. [Yet,] if love is restricted only to those things perceptible to the five senses, it can be argued that God is imperceptible to sense and cannot be pictured even in imagination, thus He cannot be loved. Negate the very essential characteristic of man, that sixth sense by which he is distinguished and which may be expressed by "intellect" (*ᶜaql*) or "light" (*nūr*) or "heart" (*qalb*) or whatever other terms you like; and yet, how wrong it is! Inward sight (*baṣīra*) is mightier than outward sight (*baṣar*).[A] The heart is more powerful in its perceptions than the eye. The beauty of concepts perceptible to the intellect is far lovelier than the beauty of forms external to the eye. Of necessity, then, the heart's pleasure in perceiving divine and lofty matters too exalted for the senses to grasp remains both more perfect and more extensive. Far stronger too is the inclination of a healthy nature and a sound mind to this [form of perception]. Love has no meaning other than the inclination to that in which a perception of pleasure resides, as will be explained in some detail. Accordingly, the love of God cannot be denied except by a person whose shortcomings relegate him to the level of the beasts, since clearly he has not passed beyond mere sense perception in any way.

Obviously man loves himself. Obviously, too, he may love someone else for his own benefit. But can a man conceivably love

[A] Cf. the contrast drawn by the Ikhwān al-Ṣafāʾ between mere outward sight which grasps external forms and the vision of God in the hereafter which is "a vision of light by light, for light, in light, from light" (*ruʾyat nūr bi-nūr li-nūr fī nūr min nūr*), *Rasāʾil*, III.282.

someone other than himself for that person's sake, and not for his own benefit? For the weak-minded this poses a difficulty; in their view it is simply unimaginable for man to love anyone other than himself, and for the other's sake, so long as the lover receives no benefit from this beyond the mere perception itself. But in truth, not only is this conceivable, it does in fact exist.

Let us then explain the causes and the categories of love.[A]

The primary object of love for every living being is its own self. Self-love signifies that there exists within one's very nature a desire to prolong one's being and to avoid non-being and annihilation; furthermore, there is a natural correspondence between him who loves and the object of his love. But what could be more perfectly in harmony with one's own self than prolongation of existence, and what could be more powerfully at variance than non-existence and destruction? For this reason, man loves continuation of existence and loathes death; and this, not merely because of what he fears after death, nor simply to avoid the agonies of death. Quite the contrary: were he to be wrested away painlessly and brought to death without either reward or punishment, even then he would not be satisfied. In fact, he would be wholly averse to that. Man does not love death and non-being except in proportion to some agony in life; however he may be tormented by an affliction, his love is for that affliction to cease. If he were to love non-existence, it would not be because it is non-existence but rather, because it contains within it a cessation of his torment. Destruction and non-being merit hatred while prolongation of existence prompts love.

Just as prolonged existence is to be loved, so too is perfected existence; the defective diminishes perfection and, indeed, lack is non-being in relation to the measure of what is lost and is a kind

[A] Here again it may be instructive to invoke the Ikhwān al-Ṣafā' and their distinction between an "inherent cause" (*ʿilla*) and an "external cause" (*sabab*); cf. *Rasā'il*, III.272. Ghazālī uses only the latter term in his discussion for reasons that will become clear: God alone is the object and the origin of all love.

of destruction in that regard. Destruction and non-being are just as hateful when they occur in the attributes and in perfection of existence as they are in themselves. When attributes of perfection exist, they too are as lovable as the prolongation of existence. This is innate through God's decree: *You will never find alteration in God's established custom.*[3] Thus, the first thing man loves is his own self, then the health of his limbs and organs, and then his property and his progeny, his associates and friends. He loves bodily health because the perfection and the continuance of his own existence are dependent on that. He loves property because it too is instrumental to the continuing perfection of his existence. The same is true of the other causes.

Now man loves these things not for their own sakes but because of their connection with his portion of prolonged and perfected existence. For this reason he loves his child, even though he does not obtain any direct advantage from him; on the contrary, he bears troubles for the child's sake because he will succeed him in existence after his own death. In the survival of his offspring there lies a sort of survival for him too. Because of his intense love for his own survival he loves the survival of the child who will supplant him; he himself cannot hope to survive forever but the child is, as it were, a part of him. In fact, were he to be offered a choice between his own death and that of his son, he would—assuming that his nature is well-balanced—prefer his own survival over his son's because though his son's survival resembles his own, it is not after all his own actual survival. The same is true of his love for his relatives and associates; that too reverts to his love of perfecting himself, for he sees himself magnified by them, made powerful by them, and adorned with their perfections. Comradeship and property, together with other external causes, are like a wing lifting man to perfection.

Perfection and prolongation of existence are things naturally loved, and necessarily so. Since the first object of love for every living creature is its own self together with the perfection and prolongation of that self's existence, and since conversely, everything counter to that is an object of aversion, self-love is the first of love's causes.[A]

The second cause of love is benevolence (*iḥsān*). Indeed, man is the servant of benevolence. Our hearts are innately disposed to love those who do us good and to hate those who do us evil.[4] The Messenger of God (may God bless him and grant him peace) said, "O my God, do not grant an evildoer power over me,[B] lest my heart come to love him!"[5] This points to the fact that the human heart irresistibly loves a benefactor and lacks the power to ward off this love. This is innate and indeed primordial to man's nature; it cannot be altered. For this same reason a man may come to love a foreigner who bears no relationship or connection to him.

Examined properly, this may be traced back to the first cause. The benefactor is one who supplies property, assistance, and other means which produce continuation and perfection of existence, not to mention the attainment of those advantages by which existence is primed. There is a difference: human limbs are loved because a perfection of existence occurs directly through them, and this is the perfection we seek. But as for the benefactor, well, he is not in his own person the perfection sought even though he may be a means to it, just like the physician who serves as a means to prolonging bodily health. And yet there is a distinction between love of health and love of the physician who is a means to health.

[A] The notion of self-love forms the lynch-pin of Ghazālī's argument. One recent commentator has, rather absurdly, gone so far as to term this "dark" and even "nihilistic"; see A. Kevin Reinhart, *Before Revelation: The Boundaries of Muslim Moral Thought* (Albany, 1995), 71. A contemporary American philosopher has, however, made self-love the basis of his own analysis of love in all its forms. Harry G. Frankfurt, in *The Reasons of Love* (Princeton, 2004), argues that self-love is not only desirable and necessary but disinterested: "Perhaps it would flirt too egregiously with the absurd to suggest that self-love may be *selfless*. It is entirely apposite, however, to characterise it as *disinterested*, in the clear and literal sense of being motivated by no interests other than those of the beloved" (82; his emphasis).

[B] That is, power to do me good.

Health is sought for its own sake; the physician is loved not for his own sake but because he is a means to health. Knowledge too is loved, as is the teacher, but knowledge is loved for itself while the teacher is loved as a cause of the cherished knowledge. Food and drink are loved, and *dīnār*s are loved as well; however, food is loved for its own sake and the *dīnār*s only as a means of getting the food. The distinction comes down to a difference of priority. Nevertheless, everything goes back to man's love for himself. Hence, anyone who loves a benefactor for his kindness loves him not essentially as he is in himself. Quite the opposite: he loves his kindness, yet this is only one of his activities. If his kindness should cease so too would the love even though the benefactor has remained as he was in himself. If his kindness lessens, love for him lessens too; if his kindness increases, love increases too. Increase and decrease affect love, correlated as they are with increase and decrease in the benefaction itself.

The third cause lies in loving a thing for its own sake, and not for some advantage arising from it outside its own nature. Rather, its innermost nature is its very advantage. This is a deep and authentic love that grows ever stronger as it continues. This is similar to the love of beauty and comeliness, for every beautiful thing is deemed lovable in the sight of him who apprehends beauty; that is due to the nature of beauty itself. The very quintessence of pleasure resides in perception of the beautiful. Pleasure is loved for itself, and not for something other than itself. Do not make the mistake of thinking that a love of beautiful forms is inconceivable except for the sake of satisfying one's appetite. Satisfaction of appetite is another pleasure entirely. But beautiful forms may be loved for themselves. Indeed, it is entirely conceivable that beauty be loved for what it is. How can this be denied? Verdure and flowing waters are loved, not so that one can drink the water or eat the verdure or derive any advantage whatsoever from them other than gazing itself. The Messenger of God (may God bless him and grant him peace) used to be filled with wonder at greenery and flowing water. Any person of sound nature seeks out the pleasure to be found in gazing on lights and flowers and birds of pretty hues with lovely patterns and symmetrical forms. Indeed, human beings dispel sorrows and cares by gazing upon such things and do not seek any benefit beyond gazing itself.

These then are the causes of pleasure. Every pleasurable thing is loved. And the mere perception of every beautiful thing is pleasure. No one can deny that beauty is intrinsically worthy of love. In fact, as has been established, God is beautiful and necessarily to be loved by anyone to whom His beauty and majesty have been disclosed. This is just as the Messenger of God (may God bless him and grant him peace) said, "God is beautiful and He loves beauty."[6]

This entails some explanation of the meaning of beauty. Know that a person held captive within the confines of the realms of fancy and sense perception might imagine that beauty has no meaning other than proportion in appearance and shape, or lovely colour—white suffused with crimson—or lofty stature, and similar qualities by which human beauty is often described. Among humans the most conspicuous loveliness is that perceptible to the eye; most of the disparities among people come down after all to individual forms. There is a widespread opinion that whatever cannot be seen or imagined or given form is impossible, and that in the case of something the beauty of which cannot be pictured, there can be no pleasure in beholding it since its beauty cannot even be conceived and thus, it is not susceptible of love. This is a blatant error. Beauty is not restricted to what can be seen, nor to symmetry of feature, nor to the intermingling of whiteness and ruddiness. For we can say, "This is a beautiful line of calligraphy," and "This is a beautiful voice," and "This is a beautiful horse." Not only that, but we can say, "This is a beautiful garment," and "This is a beautiful vessel." What meaning then might appertain to "the beauty of a voice" and "a vessel", and those other things, if beauty exists only in form? As is well known, the eye takes pleasure in gazing at a beautiful line of calligraphy and the ear in listening to fine and beautiful melodies. What then could be the meaning of a beauty that all these things have in common? This requires investigation, and yet, any investigation would be lengthy. In a work such as this, concerned with rudimentary, practical activities, it is unsuitable to fall into prolixity. Hence, we shall speak the truth succinctly.

The beauty that belongs to each thing resides in the fact that the perfection appropriate and possible to that thing be in fact present. Whenever all its possible perfections are present, a thing has its utmost beauty. If there be present but one of its perfections, then it possesses beauty in the measure in which that perfection is present. A beautiful horse is that horse that combines all that is appropriate to a horse with respect to form and shape and hue and majestic gait and readiness to lunge and pull back. Beautiful is every line of calligraphy that combines what is appropriate to calligraphy, such as proportionality of the letters, their spacing, the straightness of their order, and the beauty of their arrangement. Everything has a perfection proper to itself.[A] Its contrary may well be appropriate for some other thing. Still, the beauty of each thing lies in the perfection suitable for it alone. A man is not beautiful in the same way that a horse is beautiful; a line of writing is not beautiful for the same reasons that a voice is beautiful; vessels are not lovely through that by which garments are beautiful. And so, too, with all things.

You may object that even if these things are not visually perceptible, such as voices and [the taste of] foods, even so, they are inseparable from sense perceptions of them; indeed, they are themselves objects of sense. Indeed, the beauty of objects of sense is undeniable, nor may it be denied that pleasure comes from observing their beauty. For beauty to occur in anything other than what the senses perceive may, however, be denied.

[I reply]: Know then that beauty exists in things other than objects of sense. You might, for example, say, "This is a beautiful character," and "This is a beautiful science," and "This is a

[A] See, again, Ibn Sīnā, "Risāla fi'l-ʿishq", 475, where he speaks of the natural inclination of each being towards its own perfection (*kamāl*).

beautiful life," and "These are lovely moral traits." By "lovely moral traits" are meant knowledge and intellect, chastity, bravery, piety, generosity and manliness, and all other fine qualities. And yet, not one of these traits is perceptible to the five senses. On the contrary, they are perceived by the light of inner sight. All of these traits prompt love; the man to whom they are attributed is naturally loved by anyone who becomes aware of his qualities. One sign that the matter is so, is that our natures are innately constituted to love the Prophets (may God bless them) and the Companions (may God the Exalted be pleased with them), even though they cannot be seen directly with the eyes. Furthermore, [human nature is so constituted] to love the masters of the schools of law, such as Shāfiʿī, Abū Ḥanīfa, Mālik [ibn Anas], and others.

This can go to such an extreme that a man may overstep the bounds of passion through his love for the founder of a school of law, with the result that he is impelled to squander all his property to promote and defend his own school; it may even steal into his mind to murder anyone who criticises the *imām* and his followers. O how much blood has been spilled to promote the causes of the masters of the schools of law! Would that I knew how someone can love Shāfiʿī, for example, when he has never set eyes on his form? If he had seen him, he might not have found him attractive in form.[A] Therefore, the attraction which impels him to some excess of love must be for his inner, not his outer, form. His outer form has already turned to dust; however, he loves him solely for his inner qualities of devotion, piety, abundant knowledge, and comprehension of the fundamentals of religion, in addition to his deeds, such as spreading and disseminating the benefits of the science of the law throughout the world. These are indeed beautiful things but their beauty is not perceived except by illumined insight. Here the senses fail.

[A] Ghazālī here criticises the excesses of the followers of Shāfiʿī (d. 205/820), perhaps because, as an adherent of the Shāfiʿī *madhhab*, he had witnessed them at first hand; cf. my *Ghazali*, 9.

The same is true of a man who loves Abū Bakr al-Ṣiddīq (may God be pleased with him) and prefers him above all others, or of a man who loves, favours and champions ʿAlī (may God be pleased with him). Such a man loves through discovering the beauty of inner forms, that is, their knowledge, religion, piety, courage, generosity, and the like. Obviously, whoever loves Abū Bakr does not love his bones and flesh and skin and limbs and bodily shape since that has all perished and turned into nothingness. Nevertheless, that through which Abū Bakr al-Ṣiddīq became Abū Bakr the Truthful remains, and these are his praiseworthy qualities which are the sources of his beautiful life. Love endures because these qualities themselves persist after all bodily forms have disappeared. These qualities in their entirety may be reduced to knowledge (*ʿilm*) and to power (*qudra*). Abū Bakr recognised the true natures of things and was able to bring himself under control by restraining his appetites. All the good traits branch off from these two, neither of which the senses perceive. The location of both of them in the body is the indivisible atom. This is something too that is loved in reality even if the indivisible atom has no form, shape, or colour which could appear to the eye and make it loved for its own sake.

Hence since there can be beauty in lives—for if a beautiful life were to emerge lacking knowledge and insight, it would not command love—then, what is loved is the source of beautiful lives, that is, laudable qualities and noble virtues; all of these, however, can be reduced to the perfection of knowledge and power. This, though imperceptible to the senses, is loved naturally. So true is this that if we wish to render somebody loveable to a young man acting on his own inclinations, we have no better recourse than to describe him—whether absent or present, living or dead—at great length in terms of his bravery, generosity, knowledge, and other praiseworthy traits. To the extent that the youth believes this, he will be incapable of containing himself and will be unable not to love [that person]. So does love of the Companions (may God be pleased with them) and hatred of Abū Jahl, together with hatred of Iblīs (may God curse him), prevail by nothing else than by detailed description of virtues and vices which are themselves imperceptible to the senses. Whenever people ascribe munificence to Ḥātim al-Ṭā'ī and bravery to Khālid ibn al-Walīd, then hearts are drawn irresistibly to love them; this is not the result of seeing some perceptible form, nor does it arise from some advantage which the lover derives from them. On the contrary, when tales of justice, fairness and the bestowal of goods are told from the life of some king in certain far flung regions of the world, love for him—together with despair of any munificence on his part, simply because of the remoteness of his abode—overwhelms the heart.

Human love therefore is not limited to those who confer benefit directly; rather, a benefactor is worthy of love in himself, even if his beneficence can never reach those who love him. This is so because all beauty and all goodness are loved. The form is both outward and inward, for beauty and goodness include them both: outward forms are perceived by the outer eye, inward forms by the inner vision. He who is deprived of inner vision neither discerns them nor takes pleasure in them. He cannot love them nor be inclined towards them. But he whose inner vision predominates over his outer eye enjoys a love for inner meanings far greater than his love for any outward senses. O what a vast difference there is between him who loves a painting figured on a wall because of the beauty of its outer form, and him who loves one of the prophets because of the beauty of his inner form!

The fifth cause involves a hidden affinity between the lover and the beloved. Often love between two persons intensifies not because of beauty or some advantage, but because of sheer spiritual affinity. It is as the Prophet (may God bless him and grant him peace) said, "For those among whom there is mutual recognition there is intimacy, and for those among whom there is mutual aversion, there is divergence."[7]

We already verified this in the *Book of the Manners of Companionship*[A] when we mentioned love of God. Look for it

[A] That is, *Iḥyā'*, II.5, *K. ādāb al-ulfa wa'l-ukhuwwa wa'l-ṣuḥba*.

there since this too is one of the wondrous causes of love.

If then you reduce the types of love to five causes, they are [1] the love a person has for his own perfected and continuing existence; [2] the love for someone who does good to one by prolonging his existence, aiding in his continuance and keeping him from harm; [3] the love for someone who is good in himself to people, even if he is not good to one personally; [4] the love for everything beautiful in itself, equally whether it be in outward or inward forms; and [5] the love for someone with whom there exists a hidden, inner affinity. If you were to combine these causes in a single person, love would inevitably increase. This is like the case of a man whose son is beautifully formed, fine in character, of consummate knowledge, upstanding in disposition, kind to others as well as good to his parents—such a son is loved irresistibly and to the utmost. The strength of the love inspired by the combination of these qualities stands in proportion to the strength of these qualities in themselves. If these qualities are of the highest perfection, then love too will necessarily be at its highest.

Let us now state plainly, however, that all these causes in their fullest unity and perfection are inconceivable except in the case of God the Exalted. In reality, God alone merits love.

CHAPTER THREE

An Exposition that God Alone Merits Love

GOD ALONE MERITS LOVE. Whoever loves anyone other than God, without regard for his relationship with God, does so out of ignorance and a flawed knowledge of God. Love of God's Messenger is laudable; it is the very essence of the love of God. So, too, with love of religious scholars and the devout because that which is loved by the beloved is itself worthy of love. [Thus,] the messenger of the beloved is worthy of love, and he who is loved by the beloved is also to be loved. All this goes back to love of the original object of love and to nothing else. For those endowed with insight there is in reality no object of love but God, nor does anyone but He deserve love.

To explain this we shall go back to the five causes we mentioned and state clearly that in God these are united in their totality but in others than He they do not exist except piecemeal. In God these are reality, as we shall explain, but in others, their existence is mere fanciful supposition—metaphor pure and simple, devoid of all reality. However this be established, to those endowed with insight the very contrary of what the weak-minded imagine concerning the impossibility of love of God in any real sense has been revealed. In fact, true discernment requires that you love no one other than God.

Concerning the first cause—man's love for himself and the perfection and continuance of his own existence coupled with his hatred for annihilation and non-being, as well as any flaws to his perfection—this is the inborn tendency of every living thing and cannot conceivably be detached from it. This necessitates the utmost love for God since whoever knows himself, and knows his Lord, knows absolutely that his own existence does not occur as a result of his own nature but rather, that his existence, prolonged and perfected, comes from God and goes to God and is [sustained] by God. God is the inventor of his existence. He causes it to endure. He it is Who perfects existence by creating attributes of perfection as well as the means of obtaining them and guidance to their use. [Were God not to do this], man, as far as his own nature is concerned, would have no existence arising from himself. Quite the opposite: he would be pure nullity and sheer non-being had God not favoured him by bringing him into existence. And he would face annihilation after coming to be had God not favoured him by causing him to continue. And he would be flawed after coming to be had God not favoured him by perfecting his inner nature. In sum, nothing in existence possesses within itself the principle of its own existence except for the Self-Subsistent One Himself (*al-Qayyūm*), the Living One (*al-Ḥayy*) who subsists through His own essence while everything but Him subsists through Him.

Now if the gnostic loves his own self (and since his existence has been bestowed upon him by another, then he perforce loves Him who accorded existence to him); if, further, he knows God as Creator, Existenciator, Maker, Continuator, Subsistent in Himself and Giver of subsistence to others, and then he still does not love Him, it is due to his ignorance both of himself and of his Lord.

For love is the fruit of knowledge: it is extinguished when knowledge is extinguished; it redoubles when knowledge redoubles; it grows mighty in the strength of knowledge. For this reason al-Ḥasan al-Baṣrī (may God have mercy on him) said, "Whoever knows his Lord loves Him while whoever knows the world renounces it." How can a man love himself and not love his Lord through whom his very subsistence occurs? A man afflicted by the heat of the sun loves the shade and so will inevitably love the tree through which that shade subsists. But everything that stands in relation to God's power is analogous to the shade in relation to the tree and the light in relation to the sun. Everything consists of the effects of His power. The existence of everything follows upon His existence just as the light's existence follows upon the sun and the shade's existence follows upon the tree. And yet, to argue the contrary, the similitude has force only in relation to the understanding of vulgar folk; they imagine that light is one of the sun's effects and that light emanating from it exists because of the sun. This is pure error. To those who possess hearts it has been divulged, through revelation plainer than if they had witnessed it with their own eyes, that light comes to be through the power of God the Exalted; it is created at the encounter of the sun with dense bodies just as sunlight, its source, shape and form, also come to be through the power of God. Similitudes are meant to assist understanding but final truths should not be sought in them.

Therefore, if man's love for himself be necessary, then his love for Him through whom, first his coming-to-be, and second, his continuance in his essential being with all his inward and outward traits, his substance and his accidents, occur must also be necessary. Whoever is so besotted by his fleshly appetites as to lack this love neglects his Lord and Creator. He possesses no authentic knowledge of Him; his gaze is limited to his cravings and to things of sense. This is the world of phenomenal reality, which he shares fully with the beasts, not the transcendent world, the ground of which no one may tread except him who is close in likeness to the angels. He gazes [upon that realm] in proportion to his nearness to angelic qualities but falls far short of it in the measure of his plunge to the level of the bestial world.

The second cause of love springs from man's love for those who are good to him by helping him with money, speaking kindly to him, offering him assistance and standing always in readiness to assist him and to squelch his enemies, by rising up to ward off evils from him and, in short, by making available to him the means of attaining benefits as well as objectives for himself, his offspring, and his relatives. Such a benefactor is inevitably loved. And yet, even this obliges us to love no one but God. Whoever is truly aware knows that God and God alone is the only benefactor. I cannot even enumerate the various benefits He shows to man; no inventory could encompass them. It is as He says, *If you counted up God's favours, you could not count them.*[1] We have indicated the full extent of this in *The Book of Thankfulness.*[A]

Now we confine ourselves to explaining that human goodness is conceivable only in a figurative sense; the true benefactor is God alone. Even so, let us postulate that benefaction in the case of someone who lavishes all his possessions on you and allows you to dispose of these as you wish. You suppose that this goodness comes from him, but this is wrong. True, he does perfect his own goodness through his wealth and his power to control wealth, as well as by the compelling motivation that causes him to devolve his belongings on you. But who bestowed creation upon him? Who created his wealth? Who created his power? Who created his will and his motivation? Who made you loveable in his eyes and inclined his face towards you and prompted in his soul the notion that his own well-being in this world and the next lay in doing good to you? If not for all of these factors, he would not have given you even a grain of his property. However much God granted these impulses mastery over him and established within him the thought that his own welfare in this world and the next depended upon his lavishing his wealth upon you, he himself was compelled, he was constrained, to accede, and he was unable to resist. Nevertheless, the real benefactor is He who constrained him and forced him on your behalf, and Who gave those driving and impelling motivations power over him so that he might act. His hand was but the instrument by which God's goodness came to you. The hand's owner was coerced to act thus through a compelling force comparable to that of water racing in

[A] That is, *Iḥyā'*, IV.2, *Kitāb al-ṣabr wa'l-shukr*. For the English translation by H. T. Littlejohn see *Al-Ghazālī on Patience and Thankfulness*, Islamic Texts Society, 2011.

a stream-bed. If you think him a benefactor, or thank him, on the ground that he is a benefactor and acting autonomously, and not on the ground that he is an instrument, you are ignorant of the true state-of-affairs.

Goodness to anyone other than himself is inconceivable in man's case; indeed, goodness to any other being on the part of created beings is preposterous. A man does not spend his money for other than his own ends in spending, either for the future—and this for the sake of reward—or for the present—and this for the sake of kindliness or utility or praise or for the celebrity and repute that come with liberality and munificence; it can even represent an attempt to influence men's hearts towards submission and affection. A man does not fling his money into the sea, for there is no purpose in that; in the same way he does not toss it into another man's hand without having some purpose that redounds to him. It is that purpose that he seeks and strives to have, not you; you are not what he is striving for. On the contrary! Because you grasped his money, your hand becomes his own tool for grasping so that he may achieve his goal of good repute or praise or thanks or reward. He is therefore a benefactor to himself; he is rewarded for whatever money he has expended by a reward that outweighs money in his own estimation. Had it not been for the preponderance of that advantage in his own calculation, he would not have relinquished his money for your benefit under any circumstances whatever.

There are then two reasons as to why he deserves neither gratitude nor love. First, he was compelled by those motivations which God let overmaster him, such that he had no power to oppose. Like the prince's treasurer, he is not regarded as a benefactor just because he bestows a robe of honour on the prince's behalf upon some person to whom it has been accorded. In fact, he has been compelled by the prince to be obedient and compliant with whatever the prince may command, and he cannot oppose him. If he were separated from the prince and were acting on his own, he would not bestow [the robe]. The same is true of every benefactor: if he stood apart from God and acted on his own behalf, he would not disburse a grain of his wealth unless God motivated him and implanted within him the suggestion that his own best interest in this world and the next lay in his disbursal. Then indeed he would spend, but for that reason.

Second, he has been rewarded for what he has spent by an affluence that in his own estimation is fuller and more desirable than what he actually expended. Just as a seller is not considered a benefactor simply because he acceded a recompense which in his eyes is more desirable than what he acceded, so too with a giver: he has been compensated through reward or praise or eulogy or something else. Recompense need not be some object of material value; on the contrary, all such benefits are rewards in comparison to which money and property appear contemptible. Benefaction lies in generosity; however, generosity is the expenditure of wealth without there being any motive or share that reverts to the giver. For anyone but God this is impossible. He it is Who bestows on the worlds the goodness that befalls them, and befalls them for their own sakes, not because of some share or motive that can be ascribed back to Him. In truth, He is exalted above all motives. The words "generosity" or "goodness" are either mendacious or metaphorical with regard to anyone but God. Their application to anyone but Him is both impossible and contradictory, just as contradictory in fact as if one might term something simultaneously black and white. God is utterly unique in munificence and benignity, in generosity and in benevolence. Even if it is natural for us to love a benefactor, still a gnostic must not love anyone but God inasmuch as goodness on the part of anyone but God is unthinkable. God alone is worthy of this love. Love for anyone else should be regarded as something which man merits solely if the true meaning of benefaction as well as its true nature is ignored.

The third cause occurs when you love a benefactor for his own sake although his benefaction does not extend to you personally. This too is innate in us. For whenever some report comes to you of a pious, just, and knowing king, who is kind and compassionate to people as well as humble before them—although he be in some region of the earth distant from you—and whenever another report reaches you of a king who is tyrannous, arrogant and immoral, dishonourable and wicked—and he too dwells far from you—you discover a distinction between the two kings in your own heart. For the first king you find an inclination that is love, and for the second king a repugnance that is hatred; this, in spite of the fact that you have no hope of benefaction from the good king and are safe from any evil from the evil king, since you have no desire to travel to either of their countries. This is love of a benefactor exclusively as benefactor and not because he is a benefactor to you. This too entails the love of God. Nay, more, it makes it necessary that one love no one other than God except insofar as he may be connected with this cause.[A] God is benefactor to the totality of creatures. He lavishes loving-kindness on every class of created being. First, because He causes them to exist. Second, because He perfects them in the organs and means essential to them. Third, because He smoothes and eases their lives by creating the necessary bases of life, even when these are not strictly dictated by necessity. Fourth, because He beautifies them with excellent features and with appendages that are located where they will be most lovely; this, too, is beyond the realm of what is essential or even needed. The head, heart and liver are examples of essential bodily organs. The eye, hand and foot are examples of needed organs. By contrast, arching eyebrows, rosy lips, sparkling eyes and the rest are features whose lack impairs neither necessity nor need.

Water and food are examples of external benefits necessary for the human body. Medicine, meat and fruits are examples of needed things. The greenness of trees, the lovely forms of

[A] The notion has become part of popular wisdom; see Westermarck, *Wit and Wisdom in Morocco* (London, 1930), p. 106 (no. 290): "Love is from God and as for man (*al-ʿabd*) he is only the occasion."

luminous objects and of blossoms, the deliciousness of fruits and of foodstuffs, are examples of adornments and added graces, the absence of which does not impair either need or necessity.

These three divisions exist in every animal; indeed, in every plant; nay, rather, in every single one of the classes of created things from the pinnacle of the Throne to the deepest foundation of the world. Now, since He is the benefactor, how could anyone else be a benefactor, all the more so since that benefactor is himself merely one good thing among all the good things within God's power? For God is the creator of good as well as the creator of him who does good. He is the creator of the act of doing good, just as He is the creator of the means of doing good. Therefore, love for anyone other than Him is rank ignorance. Whoever knows this, loves no one but God.

The fourth cause is the love of every beautiful thing because of its very beauty, not because of any share one might have in it beyond sheer perception. We have already explained that this too is ingrained by nature and that beauty may be subdivided into the beauty of outer form, perceived by the physical eye, and into the beauty of inner form, perceived by the eye of the heart and the light of insight. The first beauty mere boys as well as the beasts in the field perceive but the second beauty only the lords of insight are singled out to grasp. No one who knows only the outer aspects of the life of this world may share this perception with them.

To him who perceives beauty everything beautiful is to be loved; if he is one who perceives with his heart, then that beauty becomes the love of his heart. A visible example of this is love for the prophets and the learned, as well as for those with lofty traits and pleasing characters; in fact, this remains conceivable despite any indistinctness in their faces or bodily forms. This is what is meant by the beauty of inner form. Sense does not perceive it; and yet, sense does perceive the lovely effects which emerge and delineate it in such a fashion that the heart, upon registering its presence, inclines to it and feels love for that beauty. He who loves the Messenger of God or Abū Bakr al-Ṣiddīq or Shāfiʿī loves them solely for the beauty they possess that has been made manifest to him. This is not due to any beauty in their bodily forms nor to the beauty of their actions; indeed, the beauty of their actions points to the beauty of those characteristics that are at the source of the deeds. Actions have effects which both issue from them and indicate them. Someone who sees the beauty of an author's composition or the beauty of a poet's poem—nay, rather, a painter's painting or a builder's construction—finds beautiful inner qualities disclosed to him through these visible actions, which upon inspection can be attributed in their entirety to the knowledge and ability of their the artists. Thus, when some object of knowledge is nobler and grander and more beautiful, then knowledge of it is also nobler and more beautiful. The same is true of an object of power. Whenever it is grander in degree and loftier in level, the power to accomplish it is also nobler and more exalted. Nevertheless, the most exalted of all the things that can be known is God. Hence, the knowledge that is most excellent as well as noblest is knowledge of God, along with whatever else is related to, or specified by, that knowledge. Its nobility stands in proportion to its link with Him. Therefore the beauty of the traits of the righteous, whom all hearts love naturally, may be attributed to three things.

First, their knowledge of God, His angels, His scriptures and His messengers, together with the revealed truth of His prophets. Second, their capacity for performing righteous acts both for their own sakes and for the sake of God's creatures through right guidance and good governance. Third, their aloofness from vicious practices and impure habits as well as from those appetites which divert one, when they prevail, from the time-honoured traditions of goodness and draw him onto the path of wickedness. So is it then with prophets, scholars, caliphs, and kings, all of whom are men of justice and magnanimity. Even so, how can these attributes of theirs be likened to God's attributes!

With regard to knowledge, then, we may ask: where is the knowledge of the ancients and the moderns with respect to God's knowledge which encompasses everything in a manner so surpassing of all limits that *not even the measure of a speck of dust in the heavens and on the earth eludes it*?[2] God has addressed all His creatures when He says, *Little indeed is the knowledge vouchsafed to you.*[3] On the contrary, if the inhabitants of earth and heaven collaborated to encompass His knowledge and His wisdom in setting out the details of His creation of an ant or a gnat, they would not come to comprehend even a tiny fraction thereof.[A] *They can grasp only that part of His knowledge which He wills.*[4]

Therefore, both the beauty and the nobility of knowledge are to be loved. And since knowledge in itself is an adornment as well as a perfection of him to whom it may be ascribed, it follows that no one but God should be loved. Set beside His knowledge, the knowledge of scholars is ignorance. Ridiculous would be the situation of someone who knows both the most learned and the most ignorant men of his time and still loves the most ignorant for his knowledge and abandons the most learned; this, even allowing that the most ignorant man be not wholly devoid of whatever knowledge his way of life requires. But the disparity between God's knowledge and the knowledge of creatures is even more huge than that between the most learned and the most ignorant of creatures. This is because the most learned is superior to the most ignorant only by certain limited and circumscribed fields of knowledge; it is entirely conceivable in the realm of possibility that the more ignorant man might partake of such specialised knowledge by dint of a mental effort. But the superiority of God's knowledge over all the knowledge of creatures is unbounded; the objects of His knowledge are infinite whereas the objects of creatures' knowledge are finite.

Power is perfection, lack of power imperfection. All perfection, splendour, grandeur, glory and mastery are loved, and their perception gives pleasure. A person who hears a tale of the courage of ʿAlī or of Khālid ibn al-Walīd and of other valiant men, not

[A] An analogy used often by Ghazālī; for other examples, see *Theodicy*, 46-48.

to mention their power and dominion over their enemies, feels affected with deep emotions of exultation and joy; this comes about necessarily through the mere pleasure of listening, let alone through witnessing their deeds at first hand, and prompts irresistible love in one's heart for the man so described.

Power too is a sort of perfection. Now relate the power of all creatures to the power of God. The mightiest and most powerful person, with the broadest dominions, the man most forceful in his strength and who conquers his passions and stifles the vices of his carnal soul, who combines strength over himself with strength over others—what is the utmost reach of such a man's power? In its farthest extent he has power merely over some of his own tendencies and over a few other individuals in certain matters. He has no dominion over himself in death or in life or in rising from the dead, nor over harm or benefit. Just the opposite: he cannot guard his eye from blindness, his tongue from dumbness, his ear from deafness, or his body from illness. It is hardly necessary to enumerate all those things of which man is incapable both in himself and with respect to others purely in regard to those things with which his ability stands in relationship, let alone those things with which his ability remains unconnected, such as sovereignty of the heavens with its spheres and stars, the earth with its mountains, seas, winds, thunderbolts, mines, plants and animals, and all their parts. Man has no power over even a dust speck, neither from within himself nor from others; his ability derives neither from nor by himself. On the contrary, it is God who creates him, who creates his power and who creates the instruments of his power along with all that is possible for him to do. If He gave a gnat power over the greatest and most powerful king, that gnat could destroy him. The creature has no power except through the empowerment of his Master. God says about the greatest of the kings of the earth, Dhū'l-Qarnayn[A], *We have given him dominion on*

[A] By most commentators Dhū'l-Qarnayn (see Q. xviii.83-98) is assumed to represent Alexander the Great; see *EI*[2] iv.127.

earth.[5] Still, all his power and all his might were due only to God's empowerment of him in a single corner of the world. Moreover, the earth in its entirety is just a clod in comparison with the other bodies of the cosmos; all the governments which people enjoy on earth are nothing but the dust from this clod. Even so, this grain of dust is also part of God's bounty and empowerment. Hence, it is absurd to love one of God's creatures for his ability, his governance, his empowerment and mastery, and the perfection of his strength, and not to love God for those very reasons. There is neither power nor might except in God, *the Sublime, the Mighty.*[6] He is the Omnipotent, the Vanquisher, the Omniscient, the Powerful Who folds up the heavens with His right hand,[7] while the earth and its dominions and all that is upon it remains within His grip and the forelock of all creatures lies in His grasp and in His power. If He were to destroy them to the last one, there would be no diminution of His power and reign by so much as a grain of dust. And if He were to create others like them by a thousand-fold, He would not then be incapable of further creation. Fatigue would not assail Him, nor would His inventiveness lessen.[8] There is no power and no powerful person who is not the mere result of God's power. Beauty, splendour, might and grandeur, force and dominion, belong to Him. If it be conceivable to love a powerful person because of the fullness of his power, then love for the perfection of power is unmerited by anyone other than God.

The attribute of transcendence above faults and deficiencies and of being hallowed from all vices and sins, is a requirement of love as well as one of the perquisites of goodness and beauty in their inward forms. Prophets and the righteous may be exalted above any faults or misdeeds; and yet, perfection of holiness and of transcendence cannot really be conceived except with respect to the One, *the King,*[9] the Truth, the Holy, *Possessor of Majesty and Honour*[10]. No creature, however, is without defect or flaw. Creaturely being is incapable, subjugated, compelled; indeed, it is flaw and defect personified. Perfection belongs exclusively to God. No one else possesses perfection except in the measure that

God bestows upon him. It is not even within the realm of the possible that utmost perfection be accorded to anyone other than God. In fact, though utmost perfection is but the lowest of His steps, it is still inappropriate for a creature subject to, and subsistent through, another. Perfection is preposterous with regard to anyone but God. God is unique in perfection, distanced from deficiency, hallowed of faults. To explain the various aspects of His holiness and transcendence above all defect would be lengthy. It is also among the secrets of the illuminative sciences and so, we will not dwell in detail on it.

The attribute of transcendence also means that perfection and beauty merit love (even though love's true nature is perfected solely in God). The perfection and the transcendence of anyone other than God are not absolute, but rather, stand in comparison only with whatever is more defective than it. Hence, a horse possesses perfection in comparison to a donkey, and a man possesses perfection in comparison to a horse. Even so, a fundamental deficiency is common to them all; they differ from one another only in degrees of defectiveness. He who is beautiful deserves to be loved and yet, the absolutely beautiful is the One who has no equal, the Unique who has no opposite, the Eternal who has no rival, the Self-Sufficient who has no need, the Omnipotent who does what He will and judges as He wishes without anyone to oppose His rule or revise His judgment: the Omniscient *whose knowledge not a speck of dust in heaven and earth eludes*;[11] the Vanquisher from the clutch of whose power the napes of tyrants cannot escape and from whose rule and force the necks of Caesars cannot slip free; the Eternal who has no first to His existence; the Everlasting who has no last to His perdurance; the Necessarily Existent whose mighty presence non-existence cannot encircle; the Self-Subsistent who subsists in Himself and in whom every existing thing subsists; the Almighty of the heavens and the earth; Creator of minerals, animals and plants; the Alone-in-Glory and Might; the One in rule and reign; the Possessor of goodness and majesty and splendour, beauty, power and perfection, in the knowledge of whose majesty intellects stand baffled and in whose description tongues can merely conjecture; whom the perfect knowledge of gnostics confesses its inability to know and whom the utmost prophethood of prophets affirms its failure to describe. As the master of all prophets (God's blessing upon him and upon them) said, "I cannot enumerate the praise of You: You are as You have already praised Yourself."[12]

Abū Bakr al-Ṣiddīq said, "The inability to attain perception is itself perception. Praise be to Him who made no way for His creation to know Him save through inability to know Him!"[A] Ah, I wish I knew who could deny the possibility of love of God as a reality and reduce it to mere metaphor! Does such a one deny that these descriptions belong among descriptions of beauty and of praiseworthy traits and the epithets of perfection and beauty, or does he deny God's being so described? Does he deny that perfection, beauty, splendour and might are by nature loved by anyone who perceives them?

Praise be to Him who hides Himself from the visions of the blind, jealously guarding His beauty and His majesty so that only those to whom good has first been granted by Him shall become aware—those who hold themselves distant from the dividing fire—but abandoning the lost who gird themselves in the shadows of sightlessness and who flit to and fro in the showplace of things of sense and bestial appetites. *They know the outward show of this nether life, but of the life to come they are heedless.*[13] *Praise be to God! But most men know nothing!*[14]

Love from this cause, therefore, is stronger than love for benefaction, for benefaction can increase or decrease. This is why God

[A] Ghazālī discusses this dictum also in his *al-Maqṣad al-asnā* (ed. Shehadi), p. 54: "The utmost knowledge of the gnostics is that of their inability to know. In reality, their knowledge is that they do not know Him and that knowledge of Him is absolutely impossible for them and that it is impossible that anyone know God with a knowledge that might comprehend the nature of His sovereign attributes except for God Himself." For a discussion of this passage, see my *Ghazali*, 60-61; cf. also, Ibn al-ʿArabī, *al-Futūḥāt al-Makkīya*, I.91-92, II.84-85.

inspired David (upon him be peace) by saying, "The friend I love the most is he who serves Me without expecting a gift but who gives My Lordship its due."[15] In the Psalms it says, "Who wrongs Me more than one who serves Me for the sake of heaven or hell? If I had not created heaven or hell, would I not be more worthy of obedience?"[16]

Jesus passed by a group of worshippers who were emaciated. They said, "We are afraid of hell and hope for heaven." He said to them, "You fear something created and you hope for something created." He passed by another group who said, "We worship God out of love for Him and to exalt Him because of His majesty." And Jesus said, "Truly you are God's friends! It is with you that I have been commanded to sojourn."[17]

Abū Ḥāzim said, "I am ashamed to serve God for the sake of reward or punishment, for then I would be like a bad servant who does not act if he does not fear, and like a bad worker who does nothing when he is not paid."[18]

In Sacred Tradition it says, "Let no one of you be like a bad worker who does not work when he is not paid his wage, nor like a bad servant who does nothing if he is not made afraid."[19]

The fifth cause of love is by reason of affinity and similarity. What is similar to a thing draws that thing to itself. Like is more inclined to like. For this reason, you see a young man on close terms with another young man and an adult on familiar terms with another adult. A bird will be close to its own kind and avoid any but its own kind. The intimacy of one learned man with another is more common than of a learned man with an artisan. The familiarity of a carpenter with another carpenter[20] is more common than with a farmer. This is a matter to which experience bears witness, as does Sacred Tradition. We have related this in the chapter on friendship in *The Book of Good Manners and of Friends* and one should seek it out there.

Since affinity is a cause of reciprocal love, it can have a literal meaning, such as the affinity of one youth for another under the aegis of "youth". It may be hidden such that it remains unknown, as you can see from the union of whatever they hold in common between two individuals without any consideration for beauty, acquisition of property, or the like. The Prophet (may God bless him and grant him peace) alludes to this when he says, "Spirits are armies drawn up in ranks. Those who recognise affinity with one another become intimate while those who repudiate each other disperse."[21]

This cause too makes the love of God which is necessary on account of a hidden affinity explicable neither as resemblance of form nor similarity in outward shape. Quite the contrary, [affinity] is due to secret precepts; some of these may be mentioned in books, others may not be written about but rather are to be left behind the veil of bafflement until those who tread the mystic path stumble upon them when they have fulfilled the prerequisites of the Way.

What may be mentioned, however, is the nearness of man to his Lord in those attributes which he has been commanded to imitate and in the assumption of divine moral norms as his own; as it is written, "Mould your character to God's virtues." This consists in the acquisition of laudable qualities from among such divine attributes as knowledge, righteousness, benevolence, kindness, dispensing goodness and mercy upon creatures, giving them counsel and guiding them to the truth while keeping them far from what is false—these, together with all other virtues held praiseworthy in the Law. All of this brings one close to God, not in the sense of physical nearness but rather in closeness to God's attributes.

Nevertheless, with regard to what may *not* be written down in books about the specific affinity by which humans are characterised, this is what God alludes to when He says, *And should they ask you about the spirit say, "The spirit is part of the Divine Command."*[22] He makes plain that "the Divine Command" is beyond the bounds of human intellects. Still clearer is His statement, *Then when I made him upright and I breathed of My spirit into him.*[23] It is for this reason that the angels prostrated themselves before him [*sc.* Adam].

God's statement, *I have made you a representative on the earth*, alludes to this.[24] Adam merited being God's representative only through this affinity.[A]

The Prophet (may God bless him and give him peace) also hints at this when he says, "God created Adam in His form."[25] Certain limited scholars hold the view that there is no form other than outer form perceptible to the senses. Hence, they resort to anthropomorphism and accord God corporeal form. And yet, *God the Exalted*, the Master of the worlds, *must be declared sublimely transcendent over whatever* ignorant men *believe and expound.*[26] There is allusion to this in what God said to Moses, "'I was sick and you did not visit me.' Moses replied, 'O Lord, how can this be?' God answered, 'My servant so-and-so was sick and you did not visit him. Had you visited him you would have found Me with him.'"[27]

This affinity becomes manifest only through stubborn persistence in supererogatory deeds after fulfilment of the prescribed communal obligations. As God says, "Let man not cease coming close to Me by supererogatory works, so that I may love him; for when I love him, I become the hearing by which he hears, the sight by which he sees, and the tongue with which he speaks."[28]

This is a place at which one must rein in his pen for on this subject people have diverged, some flawed individuals tending towards open anthropomorphism and others inclining towards gross exaggeration, overstepping the boundary of mere affinity into full-scale union; these latter profess incarnationism to such an extent that one of them could say, "I am God."[B] The Christians

[A] "Representative" is the original meaning of *khalīfa* ("caliph"). As Gramlich points out (654), the reference in Q. xxxviii.26 is not to Adam, but to David.

[B] A reference to Ḥallāj (executed 309/922). "Incarnationism" (*ḥulūl*) is the belief attributed to Ḥallāj and others that God Himself can become incarnate in a human individual. Ghazālī's occasional references to Ḥallāj are usually oblique; cf. also, *Mishkāt al-anwār* (Beirut, 1407/1987), 139ff, and my discussion in "Abū Ḥāmid al-Ghazālī vu par Massignon," in *Louis Massignon et l'Iran*, ed. Eve Pierunek and Yann Richard (Leuven, 2000), 51-59. Zaehner has argued—not entirely convincingly—that Ghazālī subscribed to some notion of *ḥulūl* in

err concerning Jesus (upon him be peace) when they claim that he is God. Still others say "Humanity has donned divinity" or again, "Humanity has become one with Him." Nevertheless, those to whom it has been made abundantly clear that anthropomorphism and the drawing of resemblances to God are absurd, along with union and incarnation, and to whom at the same time the reality of the mystery has been made plain, are few indeed. Perhaps it was from this vantage point that Abū al-Ḥusayn al-Nūrī was gazing when ecstasy overtook him at the poet's words:

> Forever and ever through Your love have I been
> At the stage where all hearts are lost in bafflement.

In his rapture he ran into a marsh where cane had been cut and the stalks were sticking up. He slashed both his feet and they swelled and from that he died.

Such affinity is the mightiest of love's causes as well as the strongest but it is also the rarest and the least likely to occur.

This then is what is known about love's causes. All of them are most fully manifest in God in actuality, not merely in metaphor, as well as in the supreme, rather than any lesser, degrees. Hence, to those endowed with insight, love of God, and God alone, is reasonable and acceptable, just as, by contrast, to the blind, the exclusive love of everything but God seems reasonable and allowable. Everyone who is loved for one of these [five] causes deems it conceivable that someone other than himself might be loved by virtue of sharing with him in these causes; however, such sharing is a defect in love and a fault in its perfection. No one is unique in the possession of some lovable quality; someone else exists who shares that quality. And even if he does not exist, he could exist. But God is different. He possesses qualities of the utmost majesty and perfection and there is no one who shares these with Him either actually or potentially. There is thus no element of participation in His love nor can any imperfection touch His love, just as

his later teaching; cf. his *Hindu and Muslim Mysticism*, 164ff.

no attribute of His can be shared. He is alone worthy of love in its source and in its perfection and no one can partake of this in any way with Him.

CHAPTER FOUR

An Exposition that the Noblest and Loftiest Pleasure is Knowledge of God and Contemplation of his Blessed Face and Only He who is Denied this Pleasure can Conceivably Prefer any Other Pleasure to it

KNOW THAT PLEASURES are consequent upon perceptions. A human being combines a totality of faculties (*quwā*) and instincts (*gharā'iz*). For each faculty and instinct there pertains a particular pleasure which occurs when it is obtained in accord with what the very nature of that faculty or instinct requires and for which it was created. These instincts were not compounded within man for no reason. Quite the contrary: each faculty or instinct has been compounded because of something which by its very nature it needs. Hence, the instinct towards anger was created for the purpose of vengeance and retribution; its pleasure inevitably lies in triumph and in the wreaking of revenge which are prerequisites of its very nature. The instinctual appetite for food, for example, was created so that the nourishment through which man subsists might be acquired; its pleasure lies ineluctably in acquiring that food which its nature demands. So, too, with the pleasures of hearing, seeing and smelling with their respective senses. Because of their links to sense perception, none of these can be disconnected from pain or pleasure.

In the heart too there is an instinct that may be called 'the divine light' (*al-nūr al-ilāhī*). This is in accord with God's statement,

He whose breast God has opened to Islam has a light from his Lord.[1] This may be called "intellect" (*ʿaql*) as well as "inner vision" (*al-baṣīra al-bāṭina*) and "the light of faith and certitude" (*nūr al-īmān wa'l-yaqīn*). But there is little sense in getting caught up in names since the technical terms are much too diverse. The weak-minded will suppose that there are disparities in the meanings; those with feeble intellects are prone to seek meanings in words alone. What is required is in fact just the opposite.

The heart is distinguished from the other bodily organs because it possesses an attribute which perceives meanings that are neither fanciful nor sensory; for example, its ability to comprehend the world's creation or its need for a Creator who is eternal, provident in design, wise and, in fact, describable by the divine attributes. We shall call that faculty[A] "intellect" (*ʿaql*). We do this with the proviso that the term "intellect" not be understood as it is in the disciplines of debate and disputation; the term "intellect" is widespread in those fields and because of this certain Sufis have criticised its use. But with that exception in mind, "intellect", it may be said, is the trait that distinguishes a human being from the beasts.[B] Through intellect man apprehends knowledge of God; hence, it is the most resplendent of traits and must not be disparaged.

This faculty was created so that by its use man might know the natures of things in their entirety. By its very nature the intellect demands knowledge; knowledge is its pleasure, just as the other faculties demand their particular pleasures. It is hardly a secret

[A] The term Ghazālī uses is "*gharīza*" which is normally translated as instinct.

[B] Here Ghazālī avails himself of the ancient notion of man as the "rational animal" (*ḥayawān nāṭiq*), going back to Aristotle and much invoked by the Muslim philosophers; cf., for example, Abū Zakarīyā al-Rāzī (d.ca. 313/925): "Reason is the most magnificent of God's favours to us, and it is the most useful and advantageous of objects for us. Through reason we gain precedence over speechless beasts so that we may own them, manage them, subdue them and dispose of them...In sum, reason is something without which our state would be the state of beasts, of unreasoning infants, and of the insane" (in *Rasā'il falsafīya*, ed. Kraus; Cairo, 1939, 17-18).

that there is pleasure in knowledge. This is true to such an extent that he who enjoys a connection with knowledge, however lowly its object, delights in it while he who stands allied with ignorance, however paltry the matter, suffers distress of mind. This tendency is so pronounced that man can rarely restrain himself from some challenge to his knowledge and from bragging about it even in trivial matters. For example, knowing how to play chess, despite its utter insignificance, means that a man cannot keep his mouth shut about it or refrain from offering instruction in it until he unlooses his tongue to display everything he may know about chess. This happens because there is an exuberance of pleasure in knowledge and because man feels that his nature is somehow perfected thereby.

Knowledge is one of the most specific of the attributes of lordliness (*ṣifāt al-rubūbīya*) since it betokens the utmost perfection. A man feels gratified whenever he is commended for acuity and abundance of learning; upon hearing such commendation he feels that his nature as well as his knowledge has been perfected. At this he experiences a sense of self-admiration and he takes pleasure in that as well.

It follows that pleasure in knowledge of farming or of tailoring is not comparable with the knowledge of administration of a kingdom or of ordering the affairs of men. Nor is the pleasure to be found in knowledge of grammar and poetry comparable to the pleasure of knowledge of God, His attributes and His angels, along with [knowledge of] the kingdom of the heavens and of the earth. Quite the contrary: The pleasure of knowledge is in proportion to the nobility of that knowledge; the distinction of knowledge itself is in proportion to the distinction of the thing to be known. This is so true that he who has some knowledge about the inmost thoughts of people's minds and recounts it finds a pleasure in so doing whereas the very nature of an ignorant man spurs him to seek such knowledge out. To know the inner musings of the local governor and his administrative secrets in governing is far more pleasurable than any knowledge of the inner ruminations of a peasant or a weaver. Moreover, to gain information about the secrets of the vizier and of what he has resolved to do in his vizierate is more desirable as well as more pleasurable than any knowledge one might glean of some local governor's secrets. Still better, to become privy to the inmost cogitations of the king and sultan, who has been vouchsafed power over the vizier, is more excellent as well as more pleasurable than any awareness one might have of a mere vizier's secrets; a man's satisfaction in that knowledge together with his hot pursuit to unearth it are far more intense, just as his love for it is greater because the pleasure he takes in it is even more tremendous.[A]

From this it should be clear that the most pleasurable form of knowledge is the loftiest and that its loftiness is commensurate with that of the object to be known. If there should exist among knowable objects any that is most exalted, most perfect, loftiest and most immense, knowledge of that object will then be the most pleasurable form of knowledge—and that, necessarily—as well as the most illustrious and most excellent. Ah, would that I knew in all of existence any knowledge more majestic, more sublime, nobler, more perfect and more august than that of the Creator of all things, of Him Who perfected and embellished them, Who bestowed beginning upon them as well as recurrence, Who conferred order and rank upon them! Could any presence in sovereignty and perfection and beauty and splendour be conceived more stupendous than the presence of Lordship whose majesty no precepts encompass and the marvels of whose states the epithets of no wordsmiths contain?

If you do not doubt this then you must also not doubt that to become privy to the secrets of lordliness and to know the order

[A] This passage may reflect Ghazālī's own earlier experience when he enjoyed the close patronage of the powerful vizier Niẓām al-Mulk (assassinated 485/1092) and served as a liaison between the Abbasid caliph and the Seljuq Sultan, often shuttling between both courts; see my *Ghazali*, 5, 31, for further references.

of the divine decrees encompassing all existing things is the most sublime of all forms of knowledge, both mystical and profane, as well as the most pleasurable and excellent; it is the most desirable and the most apt of all the knowledge that souls can apprehend when they themselves assume the perfection and beauty by which it is characterised. It is also the worthiest knowledge through which gladness, joy and bliss may be augmented.

Clearly, then, knowledge is pleasurable and the most pleasurable knowledge is the knowledge of God, His attributes, His actions and His providential design in His realm from the highest limit of His throne to the farthest boundaries of both the worlds. Moreover, the pleasure of knowledge is stronger than other pleasures; stronger, that is, than the pleasures of appetite, anger, or the rest of the five senses. Pleasures after all are varied in type; such as the difference between the pleasure of sexual intercourse and that of listening, or between the pleasure of knowledge as opposed to that of governing. These differ also by being weak or strong, such as the distinction between the pleasure of lust in someone aroused for intercourse and the pleasure of one listless from satiety of appetite. Or it is like the difference between the pleasure of gazing on a lovely face of surpassing beauty and that of looking upon a face inferior to it in loveliness.

You come to know the most dominant of pleasures because it is preferred over others. He who chooses gazing on a lovely form and enjoying the sight of it over inhaling sweet perfumes knows that that is more pleasurable in his own eyes than sweet perfumes. So, too, when food is brought at mealtime and yet, the chess player continues to play and forgoes eating—by this one may know that for him the pleasure of victory in chess is stronger than the pleasure of eating.

This then is a truthful measure for discovering the preponderance of pleasures. Now, however, let us step back a bit and recapitulate. Pleasures are divisible into: *Outer*, for example, the pleasures of the five senses; and *Inner*, for example, the pleasure of ruling or of winning or of magnanimous acts or of knowledge, and so forth, since such pleasure does not accrue to eye or nose or ear or touch or taste.

In those endowed with perfection the inner senses are dominant over mere outer pleasures. If a man were to choose between the pleasure of a plump chicken and an almond pastry,[A] on the one side, and the pleasure of ruling and conquering enemies and attainment of some degree of political mastery, on the other, and he were a man of coarse aspirations, dead of heart and ruled by bestial tendencies, he would choose the meat and the pastry; however, if he possessed lofty aspirations and a perfected intelligence, he would choose governing, and hunger, even if endured for many days, would seem a trifle. His choice shows that he considers governing more pleasurable than good food. Indeed, he who has not cultivated his inner senses is defective, like a young boy or someone whose inner strengths have been exhausted, an imbecile; for such as these to choose the pleasure of food over that of governance is far from improbable.

Now just as the pleasure of governance and of noble deeds is dominant over him who has passed beyond the defects of boyhood, as of idiocy; so, too, the pleasure of the knowledge of God and awareness of the beauty of the presence of lordliness and of gazing upon the mysteries of divine ordainments is a pleasure more intense than governance, itself the highest of pleasures prevailing over creatures. The utmost expression of it that may be uttered is that *souls do not know what delights have been concealed for them.*[2] Indeed, "He has laid up for them that which no eye has seen and no ear heard and which has not penetrated any human heart."[3]

He alone knows this who has tasted both pleasures. Without doubt he will choose retirement and solitude, thought and recitation, and will dive into the seas of mystic knowledge and abandon governance. He will despise those whom he governed because he

[A] The almond pastry is *lawzīnaj*, made with almond oil and similar to *qaṭā'if*; cf. Dozy, II.565.

knows the nullity[A] of his own governance, as of those over whom he once governed, and because he knows too that he has been tainted thereby with turbid impurities from which he cannot conceivably be free. He knows that he is liable to be cut off by death which comes inescapably even when *the earth takes on its embellishments or is adorned, and although its inhabitants imagine that they are powerful over it.*[4] By comparison, knowledge of God and cognizance of His attributes and acts and of the order of His rule from the steepest heights to the lowest depths are pure of rivalry and of all impurities; to those who arrive, one after another, knowledge is spacious; because of its abundance no one is cramped. The breadth of the knowledge of God is only comparable with the heavens and the earth; it leads the gaze beyond all measurable quantities, for its extent is infinite. The gnostic ceaselessly acquires such knowledge in paradise, the breadth of which is that of the heavens and the earth; in those gardens he revels and picks their fruit, he sips from their cisterns. He is safe from any cessation since the fruits of this garden are neither finite nor forbidden. This pleasure is everlasting, death does not sever it, since death does not destroy the substrate[B] of knowledge of God. Its locus is the spirit which is a divine and heavenly thing; death alters only its circumstances and cuts off its activities and impediments. Death frees it from its captivity but as for annihilating it? Certainly not! *Never think that those who were slain in the cause of God are dead. They are alive, and well provided for by their Lord; pleased with His gifts and rejoicing for those they left behind, who have not yet joined them.*[5]

Do not imagine that this refers exclusively to those killed on the battlefield; with every breath the gnostic gains the rank of a thousand martyrs. In Sacred Tradition it is reported that, "A

[A] Arabic *fanā'*, a Sufi technical term meaning "annihilation of self", here used in the sense of "emptiness" or "transience".

[B] Ghazālī employs the theological term *maḥall* or "substrate", i.e., that underlying essence in which an "accident", e.g., whiteness or tallness or the like, resides.

martyr in the hereafter longs to be returned to this world so that he may be killed all over again because of the magnitude of the reward for martyrdom which he beholds."[6] "The martyrs yearn to be religious scholars when they behold the high rank which they see these latter receive."[7]

All the regions of the kingdom of the heavens and earth are the gnostic's arena which he occupies whenever he wishes without any need for bodily movement. Through his knowledge of the beauty of the realm he finds himself *in a garden the breadth of which is the heavens and the earth.*[8] Every gnostic possesses this without any crowding of one upon another. True, they differ in the scope of their exaltation to the measure in which the vastness of their speculative ability and the scope of their mystical knowledge may differ. They constitute ranks in God's presence though the difference in their ranks is beyond all enumeration.

Clearly, then, the pleasure of governance, which is inner, is more powerful in the peaks of its perfection than all the pleasures of sense; clearly, too, this pleasure does not accrue to the beast, the child, or the imbecile. And yet, knowledge of God, His attributes and actions, together with the realm of His heavens and the mysteries of His rule, offers a pleasure greater than that of governance; he who has attained, and tasted, a certain degree of knowledge knows this. Of somebody who has no heart this cannot be affirmed since the heart is the seat of this power. To assert to young boys that the pleasures of sexual intercourse are superior to those of playing with a polo stick is impossible, just as it is to assert to the impotent that sexual pleasure is superior to the pleasure of sniffing violets; the impotent man has lost the ability by which he could perceive this pleasure. But he who is unimpaired by impotence and who possesses an intact sense of smell perceives the difference between the two pleasures. On this there remains nothing but to say: He who has tasted knows.[A]

[A] Arabic: *man dhāqa ʿarafa*. For the importance of "taste", or direct unmediated experience, in Ghazālī's later thought, see *Munqidh* (ed. Jabre), esp. 41-45;

Even if seekers after knowledge do not concern themselves with pursuit of the knowledge of divine things, they may still catch a scent of this pleasure through disclosure of the difficulties, and solution of the perplexities, in their own endeavours, which their zealous pursuit intensifies. For these pursuits too are sciences and bodies of knowledge, even if their objects be not as noble as the objects of divine knowledge. But he who lingers in thought on knowledge of God—he to whom the mysteries of God's realm may be revealed, however slightly—discovers within his own mind a bliss in which he exults and an astonishment at himself and his own existence as well as at the potential vastness of his own capacity for joy and bliss. Only through taste can this be grasped. To treat the matter of taste anecdotally would be of little use. Still, even this measure should alert you to the fact that knowledge of God is the most pleasurable of all things and that there is no pleasure superior to it.

Abū Sulaymān al-Dārānī said, "God possesses servants whom neither their dread of hell nor their hope of paradise distracts from Him; how then could this world distract them from God?"[9] In this vein too one of the brothers of Maᶜrūf al-Karkhī said to him, "Tell me, O Abū Maḥfūẓ, what stirred you to serve God and to sever your bonds with creatures?" Maᶜrūf remained silent. The brother then asked, "Was it remembrance of death?" Maᶜrūf said, "What is death?" The brother asked further, "Was it remembrance of the tomb and of the *barzakh*?"[A] Maᶜrūf replied, "What are the tomb and the *barzakh*?" The brother asked then, "Was it dread of hell and hope of heaven?" But he answered then, "What is all that?

for a discussion, see my "The Taste of Truth: The Literary Structure of the *Munqidh min al-ḍalāl* of al-Ghazālī" in *Islamic Studies presented to Charles J. Adams* (Leiden, 1991), 129-148.

[A] *Barzakh*, a word derived from Persian, denotes the intermediate realm, a kind of limbo, in which the dead await resurrection at the Last Judgement. Cf. *EI*², 1.1071; for a discussion, see Ragnar Eklund, *Life between Death and Resurrection according to Islam* (Uppsala 1941), 85 & 147ff., and my article "Purgatory (Islamic)," in *Dictionary of the Middle Ages*, ed. J. Strayer, x.214-215.

There is a King who holds everything in His hand. If you love Him, then He causes you to forget all else, and when there is a relationship between Him and you, He replaces all of that for you."

About Jesus it has been reported that he said, "When I see a rich man occupied with seeking for God, I strive to make him renounce everything but Him."[10]

One of the masters saw Bishr al-Ḥāfī in a dream and said, "What are Abū Naṣr al-Tammār and ᶜAbd al-Wahhāb al-Warrāq doing?" Bishr replied, "I left them both an hour ago eating and drinking in God's presence." I said, "And what about you?" Bishr answered, "God knows how little I crave food and drink and so He granted to me to gaze upon Him instead."

It was reported of ᶜAlī ibn al-Muwaffaq that he said, "I saw in dream as though I had entered paradise. There I beheld a man seated at a table. Two angels, on his right hand and on his left, were popping little titbits into his mouth from all sorts of luscious delicacies while he feasted. Then I saw another man standing at heaven's door; he was scrutinising people's faces. One he admitted, another he sent away. Then I passed beyond both of them into an awesome sanctuary of heaven and in the pavilion of the Throne I saw a man who was gazing fixedly and without blinking in contemplation of God. So I asked Riḍwān,[A] 'Who is this?' And he replied, 'This is Maᶜrūf al-Karkhī who worships God neither out of fear of His hellfire nor out of longing for His garden but rather, out of love for Him. Therefore, God permits him to gaze upon Him until the Day of Resurrection.' He mentioned that the first two men were Bishr ibn al-Ḥārith and Aḥmad ibn Ḥanbal."[11]

For this reason Abū Sulaymān al-Dārānī said, "He who is occupied with himself today will be occupied with himself tomorrow as well, whereas he who is occupied with his Lord today will be occupied with his Lord tomorrow."[12]

Sufyān al-Thawrī said to Rābiᶜa, "What is the inner truth of your faith?" She replied, "I do not serve God out of fear of His

[A] Riḍwān is the angel in charge of Paradise.

fire nor out of love of His garden, for then I would be like a bad worker who works only when he is afraid. Quite the opposite, I serve Him out of love and longing for Him." She recited a poem on the meaning of love:

I love You with a double love: a love that is sheer passion
and a love that is only because You are worthy of love.
As for the love that is passion, it is my immersion
in remembering You and in forgetting what is not You.
As for that love of which You are worthy,
it is Your lifting the veil so that I see You.
I deserve no praise for one love or the other
but You merit praise for them both.[13]

Perhaps by "love of passion"[14] she means love of God because of His goodness to her, as well as for His bestowal upon her of the bounties of this life; while by the "love because He merits it", she means love for His beauty and majesty which have been revealed to her. This is the superior, and the mightier, of the two loves.

The pleasure of looking upon the beauty of lordliness is that which the Messenger of God (may God bless him and grant him peace) expressed when he said while speaking about his Lord, "I have amassed for My righteous servants that which eye has not seen, ear has not heard, nor the mind of man conceived."[15] Certain of these pleasures may be bestowed in advance in this world to someone whose purity of heart has reached the farthest limit. This is the reason why one of the gnostics remarked, "I do not find God's presence so I say 'O Lord!' or 'O God!' and I find that weightier upon my mind than mountains because one calls from behind some barrier; and yet, did you ever see anyone shouting to a companion seated with him?"[A] Another said, "Whenever a man

[A] According to Zabīdī, "A call is made only to someone who is not present. But who is the one whom his seated companion might call out to?" He notes that in a Sacred Tradition, God calls Himself the seated companion of Moses: "O Mūsā, I am the seated companion of him who remembers Me (*anā jalīs man*

reaches the limit in this knowledge, people cast stones at him;" that is, his discourse goes beyond the limit of their comprehension and so they consider what he says a transgression or a blasphemy.[A]

The sole and ultimate object of all gnostics is to arrive at an encounter with God, for it is the delight of their hearts since *no soul knows what delights have been stored up for them.*[16] When these delights appear, cares will be wiped away together with all desires; the mind will be immersed so utterly in felicity that were the blessed to be cast into fire, they would not feel it in their ecstasy. Were all the pleasures of this world to be spread out for them at that moment, they would not spare them a glance because they possess consummate bliss and that utmost joy which is limitless.

I wish I knew how a person who grasps only the love of sense objects might come to understand the pleasure of gazing upon His face—He who has neither shape nor form—and I wish I knew what significance lies in God's promise to bestow such pleasure upon His servants, pleasure which He Himself calls the supreme felicity! Whoever knows God knows also that the fragmentary pleasures attached to all the various appetites are subsumed under this supreme pleasure. As one of God's lovers has remarked:

My heart had scattered affections
but I have fused my passions into one
since my eye has beheld You.
He whom I used to envy now envies me
and I have become master of men since I mastered myself.
To others I abandon both world and belief
for I am rapt in remembrance of You,
my only world and my belief![B]

dhakaranī)." *Itḥāf* IX.578, l.7ff. The point is that for those who love God, He is too near to be called or shouted to.

[A] Probably a veiled allusion to Ḥallāj.

[B] Verses possibly by Ḥallāj; cf. L. Massignon, *Le Dīwān d'al-Hallāj*, 37, and *Dīwān al-Ḥallāj*, ed. Kāmil Muṣṭafā al-Shaybī, 67.

And another said:

Separation from Him is more terrible than His fire;
attaining Him is sweeter than His paradise.

By this they mean to express a preference for the heart's pleasure in knowing God over the pleasures of food, drink and sex. Paradise is the source of the pleasures of the senses but the heart takes its pleasure in the encounter with God alone.

We have already mentioned one example of the way in which people differ in their pleasures. In his earliest impulses and judgment, a boy displays an instinct for pleasure in games and play. In his opinion these are more enjoyable than other things. Later, he takes pleasure in dressing and in wearing finery and in riding horses; at that stage, he is contemptuous of the pleasures of play to which he had once been so inclined and had loved. Still later he begins to manifest the beginnings of a pleasure in sex and an appetite for women; now he forsakes all that came before for the sole pleasure of attaining women. Afterwards appear the pleasures of command and high status and acquisitiveness.[A] These are the final pleasures of this world as well as the highest and the most compelling. As God says, *the life of this world is nothing but game and show and frippery and swaggering rivalry among yourselves...*[17]

After these, other instincts manifest themselves through which he may grasp the pleasure of knowing God and His acts. At this point he starts to feel scorn for all that came before since that which comes later is stronger. This is the ultimate pleasure since the love of play appears with the onset of judgment; a love of women and of apparel at the onset of the age of majority; a love of directing affairs after the age of twenty; and a love of knowledge around the age of forty. This is the final stage. Just as a boy makes fun of someone who gives up games to busy himself with

[A] "Acquisitiveness" or more literally, "increase" (*takāthur*), is explained by Zabīdī as denoting the "increase of goods and of children" (*al-amwāl wa'l-awlād*), *Itḥāf* IX. 579, line 4.

dallying with women or to pursue active public life, so too do leaders laugh at someone who forsakes ruling to concern himself with knowledge of God. The gnostics say, "If you sneer at us, so shall we jeer at you, as in *you scoff but you shall know*."[18]

CHAPTER FIVE

An Exposition of Why the Beatific Vision in the World to Come Surpasses Knowledge in this World

KNOW THAT SENSE perceptions are divisible into that which pertains to the imagination, such as imagined forms, bodies of various colours, and the shapes of individual animals and plants; and into that which does not pertain to imagination, such as God's nature and all that is incorporeal, such as knowledge, power, will, and the like. Whenever one looks at another person and then shuts his eyes, he discovers that person's form present in his imagination as though he were looking at him. But if he opens his eyes and looks again, he perceives a difference between the [image and the person]. This difference is not attributable to some disparity between the two forms: the form seen is congruous with the form imagined. The difference resides solely in enhanced distinctness (*wuḍūḥ*) and disclosure (*kashf*); the form seen is more consummately disclosed and made distinct. This is like seeing a person at dusk before the diffusion of daylight and then seeing him in full light: the only difference between the two circumstances is an increase in visibility. Hence, whenever imagination is prior in perception, sight perfects and completes the imagination's perception. This is the most complete disclosure and for that very reason is called "vision", not because it is located in the eye. Quite the opposite, in fact: Had God created this perception of total disclosure in the forehead or chest, for example, it would still deserve to be called "sight" (*ru'ya*).[A]

[A] For this line of counterfactual reasoning, which goes back to Galen and

Chapter Five

Since you now understand this about objects of imagination, know also that objects of knowledge unendowed with form may be present in the imagination because it knows and apprehends them in two stages. One of the stages is preliminary while the other is perfective; again, the difference between them is one of greater disclosure and distinctness, as in the case of the imagined and the seen. The second stage, in comparison to the first, is termed "direct witness" (*mushāhada*) and "encounter" (*liqā'*) and "sight" (*ru'ya*). Such a designation is apt: seeing is called seeing because it represents the utmost disclosure. Just as God's "custom" entails that shutting the eyes prevents complete disclosure by sight and that the barrier between seeing and seen be removed for vision to occur—for so long as it is not removed, perception of the actual remains mere fantasising—so, too, God's custom requires that the soul, while hindered by bodily accidents (and as long as the urgings of the appetites, with all their human tendencies, have not been mastered), for so long will the soul not attain the visionary encounter of those knowable objects that lie beyond mere fancy.[A] On the contrary, our present life itself obstructs vision and necessarily so, just as the eyelids veil the vision of the eyes.

Even so, a disquisition on life as hindrance would be lengthy; nor is it really pertinent to this aspect of knowledge. This is why God said to Moses, *You will never see Me.*[1] And He said, *Eyes will not see Him*[2] in this world. Certainly, it is true that the Messenger of God (may God bless him and grant him peace) did not see God on his night journey.[B]

his *De usu partium*, see *Theodicy*, 48ff. For further examples, see pseudo-Ghazālī, *al-Ḥikma fī makhlūqāt Allāh* (Cairo, 1352/1934).

[A] For God's "custom" (*ʿādat Allāh*), see Ghazālī's *Tahāfut al-falāsifah*, ed./tr. Marmura, esp. 170ff.; also, the discussion in my *Ghazali*, 77-86. The notion as adopted by Ashʿarite theology held that all secondary causality is in reality merely God's "custom" or "habit" in governing the world and could be otherwise at any instant.

[B] This refers to the *miʿrāj* of the Prophet; see Q. xvii.1: *Glory be to Him who made His servant go by night from the Sacred Temple to the farther Temple whose*

But when the veil is lifted by death, the soul remains spotted by the muddy flecks of this world nor is it wholly free of them even when separated. Indeed, there are souls upon which filth and rust have accumulated like a mirror whose surface has been marred by a stubborn incrustation of smut. Such souls remain insusceptible to scouring and polishing; they have been veiled from their Lord forever.[A] We seek refuge with God from that! Others have not yet reached the terminal stage of rust and dirt and cannot avoid purification and polishing. Such a soul is consigned to the Fire that consumes the filth that dirties it; exposure to the Fire is proportional to that soul's need for purification. The least span is a fleeting moment; for a believer, the longest span is seven thousand years, according to Sacred Tradition.

No soul can journey from this world without some dust and muddiness, however slight, accompanying it. That is why God says, *There is not one of you who shall not pass through it: such is the absolute decree of your Lord. We will deliver those who fear Us, but the wrongdoers shall be left there on their knees.*[3] Every soul may be sure of coming to the Fire though it will not remain sure of emerging from it. When God has finished cleaning and purifying the soul and when what has been foreordained has reached its term[4] and when all that Revelation has promised—full accounting (*ḥisāb*), presentation (*ʿarḍ*), and the like—has been brought to conclusion, and one is at the point of being worthy of paradise—and that, to be sure, is an obscure moment of which God has notified none of His creatures; it will come to pass after the resurrection, though the moment of resurrection itself is yet unknown—at that point, a man will be intent on his spiritual cleanliness and purity from blemishes until not even a speck of dust darkens his countenance.

surroundings We have blessed, that We might show him some of Our signs. See also *EI*[2] VII.97ff.

[A] See Q. LXXXIII.15: *on that Day they* [the unbelievers] *shall be those veiled from their Lord.*

This is because God (Great and Glorious is He!) will manifest[A] Himself within him to such an extent that the revelation of this Self-manifestation will stand in relation to what he now knows like the clarity which a mirror reveals in comparison to the merely imagined.

This eye-witnessing (*mushāhada*), this manifestation (*tajallī*), are what is termed "vision" (*ru'ya*). Vision therefore is genuine; with the proviso, however, that this is not to be understood as the imagination's habit of completing some imaginary entity represented in the mind and specified as to direction and position in space. The Lord of Lords is utterly transcendent and exalted above that. And actually, the opposite is true: Just as you know God in this world with a knowledge both real and entire, without either fantasy or mental representation or surmise of form and shape, so too will you behold Him in the world to come. I can even claim that the knowledge here available, in this world, in its very essence needs to be perfected, brought to consummate clarity and transformed into direct seeing. There is no difference between direct seeing in the next world and that which can be known here, except in a magnification of disclosure and lucidity, as we expressed earlier by analogy with the perfection of imagination through sight itself. In knowledge of God, there is no assertion of form and mode. Likewise, in the completion of that knowledge by direct seeing and by ascension into the utmost clarity of disclosure is there neither form nor mode; that [perfected seeing] differs in essence only in magnitude. In the same way, visible form remains imaginable to the eye; the actual seeing differs only in intensity of disclosure. God (He is exalted) refers to this when He says, *Their light will shine in front of them and on their right, and they will say: "Lord, perfect our light for us..."*[5]

[A] Ghazālī uses the term *tajallin* to denote God's self-manifestation in creation; the term will be picked up and developed intensively by Ibn al-ʿArabī over a century later. See William C. Chittick, *The Self-Disclosure of God* (Albany, 1998), esp. 47ff.

Accordingly, only those who are gnostics in *this* world will succeed in attaining the level of contemplative vision; for knowledge is the light which in the next world will be converted to direct apprehension, just as the pit of a fruit is converted into a tree and the seed into a crop. How can somebody who lacks fruit-pits get fruit from his land? And how can he who does not sow seed reap a crop? So, too, how can he who does not know God in this world see Him in the next? Knowledge exists at disparate levels; so, too, does illumination. Disparity in illumination stands in correlation to disparity in knowledge. In the same way, plants differ in relation to the difference of their seeds; they are necessarily various in abundance or scarcity, excellence or strength, and in their weakness too.

This is why the Prophet (may God bless him and grant him peace) said, "God revealed Himself to people at large but to Abū Bakr specifically."[6] It must not be supposed that anyone other, anyone lesser than, Abū Bakr discovered in contemplation and in vision what Abū Bakr discovered. On the contrary, he shall find no more than a tenth of a hundredth part thereof in so far as his knowledge in this world is a tenth of a hundredth. But since Abū Bakr excelled other people through the mystery hidden within his heart, his superiority remained necessarily in his breast in a form of illumination in which he stood alone. And just as in this world you see someone prefer the pleasures of ruling over those of eating and having sex, and you see someone else prefer the pleasures of knowledge and understanding of the kingdom of the heavens and the earth, together with other divine matters, over that of ruling, as well as over those of food and sex; so, too, in the world to come are there people who prefer the pleasure of gazing on the face of God over the bliss of paradise itself, the bliss of which is tantamount to that of eating and drinking. These people are in their very natures those whose circumstances in this world are as we have already described them; namely, they prefer knowledge and study of the divine mysteries over the pleasures of sex and food and drink whereas others are wrapped up in these. Thus, when it was said to Rābiᶜa, "What do you say about paradise?" she replied, "The neighbour, then the home."[A] She went on to explain that within her heart there was no concern for the Garden but rather, for the Lord of the Garden. No one who does not know God in this world will see Him in the next. No one who does not find pleasure in knowledge in this world will find pleasure in gazing [on God] in the next world; in the next world no one is granted renewed familiarity with that with which he has not been conversant in this world. No one shall harvest but what he has sown. No man shall be raised up except in that condition in which he died, and no man will die except in accord with how he has lived. The knowledge that will accompany him will be that in which he delighted solely for its own sake and yet, it will be transformed into actual seeing by the lifting of the veil so that his pleasure in it will be redoubled, just as the lover's delight redoubles when his beloved's form, as he imagines it, gives way to an actual glimpse of that form; indeed, that is his utmost delight. The goodness of paradise resides solely in the fact that each possesses what he most desires. Whoever desires nothing beyond the encounter with God (Exalted is He) takes pleasure in nothing but this; he may even suffer in other pleasures. Since the bliss of paradise lies in proportion to one's love of God, and the love of God is in proportion to one's knowledge of Him, the very basis of all felicity, therefore, is that knowledge which Revelation enunciates as belief.

Of course, you may object, "If the pleasure of sight stands in some relation to that of knowledge, why this is a paltry thing, even if doubled, since the pleasure of knowledge in this world is feeble; even doubling it to the nearest limit would not enable it

[A] Zabīdī (*Itḥāf* IX.582, line 26) gives variants on this saying (*al-jār thumma al-dār*), variously attributed, e.g., "The companion before the road," or "The provision before the journey," etc. Rābiᶜa's dictum means that it is the presence of God ("the neighbour") that is to be sought rather than paradise as such. The proverb is still current; see E. Westermarck, *Wit and Wisdom in Morocco* (London, 1930), p. 104 (no. 271): "Choose the neighbour before the house, and the companion before the road."

to become so strong that one could consider the other pleasures of paradise contemptible." But know that such slighting of the pleasure of knowledge occurs among people without knowledge. How could somebody without knowledge grasp its pleasure? How can a man scarcely concerned with knowledge, and whose mind is burdened by worldly attachments, grasp its pleasure?

In their knowledge, cogitations and intimate colloquies with God (Exalted is He), the gnostics possess pleasures such that if paradise were to be spread out before them in this world, they would not exchange these pleasures for those of the whole of heaven. In its consummate perfection this pleasure is utterly incommensurate with the pleasures of encounter and vision, just as there is no real comparison between the pleasures of imagining the beloved and of actually seeing her. Likewise, the delight of sniffing the odours of delicious foods is incommensurate with actually tasting them; so, too, the pleasure in the touch of a hand is not commensurate with the bliss of sexual union.

A demonstration of the huge disparity between them is possible only by means of analogy. Hence we could argue that in this world the joy of looking on the beloved's face falls under several headings. First comes the perfection, or lack thereof, in the beloved's beauty, for pleasure necessarily consists in gazing upon the most beautiful and the most perfect. Second is the force of love and desire and passion; for the delight of one whose erotic desire is most intense is dissimilar to the delight of one whose passion and love are weak. Third comes the perfection of perception. The pleasure someone takes in looking at the beloved in darkness or behind a fine veil or from far away, is incomparable to the pleasure of him who perceives up close, without a veil, and in the full splendour of the light. The sensation of pleasure in sexual intercourse with a woman who is clothed is not at all equal to the sensation with one unencumbered by a garment. Fourth comes the profusion of obstacles to the one yearned for, together with heart-consuming agonies. The delightedness of a healthy and relaxed man deprived of gazing upon his beloved is not comparable to the delightedness of an anxious and fearful man, or of a sick and suffering man whose mind is absorbed in grave and weighty concerns. Now take the measure of a lover of diminished passion who peers upon his beloved's face from behind a veil and at such a distance that her true appearance stands unrevealed. Imagine him next in a situation in which scorpions and hornets swarm together to afflict and sting him and distract his mind; even in this state he is not devoid of some pleasure, namely, that of seeing his beloved with his own eyes. Suppose now that suddenly still another circumstance erupts: her veil is ripped asunder, effulgence blazes upon her and all his torments are swept away until he grows blissfully tranquil while mighty desire and exuberant love simultaneously pounce upon him to the full. Consider how his pleasure would be redoubled; no measurable proportion would remain between his first state and his last. Now understand the analogy to the pleasure of knowledge. The thin veil is a likeness of the body and man's immersion within it. The hornets and scorpions represent analogues of the passions that overmaster him, such as hunger, thirst, anger, grief and melancholy. Diminished passion and love are a likeness of the soul's insufficiency in this world and the defectiveness of its yearning for *those on high*[7] while turning its gaze towards the *lowest of the low*.[8] In the same way, a boy is unable to consider the pleasure of ruling as his glance keeps turning towards play with a sparrow.

Even if the gnostic's knowledge in this world is firm, still he may not be spared such troubling confusions; and in fact, he cannot conceivably be entirely free of them. Of course, in certain circumstances these hindrances may lessen and abate; out of the loveliness of his knowledge, assuredly something will emerge to astonish his intellect and intensify his pleasure so that his mind may be cleft asunder by its sublime might. But even that is like the dazzle of lightning that rarely lasts.[A] Instead, distractions, stray

[A] For another use of this simile (which may owe something to Q.II.20), see Maimonides, *Guide of the Perplexed*, tr. S. Pines (Chicago, 1963), I. 7: "We are like

thoughts and notions will arise to perplex and ruffle him; this is a continual inevitability in our mortal life. Our pleasures undergo incessant disturbance until we die; life whole and good comes to us only after we die. The only authentic life is in the hereafter: *It is the life to come that is the true life, if they but knew it.*[9]

Whoever attains this level loves the encounter with God. He loves death and does not avoid it, except in so far as he hopes to keep on perfecting his knowledge. Knowledge is like a seed while the ocean of knowledge is without a shore; to encompass the quintessence of God's majesty is impossible. Whenever knowledge of God, His attributes and acts, and the mysteries of His dominion, increases and grows strong, felicity in the hereafter increases as well and it too becomes mighty; even so, when the seed is excellent and copious, the crop is abundant. And yet, it is not possible to obtain this seed except here in this world, nor is there any sowing except on the elevated slopes of the heart, though the harvest be only in the world to come. This is why the Messenger of God (may God bless him and grant him peace) said, "The best happiness is a long life in service to God."[10] Knowledge is perfected and broadened only in a long life through perseverance in thought, assiduity in mental effort, aloofness from the impediments of this world, and fierce concentration on the quest; but this, of necessity, demands time. He who loves death loves it because he sees himself firmly fixed in knowledge and in possession of the furthest point prepared for him. He who dislikes death dislikes it because he is always hoping for some further increase in knowledge that will come to him through longer life; he sees himself as cut off from what he could attain, and which escapes him, unless he could have lived longer. This is the reason for the dislike—as well as for the love—of death among the learned.

someone in a very dark night over whom lightning flashes time and time again." According to S. Pines, Maimonides took the image from Ibn Sīnā's late work *al-Ishārāt wa'l-tanbīhāt*; cf. Abrahamov, *Divine Love*, 160, n.90. Maimonides published the *Guide* in Judaeo-Arabic in Cairo in 586/1190, some 80 years after Ghazālī's death; it is well known that Maimonides had read Ghazālī.

By contrast, ordinary people consider death merely a curtailment of their worldly appetites; if these could be extended, they would love to live on but when these appetites are restricted, they long for death. All of this is deprivation and loss at whose root lie ignorance and heedlessness. Ignorance and heedlessness are the sources of all misery; knowledge and awareness are the bases of all felicity.

You already know the meaning of love and of passion through what we have mentioned earlier.[A] Indeed, the latter is a strong over-brimming love. You also know the meaning of pleasure in knowledge, as well as the meaning of vision, and of pleasure in vision, which is, as you now know, the most pleasurable of all things to those endowed with intelligence and self-mastery. It may not be so for those who are lacking in understanding, just as governing is not more pleasurable than eating in the opinion of teenagers.

Still, you might inquire whether the locus of this vision in the hereafter is the heart or the eye. People have different opinions on this subject; however, the masters of inner perception pay no attention to this divergence of views nor do they even consider it. Quite the opposite: the man of intellect eats greens and does not inquire as to the plant from whence they sprang.[B] Whoever craves a glimpse of someone whom he ardently desires is so engrossed by ardour that he does not stop to consider whether the emotion takes shape within his eye or his forehead. Rather, he strives to see and to pleasure in seeing, whether that occurs in his eye or in some other organ. To be sure, the eye is the locus and the receptacle; [yet in itself] it possesses neither reflection nor discernment. The truth is that the everlasting power is immensely broad; and should not be judged by any deficiency of either [reflection or discernment]. This remains within the realm of admissibility, but as for

[A] Ghazālī here distinguishes between *maḥabba* (love) and ʿ*ishq* (passion).

[B] Zabīdī comments, "He takes a gift and does not ask about the giver." *Itḥāf* IX.585, line 10.

the actual state-of-affairs in the hereafter with regard to what is possible, well, this may be grasped only through hearing.[A]

The truth is that which has become manifest to the People of Tradition and Community[B] in the form of proof-texts from Revelation; namely, that this has been created in the eye so that the words "sight" and "contemplation" and the other words occurring in Revelation might apply to what is outwardly manifest therein, for to remove external meanings except under necessity is not permissible. But God is supremely knowing!

[A] By "hearing" (*samʿ*) he means "tradition".

[B] *Ahl al-sunna wa'l-jamāʿa*, the standard formula for mainstream Sunnī believers.

CHAPTER SIX

An Exposition of the Factors that Strengthen Love of God

KNOW THAT THE happiest people are those who are strongest in their love of God. The very significance of the hereafter is to abide eternally with God and enjoy the bliss of encountering Him. For a lover no greater felicity exists than to spend eternity with his Beloved after long yearning for Him, and to be able to gaze upon Him uninterruptedly for ever and ever without distraction or impediment, without either chaperone or rival, as well as without any fear of cessation.[A] This bliss is in proportion to the force of the love: when love increases, pleasure increases too. A person may obtain God's love only in this world, and while he is still in it; a believer cannot be separated from the source of love because he is not separated from the source of knowledge.

As for the power of love and its dominion, reaching as far as the utter wantonness known as erotic passion,[B] that is something from which the many are sundered. Indeed, it comes to pass through only two things. The first of these is the severance of worldly ties and the expulsion from the heart of love for anything other than God. The heart is like a vessel which cannot accommodate vinegar so long as it has not been emptied of the water in

[A] The figures of the chaperone and the rival are commonplace in Arabic love poetry; cf., for example, Ibn Ḥazm, *Ṭawq al-ḥamāma*, tr. A. J. Arberry, *The Ring of the Dove* (London, 1953).

[B] Again, the term used is *ʿishq* as opposed to *ḥubb* used above.

it. *God did not make for man two hearts in his body.*[1] Love's perfection means that a man love God with his whole heart. As long as he turns to something other than God, a corner of his heart will be preoccupied with other than Him, and to the measure that he is diverted by other than God, will his love be lacking. Whatever measure of water remains in the container is the measure of the vinegar poured into it that will be missing. God alludes to this exclusivity and restrictiveness when He says, *Say 'God!' Then leave them to amuse themselves with foolish chatter*[2] and also when He says, *As for those who say: Our Lord is God, and take the right path to Him.*[3] This is what it means when you affirm: "There is no God but God." In other words, there is no one to worship (*maʿbūd*) and no one to love (*maḥbūb*) other than Him.

For every beloved is to be worshipped. The worshipper is the one who is bound, the beloved is the one to whom he is bound. Every lover is bound by what he loves. This is why God says, *Have you considered the man who has made a god of his own appetite?*[4] The Prophet (may God bless him and grant him peace!) said, "The most hateful god who is worshipped on earth is appetite.[A]"[5] He said (may God bless him and grant him peace), "Whoever says sincerely 'There is no God but God' enters paradise."[6] Sincerity means devotion to God with a pure heart in which there remains exclusively worship for God alone; for God and God alone has become the heart's beloved, the heart's worship and the goal of the heart's quest. For a person in this situation the world is a jail; it blocks him from seeing his beloved with his own eyes. Death betokens release from jail and an eternity with the beloved. What is the state of someone who has only one beloved, for whom he has long yearned and from whom he has long been barred, when all at once he finds himself sprung from prison, in unhindered access to the beloved and at blissful ease for all eternity!

[A] By "appetite" (*hawā*) is here meant the entire range of sensual passions but the term is sometimes used interchangeably with *ʿishq*; see Giffin, *Theory of Profane Love*, 95.

Chapter Six

One cause of a feeble love for God in human hearts is the strong love for this world, comprising love of family and possessions, children and relatives, property and livestock, orchards and gardens. Someone who delights in lovely bird songs and the fresh breeze of the morning is still attached to the pleasure that comes from loving the world and so his love for God has been weakened. To the degree in which he is on intimate terms with this world, to that degree does his intimacy with God grow less. Nothing is gained from this world without a corresponding loss in the world-to-come, and necessarily so: a man who approaches the east unavoidably distances himself from the west by the same degree. A man with two wives cannot gladden his first wife's heart without at the same time causing pain to his second; this world and the world to come are both wives of one man and are like east and west.[A] This awareness is plainer than eyesight to those with hearts.

The way to uproot this-worldly love from the heart is to set out on the path of renunciation (*zuhd*), to cleave fast to patient endurance (*ṣabr*) and to let oneself be led to both renunciation and endurance by the reins of fear (*khawf*) and hope (*rajā'*). What we have already stated with respect to repentance, endurance and renunciation, fear and hope, are prerequisites by which one may acquire one of the two fundamentals of love; namely, to empty the heart of all that is not God, the first step of which is to believe in God, the Last Day, the Garden and the Fire. Fear and hope then branch off and repentance and patience sprout from them. These lead to renunciation, here and now, of possessions, status, and all worldly fortunes. Through these stages one may then purify the

[A] The notion of an equilibrium of gain and loss between this world and the next occurs throughout Ghazālī's later works; cf. also *al-Qusṭās al-mustaqīm* (Beirut, 1959), 69; *Theodicy*, p. 64-65. He probably derived it from Makkī, III.40: "Loss in this world is gain in the hereafter; gain in this world is loss in the hereafter." Sulamī attributes it also to Abū Sulaymān al-Dārānī (71, line 2); there is an analogue in the New Testament parable of Dives and Lazarus (*Luke* 16:19-31).

heart from all that is not God; and then the heart widens until the knowledge and love of God descend into it. All these are preliminary to purification of the heart which is itself one of love's pillars. The Prophet (may God bless him and grant him peace) alludes to this when he says, "Purity is half of faith."[7] We mentioned this at the beginning of *The Book of Ritual Purity*.[A]

A second cause of powerful love is extensive knowledge of God which overmasters the heart. This comes after the heart has been purified from all worldly distractions and connections, and is analogous to the sowing of seed in the earth after it has been cleared of grass. This is the second half. From this seed the tree of love and knowledge is born. This is the good word with which God struck an analogy when He said, *Do you not see how God compares a good word to a good tree? Its root is firm and its branches are in the sky.*[8] Another allusion occurs in His words, *To Him the good word ascends*—and this is knowledge—*and the good deed exalted.*[9] Right action is, as it were, the bearer and the servant of this knowledge.[10]

Right action lies wholly and exclusively in purification of the heart; first of all, from this world and then, in continual purification. Action is willed only for the sake of mystic knowledge (*maʿrifa*). Knowing how to carry out the action is meant only for the sake of the action. Knowledge is at once the first and the last. To begin, there is knowledge of practical dealings and its purpose is to [know how to] act. The purpose of practical dealings [themselves] is to purify and cleanse the heart so that truth may become manifest within it and so that it may be adorned with the privileged knowledge of hidden things. Whenever this secret knowledge occurs, love follows necessarily upon it. Just so, when a man of well balanced temperament glimpses what is beautiful and perceives it with his external eye, he loves it and is drawn to him; when he loves it, pleasure ensues, for pleasure, of necessity, is consequent on love, while love, of necessity, is consequent

[A] See *Kitāb al-ṭahāra*, *Iḥyā'* (Beirut, 1996), I.150: *al-ṭuhūr niṣf al-imān*; and *Itḥāf*, II.303, line -3.

upon knowledge. Only he who has cut out of his heart the entanglements of this world can come to this knowledge through lucid cogitation, unceasing recollection, profound diligence in the quest, and continuous contemplation of God and His attributes together with the kingdom of His heavens and all His other creations.

Those who arrive at this stage may be divided into the strong (whose primary knowledge is of God: only later, and through Him, do they know others); and the weak (whose primary knowledge is of His acts: only then do they rise from there to the Agent).[A] God alludes to the former when He says, *Does it not suffice that your Lord is the witness of all things?*[11] Also when He says, *God bears witness that there is no God but Him.*[12] Hence the notion of one Sufi who when asked how he knew his Lord replied, "I know my Lord through my Lord; were it not for my Lord, I would not know my Lord."

God alludes to the second group when He says, *We will show them our signs in all the regions of the earth and in their own souls, until they clearly see that this is the truth.*[13] Also when He says, *Will they not contemplate the kingdom of the heavens and the earth?*[14] And again, when He says, *Consider what is in the heavens and the earth!*[15] He says as well, *Who created seven heavens, one above the other. You will see no flaw in the creation of the Merciful. Look then, can you see a single fissure? Cast your glance again and yet again: your glance will come back to you tired and weak.*[16] This way is easiest for most people as well as being the broadest for those who tread the mystic path. In the Qur'ān, there are numerous appeals to this in the commands to reflect, to think, to consider and to contemplate signs beyond measure.

You may object, "Both ways are problematic. Explain to us

[A] Zabīdī comments, "The strong never see anything without seeing God at the same time. Some of them even augment this; thus, one said, 'I never see anything without seeing God beforehand,' for among them are those who see things through Him; by contrast, the weak see things but see Him only by means of things." *Itḥāf*, IX.588, lines 2-3.

which of the two enables one, with God's help, to obtain knowledge and thereby come to love." Know that the highest way is by calling God as witness for all creation. This, however, is obscure; any discussion of it surpasses most people's comprehension. Therefore, there is no point in even bringing it up in books.

As to the lower and easier path, it is not wholly beyond the grasp of the understanding; people fail to comprehend it only by being averse to reflection or because of their involvement in worldly passions and their own fortunes. Nevertheless, we are precluded from discussing this by the sheer extent and abundance of the subject matter; its further ramifications are also beyond all measure. There is no speck of dust from the supernal heavens to the boundaries of both worlds that does not contain within itself prodigies of wondrous significance to indicate the perfection of God's omnipotence and wisdom and the farthest reach of His majesty and might.[A] These are infinite. *Indeed, if the oceans were ink for the words of my Lord, the ocean would dry up before my Lord's words could be exhausted.*[17] To plunge in is to be submerged in the currents of the sciences of illumination. It simply is not possible to skim over the surface of this by knowing practical dealings alone. Even so, to hint succinctly at a single instance, if only to prompt awareness of its nature, is possible. Thus we say that the simplest of the two paths is that of contemplation of God's deeds; let us speak then of these and set the higher path aside.

Many are the acts of God, but let us search out the least, the simplest and the tiniest of them and contemplate their wonders. Earth, with everything it contains, is the least of the creations. By "least", I mean in comparison to the angels and the heavenly realm when you peer into it with regard to volume and magnitude in its individual bodies. The sun, despite its apparently small mass, is some 160 times the size of the earth. Now consider the earth's littleness in comparison to the sun, then consider the sun's littleness in relation to the sphere in which it is established; the sun bears

[A] For a discussion of this topos, see my *Theodicy*, 38ff.

no comparison with that sphere, since it is in the fourth heaven which itself is small in relation to the seven heavens that surround it. But the seven heavens themselves are like a ring in a trackless desert in comparison to the Seat of God, and the Seat itself stands in the same relation in comparison to God's Throne.

This then is a peek at the outer aspect of individual entities with respect to their sizes. How contemptible is the whole earth in comparison to these! How small is land compared to the oceans! The Prophet (may God bless him and grant him peace) said, "The earth is to ocean as a stable is to earth."[18] Observation and experience corroborate this: it is well known that the portion of land not submerged by water is like a little island in relation to the entire earth.

Now turn your gaze towards man—created from the dust that is a portion of the earth—and towards the other animals and consider how tiny they all are in comparison to earth. Better yet, set all that aside. The smallest animals we know are gnats, ants and the like. Consider how small the gnat is.[A] Reflect with alert intellect and steady thought. Observe how God created the gnat in the shape of the elephant, the biggest of beasts: He created a trunk for it like the elephant's trunk, and He created other organs for it too, though on a smaller scale, such as He created for the elephant, with the addition of two wings. Consider how He apportioned its external organs and made its wings sprout; how He drew out its hand and its foot and opened up its hearing and sight. Inside the gnat He arranged organs of nutrition alongside instruments He did not provide for other animals. He compounded inside it particular nutritive, attractive, defensive, retentive, and digestive

[A] For the gnat see Q. II.26: *God does not disdain to give a parable about a gnat.* For an extended discussion of the gnat (*baʿūḍ*) as a repository of divine wisdom, see *Theodicy*, 45ff. For the common features of gnats and elephants, see Jāḥiẓ, *Kitāb al-ḥayawān* (ed. Hārūn), VII.169. There is a discussion in the *Rasāʾil* of the Ikhwān al-Ṣafāʾ, to which Ghazālī may be indebted; for a translation, see L. E. Goodman and R. McGregor, *The Case of the Animals versus Man Before the King of the Jinn* (London, 2009), 79.

faculties which He did not compound for other animals.

So much for the gnat's external form and features. Next consider its endowments, how God equipped it for its own proper nourishment, causing it to know that man's blood is its food. Consider then how He gave it a means of flight towards man; how He created a long pointed trunk for it; how He guided it to the pores of human skin where it could poke its trunk; how He gave it strength to stick its trunk inside and taught it to suck and swallow blood; how He created the trunk in hollowed delicacy so that the thin blood might flow inside it and then arrive at its belly and from there spread to its other organs and nourish them! How did He make it aware that man would aim his hand at it and instil stratagems of escape inside it, with equipment always at the ready? Thus for the gnat He created a sense of hearing by which it could perceive the faint movement of a hand, even when quite far, and leave off sucking and escape, only to return later, when the hand is again at rest.

Next consider how He created two pupils for the gnat so that it sees the places where it might feed and aim for them—and this, despite the tiny mass of its head. Observe that the pupil of every animal is small. Because it is so small the gnat's pupil cannot accommodate eyelids; but eyelids act as polishers of the looking glass of the pupils against motes and dust, and so God created pairs of hands for gnats and flies. If you watch a fly you will see it continually rubbing its pupils with both hands. For man and the larger animals He created eyelids such that one closes over the other while their corners are pointed so that dust clinging to the eye is collected and pushed to the tips of the lashes. He created black eyelashes to gather the brilliance of the eye and He appointed them specifically for sight as well as to beautify the form of the eye. The eye meshes the lashes together when dust is stirred up; then the eye peers out from behind the window-grid of the lashes whose interlacing blocks the dust from entering, but without hindering vision. For the gnat, however, He created two eyes that are kept polished without eyelids and He gave the gnat the know-how to burnish its eyes by using its hands. Because its sight is weak it swarms at the lamp; its vision is weak, so it searches for daylight. When the poor thing spots the glow of a lamp by night, it thinks it is in a darkened house and that the lamp is an opening in the dark house to an illumined spot. Thus, it ceaselessly seeks brightness and hurls itself at it; when it passes beyond and sees dark again, it thinks it has not found the opening and that it did not direct itself in the right way. So it keeps coming back until it is burned up in the flame.

Perhaps you imagine this happens because of the gnat's ignorance and shortcomings. If so, you should know that man's ignorance is still greater than the gnat's. Even more, the way humans bow down to worldly appetites whenever the glitter of the passions flashes, merely to lay bare their outer aspect, resembles the way moths swarm into a fire. Man does not realise that beneath these passions, despite their outward appearances, lies a steeped and lethal poison; even so, man flings himself unceasingly upon them until he is engulfed and bound by them and then is destroyed everlastingly. O would that man's ignorance were the ignorance of moths! Dazzled by outer brightness moths are burned but are purified in an instant whereas humans remain in the fire of hell for ever and ever, or at the very least for a long drawn out spell![A] This is why the Prophet (may God bless him and grant him peace) used to cry out saying, "I am holding you back from hellfire even though you swarm into it as moths swarm!"[19]

This is but a single wondrous gleam from all the marvels which God has made in the tiniest animals. There are such marvels within them that if the first and the last[B] were to work together to grasp the nature of a gnat, they would be incapable of understanding its essential reality. Nor would they learn even obvious matters from its external form. As for the hidden aspects, why,

[A] The question of whether punishment in hell was eternal or not was debated by Muslim theologians and there was no firm consensus.

[B] Meaning: all people from the beginning to the end of creation.

these inner meanings God alone can know. For all that, there are within every animal and plant marvels that distinguish it and in which no other animal shares.

Consider the bees and their prodigies, and how God inspired them to take their houses *in the mountains and in the trees and in the hives which men will build.*[20] Consider how He brought forth from their spittle wax and honey, one of which He made for illumination and the other for healing.[21] If you reflect upon the wonders of their activities in feeding on blossoms and flowers, their wariness of impurities and unclean things as well as their obedience to one of their number, their prince, who is the greatest among them, and how God made their prince subject to Him in justice and equity such that he kills any of them that fall into uncleanness at the very gate of the hive—if you consider all this, truly you will be astonished![A]

If you possess insight into your inmost self, if you are past caring for your gut and your sex, as well as your enmity for your rivals and partiality for your friends, then set that all aside and observe how the bees build their dwellings out of wax and how out of the totality of possible shapes they select the hexagonal. They do not construct a circular, a rectangular or a pentagonal house but rather, one with six sides; this, because of a feature specific to hexagonal form which even the geometer's mind cannot grasp. The most spacious and encompassing of forms is the circular and whatever resembles it; by contrast, the rectangular creates wasteful corners. Now the bee itself is rounded and elongated in shape and so it eschews the four-sided in order not to squander the corners which would remain empty. If, however, it were to construct its houses rounded in form, useless cavities would remain outside the dwelling; round forms joined together

[A] Like most ancient and mediaeval authors, Ghazālī seems unaware of the role of the queen bee in the hive; perhaps, in this instance too, following the *Rasā'il* of the Ikhwān al-Ṣāfa'; cf. *The Case of the Animals, op.cit.*, 232-237, 242-244.

do not merge in complete contiguity. But no form endowed with angularity comes close to the hexagonal in evenness. All of them press together when joined so that after the individual cells are connected, no opening remains that is not hexagonal, such is the peculiarity of this shape.

Consider then how God has inspired the bee, despite its smallness, with His kindness and providential care for its existence and whatever it requires to enjoy its life. Glory be to Him! How great is He and how capacious His loving-kindness and benignity! Now take to heart this trifling glimmer from one of the least considerable of creatures and set aside the marvels of the kingdom of the heavens and the earth. Indeed, the measure that our limited comprehension can attain consumes our lifetimes without leading to clarity. Between what our learning may encompass and what the knowledge of scholars and prophets encompasses there is not even a relation; nor is there any relation between that which the knowledge of all creatures comprehends and that which God in His knowledge exclusively commands. Quite the opposite, in fact: The knowledge creatures possess does not even merit the name of knowledge alongside the knowledge of God.

Thus, through reflection upon this and upon analogous instances, knowledge increases that leads to the smoother of the two paths. As knowledge increases, love increases. If you seek the bliss of meeting God, cast this world behind your back and plunge your life into constant litany and prolonged meditation.[A] Perhaps in that way you will gain a little measure; for to gain even that tiny bit is to gain a great and endless realm.

[A] Ghazālī often uses such rhyming formulae (here, *dhikr* and *fikr*) for emphasis.

CHAPTER SEVEN

An Exposition of Why There are Disparities Among People with Respect to Love

KNOW THAT BELIEVERS participate in the ground of love (*aṣl al-ḥubb*) because they share in the ground of belief (*aṣl al-īmān*). Nevertheless, they differ because of disparities among them in knowledge and in love of this world; for things differ only through the disparity in their causes. Most people retain nothing about God beyond His attributes and names which clink upon their ears until they snatch them up and remember them. They may fantasise meanings for them from which the Lord of Lords is to be deemed utterly exalted; they may also, without grasping the true nature of God's attributes and names, not imagine some false meaning but rather, believe them with sincere assent and affirmation, involve themselves in right action and forgo further inquiry. These latter are people of sound belief from among the companions of the right hand[A] whereas those given to idle fantasising are those who stray into error. Those gnostics who know the true nature of things, however, are those who have been brought near to God. God mentions the circumstances of these three groups when He says, *Thus, if he is favoured, his lot will be repose and plenty, and a garden of delight.*[1]

But maybe you are someone who understands these matters only by way of example; let us then give an example of disparity

[A] See Q. LVI.90-91: *If he is one of those on the right hand, he will be greeted with "Peace be to you!" by those on the right hand.*

in love. Shāfiʿī's followers have a love for Shāfiʿī in common. They include both jurists and common folk because all share knowledge of his virtue and religious devotion together with his exemplary life and laudable traits. The common man, however, knows his distinction in a general manner whereas the jurist knows it in specific detail. The jurist's knowledge is more comprehensive and so his admiration and love for him are more intense.

Someone who considers a writer's work and both appreciates and recognises its excellence, loves him as a matter of course; his heart inclines to that writer. If he sees another of his works that is better and more wonderful, his love doubles accordingly since his knowledge of the author's distinction has also doubled. Just so, a man believes that a poet is superb and loves him for it. Whenever he hears of some surpassing instance of skill amid the prodigies of that poet's verse and art, his knowledge of him grows as does his love. So is it with other arts and virtues. The common man may hear that so-and-so is a writer and that he has written an excellent work, but he does not know what is in the work and so his knowledge of it is general; his inclination towards him is correspondingly general. The discerning reader, by contrast, investigates those writings and learns of their marvels and doubles his love because the marvels of craft and composition in the making of verse are signs of their maker's perfect qualities.

The world in its totality is the handiwork—the writing—of God. The common man knows and believes this, but the discerning observer studies the minute particulars of God's craftsmanship in this world until he perceives in a gnat an example of the prodigies of His craft such that his mind is bedazzled and his reason cast into confusion. As a result, God's might and majesty and the perfection of His attributes are magnified within his heart, and his love for Him increases. As he grows in knowledge of the wonders of God's handiwork, he deduces God's grandeur and majesty as Creator; his knowledge of Him grows alongside his love. The sea of this knowledge—by which I mean knowledge of the marvels of God's artistry—is without a shore. Surely then disparity among men of knowledge in this matter of love is also immeasurable.

One reason that love varies lies in the difference of the five causes for love which we have already mentioned. For example, he who loves God because He is kind and bountiful to him and does not love Him for Himself, may be weak in his love since it alters when that kindness alters; his love in circumstances of affliction is dissimilar to his love in conditions of contentment and abundance. He who loves God for Himself and because He merits love by reason of His perfection, beauty, glory and might does not differ in his love when God's kindness to him alters.

These reasons, among others, cause disparities among people in their love. Disparity in love occasions a difference in bliss in the life to come. For this reason God says, *The hereafter has greater honours and is more exalted.*[2]

CHAPTER EIGHT

An Exposition of Why the Human Understanding Is Unable to Know God

KNOW THAT GOD is the most manifest and the most lucent of existing things. This implies necessarily that knowledge of God be primary and *a priori* for human understanding, as well as pre-eminently plain and simple to the intellect. Yet, you may see the matter differently and so, some explanation becomes unavoidable.

We declare that He is the most manifest of existents as well as conceptually the most exalted; but this you will not understand except through analogy. Thus, when we see somebody writing or sewing, his being alive before us is the most obvious of existing things. His life, knowledge and ability, and his will to sew, are plainer to our sight than his other outer and inner qualities. His inner qualities, such as his appetite, his anger, his temperament, his health or sickness, and all the rest, we simply do not know. Of his outer qualities, some we know while about others we may be dubious, for example, how tall he is or the difference in his skin colour and the like. Even so, his life, ability, knowledge, will, as well as his being a living creature, are evident to us; they are evident without our sense of sight becoming involved with his life, power and will. Such qualities are not susceptible to sense perception through any of the five senses. Therefore, his life, power and will cannot be known except through his action of sewing and the movement of his hand.

Now if we were to look at everything else in the world except him, we would not by that method be able to learn of any of his qualities. Thus, there is but one indicator of all that pertains to him, even if that is glaringly obvious. Consequently, you ineluctably bear witness to the existence of God, and to His power and knowledge and other attributes, whenever you see and perceive with your inner and your outer senses, whether what you perceive be stone or clay, plant, tree and animal, sky, earth and star, dry land and sea, fire and air, substance and accident. Our primary testimony of Him lies in our very selves, in our bodies, our physical characteristics, in the fluctuations in our circumstances, in the modulations of our hearts and in all the various phases of our movements and our repose. What is plainest to us, what we know best, is our own self; after that, we know the perceptions we form with our five senses and after these, those instant apprehensions which our intellect and insight fashion for us. Each one of these immediate apprehensions[A] consists of a single object perceived, a single witness and a single sign. All things in the world are articulate witnesses and signs testifying to the existence of their Creator, Arranger, Enabler, and Mover; they point to His knowledge, power, loving-kindness and wisdom.

Perceptible existents are innumerable. Now if the life of the man who writes is plain to us, even if there is only a single indicator to it (namely, that we perceive it by the movement of his hand), then how can He not be manifest to us since nothing in existence can be conceived, either inside or outside our own selves, that does not bear witness to Him and His might and majesty? All the more so since every speck of dust proclaims with the very tongue of its actuality that its existence derives not from itself, nor its motion from its own substance, but rather, that it requires a creator and a mover. The very composition of our own limbs bears witness to this, before all else, as does the harmonious configuration of our bones, muscles and nerves, not to mention the very follicles of our hair and the shapeliness of our extremities, together with all our inner and outer parts. We know that these did not assume their

[A] Arabic *mudrakāt*, i.e., what we grasp directly and immediately.

own harmonious linkages by themselves, just as we know that the hand of a man writing does not move by itself. Nevertheless, since there abides in existence nothing apprehensible, perceptible, and cognoscible, nothing visible or invisible, that is not testimony to, and acknowledgement of, the grandeur of His self-manifestation, our intellects, yet overwhelmed with radiance, are too dumbfounded to grasp it.

There are two reasons why our minds fail to comprehend this. One of these is its very hiddenness and subtle concealment (no examples need be given here); the other is its extreme obviousness. Thus, just as the bat sees by night but not by day, not due to any obscurity in daylight or its luminance, but because of the weakness of its eyesight (for the bat has feeble vision), so the sun's light dazzles it at dawn. The force of the sun's appearance combined with the bat's poor vision is the reason for its impaired sight. It does not see anything unless the brightness is tinged with shadow and the sun's blaze dims.[A] Our own minds are weak in just the same way. The beauty of God's presence is utterly radiant and effulgent; it immerses and encompasses utterly. Not a single atom in the realms of heaven and earth eludes that presence. Its very manifestation thus becomes the cause of its hiddenness. Glory be to Him who is veiled in the radiance of His own light and concealed from both inner and outer vision by His own self-revelation!

Do not wonder at this concealment by means of manifestation. Things are explicable by their contraries.[B] That whose existence is so generalised as to have no contrary is hard to grasp. If things were to differ such that one was indicative while another was not, the distinction would be apprehensible straightaway; but because things participate in signifying one and the same order, the matter becomes ambiguous. One example of this is sunlight

[A] Zabīdī cites the verse of poetry: "Just as day augments human vision with light and blinds the eyes of the bat..." *Itḥāf* IX.597, line 2.

[B] *Al-ashyā' tustabāna bi-aḍādihā*: this dictum, much loved by later Sufism, has an ancient history; cf. *Theodicy*, 65-67, for further discussion and sources.

dawning upon the earth. As we know, that is one of the accidents that occurs on earth and which disappears when the sun goes down.[A] But if the sun were to shine continuously and not set, we would conclude that bodies have no aspect other than their hues, which are black and white and the like; we would not see anything but blackness in the black and whiteness in the white. We do not perceive luminance in itself. Only when the sun sets and places darken do we see that there is a difference between the two aspects [light and darkness]. From that we come to know that bodies may be illumined by light and characterised by a trait they no longer possess when the sun sets. And so we come to know light's existence by its non-existence. We would not have learnt about it without tremendous difficulty had it not ceased; this is because we see forms as similar and undifferentiated both in darkness and in light. Thus, though light is the most evident of the perceptible things and other objects are perceived by its means, its own existence [is not recognised]; for it is not evident in itself but only as it becomes manifest through some other thing.

Consider how its existence would be considered obscure because of its [very] obviousness were it not for the occurrence of its contrary! Thus, does God make things manifest and thus through Him do all things become clear. If He were to cease to be or withdraw into hiddenness or alter, the heavens and the earth would collapse; the phenomenal as well as the transcendental realm would be nullified and the distinction between both states would be graspable. If one thing were to exist through Him and another through some other, the distinction between the two would become perceptible in its very signification. And yet, His signifying action is generalised within things to point to a single order. His existence is everlasting amid shifting circumstances; anything counter to this is impossible. The very intensity of His self-manifestation necessarily occasions concealment.

[A] By "accident" (*ʿaraḍ*) is meant that which is not an essential component: neither sunlight nor darkness is intrinsic to earth.

This is the reason why human understanding falls short. But he whose inner vision (*baṣīra*) is forceful and whose vigour has not been sapped remains in a state of inner equilibrium, seeing God alone. He does not acknowledge anyone other than Him. He knows that God alone exists and that his own actions are merely one of the results of God's omnipotence, for these are consequent upon Him; they have no existence in reality apart from Him. Existence belongs only to the One, the True, by Whom all actions come to be; and his own state arises from this too. He does not consider a single act without seeing God the Agent within it; he looks beyond any action with regard to whether it occurs through the agency of heaven and earth, animal or tree. No, indeed, he considers any act to be the creation of the One, the True. So his gaze does not pass from Him to someone other than Him! He is like someone who considers a person's poem or calligraphy or composition and sees in it the poet and the author. He sees his effect as his effects and not inasmuch as they are ink and gallnuts and ruled lines impressed upon a blank page; nor does he make a practice of taking anyone other than the author into consideration.

The whole world is God's composition. Whoever looks at it as the act of God and knows it as God's act loves it, inasmuch as it is God's act, regarding nothing but God and knowing nothing except through God and loving nothing but Him. Indeed, the true proponent of God's oneness is he who sees only God. He does not look at his own self as his own self but purely as God's servant. Of him it may be said that he has been annihilated in God's oneness; and that he has died away from his own self. There is allusion to such a one in the remark of him who said, "We were with our selves but then we absented ourselves from our selves and so we remained, but without 'we.'"[A]

[A] This refers to the aforementioned notion of *fanā'*, "annihilation of self;" see *Luma*ʿ, 213-15. Its counterpart is *baqā'* ("remaining") which denotes the higher state of transfigured return to the phenomenal world after extinction of the individual self and which is alluded to in "and so we remained,

These matters are known to those endowed with discernment but remain problematic for those whose comprehension is weak because of the inability of religious scholars to clarify and explain them through clear and comprehensive terms that bring them within human understanding. Of course, it may be because of their [the religious scholars'] preoccupation with themselves and their conviction that any such exposition does not concern others than themselves.[A] This is the reason for the failure of human minds to know God. Added to this is the fact that a person [instinctively] grasps all the perceptions that bear witness to God only in youth when reasoning is absent; thereafter, bit by bit, inborn reasoning begins to appear. Seriousness of purpose becomes subservient to the fulfilment of appetites. A man may become habituated and accustomed to his own perceptions and sensations; and so, through long familiarity, their impact no longer has an effect. Thus, when he unexpectedly comes across a strange animal or plant or some miraculous action of God that disrupts habit wondrously, his tongue proclaims its acknowledgement quite naturally and he exclaims, "Glory be to God!" This, even though the whole day through he sees himself and his own limbs, as well as other familiar animals, all of which are decisive proof-signs. He does not sense their power of witness because of his long familiarity with them.

Imagine someone born blind who reaches the age of reason and has the covering lifted from his eye, so that his sight extends to the heavens and earth, the trees and plants and animals—unexpectedly

but without 'we'" (*fa-baqaynā bi-lā naḥnu*). Introduction of the concept into Sufism is usually attributed to Abū Yazīd al-Bisṭāmī (d. 264/874 or 264/877-8); see *EI*², I.162-3, and Zaehner, *Hindu and Muslim Mysticism*, 93-134. Zabīdī cites the theologian Saʿd al-Dīn al-Taftāzānī (d. 792/1390) who connects the notion with "incarnationism" (*ḥulūl*); cf. *Itḥāf* IX.598, *paen.*, with reference to *Sharḥ al-Maqāṣid* (Istanbul, 1277), II.51ff.

[A] Another of Ghazālī's disparaging comments on the *ʿulamāʾ* which occur throughout the *Iḥyāʾ*.

and at a single stroke.[A] You might fear for his reason, dazzled by his intense wonder at the witness these marvels bear to their creator.

This reason, among others, combined with absorption in appetites, blocks people from the illuminative way, with its sapiential lights, and keeps them from swimming in those wide seas. In seeking out knowledge of God most people are like the baffled man about whom the saying was coined, "When he is mounted on his donkey, he keeps looking for his donkey." Transparent things become abstruse when they are sought for. The secret of this matter may be verified. For this reason, it has been said:

> It has shone forth, and is not hidden from anyone
> Except for the man born blind who does not recognise the moon.
> And yet, it is secret in that it shines forth as veiled.
> How can he who is blindfolded by convention acknowledge it?

[A] Ghazālī uses the same example in his *Tahāfut al-falāsifa* (ed./tr. Marmura), 171–172.

CHAPTER NINE

An Exposition of What Longing for God Means

KNOW THAT WHOEVER denies the reality of God's love must deny the reality of longing. Longing is inconceivable except for a beloved. But we affirm the necessity of longing for God and that the gnostic is compelled to it due to the lights of inner vision in contemplation and following Traditions. What we said earlier in affirmation of love should suffice for the affirmation of longing. Every beloved in his concealment must become an object of longing. A beloved who is present and attained cannot be longed for because longing seeks, and yearns to seek, for something, whereas that which is already found is not sought.

Even so, it should be explained that longing is inconceivable except for something that is perceptible in one aspect while remaining imperceptible in another. The utterly imperceptible cannot be an object of longing. He who does not see a person, or hear him described, cannot conceive a longing for him; if he does not perceive his perfection, he does not long for him. The most perfect perception is visual. Now someone who contemplates his beloved and gazes incessantly on him cannot conceive of longing. But longing is connected solely with what is perceptible under one aspect and imperceptible under another; it falls under a dual aspect that may be clarified only by examples drawn from the realm of visual experience. So, for example, we say, "A man whose beloved is absent but in whose heart an image remains, longs to complete that image by direct sight." But if his remembrance and image and knowledge of the loved one vanished from his mind, so that he forgot him, he could not conceive of longing for him. If he were to see him again, he would not conceive of longing for him the instant he glimpsed him. His longing denotes an inner yearning to perfect his imagination. Likewise, he might spot him in shadow when the true nature of his form would not be fully apparent; he would then long to consummate his view and perfect the disclosure of his beloved's form by casting light upon him.

Secondly, he might see the face of his beloved but not his hair, for example, or the rest of his lovely features; so he longs to complete his view. Even if he does not see any of these features and cannot retain an image of them in his mind that then emerges into sight, he still knows that he has a beautiful limb or limbs, even if he does not directly scan their beauty in all their details; and so he longs to have revealed to him what he cannot see.

Both these aspects are conceivable with respect to God; indeed, acceptance of them is incumbent on every gnostic. Divine matters are not always perfectly plain to gnostics even when these matters are themselves utterly clear. Rather, the gnostic seems to stand behind a fine veil that is not fully transparent; it is blemished by the specks of vain imaginings. In this world, the processes of mental representation never cease producing images and similitudes of all knowable objects. To the gnostic, these are blotches and blemishes; worldly distractions adhere to them. Complete clarity comes about through direct vision and the perfected radiance of revelation, but this happens only in the hereafter. This must necessitate longing: it is the farthest point which gnostics love most.

This is one of the two types of longing: to wit, that that in which there is some clarity be made consummately clear.

The second is that divine matters are infinite and unbounded; to every person only a few are disclosed while infinitely many remain obscure. The gnostic knows that these exist and are known to God. He realises that those knowables that elude his comprehension are more numerous than those that are present to him.

He yearns incessantly to acquire some primary, as-yet-unattained knowledge of all remaining things knowable and which he knows not in the least, either clearly or even dimly.

The first yearning comes to fulfilment in the next world, in the sense that is termed 'vision', 'encounter' and 'witnessing with the eyes'. Such longing cannot conceivably be appeased in this world. Ibrāhīm ibn Adham was one who yearned. He related, "One day I said, 'O Lord, if You give peace of heart to anyone who loves You before he meets You face to face, then give that peace to me, for a dreadful restlessness is destroying me.' He went on, "In a dream I saw that God stood me in His presence and said to me, 'O Ibrāhīm! Are you not ashamed to ask Me to give you what will appease your heart before you meet Me? Is he who yearns ever at peace in his heart before he meets his love?' I replied, 'O Lord, I am lost in love of You and have no idea what I say. Forgive me and teach me what to say.' God answered, 'Say: "O my God, make me content with Your decree, give me endurance against Your adversity, grant me gratitude for Your magnanimity!"'"[1] Longing like this will be appeased only in the world-to-come.

The second longing appears to have no end, either in this world or in the next, since any end would imply that in the next world God's majesty and His attributes, His wisdom and His acts, as they are known to God Himself, would be disclosed to man. This is impossible because such knowledge is infinite. Hence, man remains constantly aware that something in the divine beauty and grandeur remains irreducibly inexplicable. His longing can never be stilled—all the more so when he sees how many levels there are above and beyond his own level!—but he yearns to consummate his union by arriving at the root of union. For this reason, he discovers pleasurable longing in which no pain appears. And it is very probable that the twin graces of disclosure and contemplation continue infinitely, just as bliss and pleasure keep increasing forever and ever. Any pleasure consisting of ever-freshened and blissful delight diverts one from the sensation of longing for the unattainable.

Of course, this presupposes that disclosure of that which cannot be disclosed in this world will actually be possible [in that world]. Were it not given unstintingly, bliss would reach a limit and not be augmented; as it is, that bliss continues everlastingly. God's statement, *Their light will shine in front of them and on their right, and they will say: 'Lord, perfect our light for us and forgive us'...*[2] supports this sense: bliss is the perfection of light notwithstanding any [prior] light gained in this world. Alternatively, what is meant here is a perfection of light quite distinct from illumination in this world, that is, an illumination in need of increased perfection and radiance; for the meaning here lies in its completion.

God's statement, *"Wait for us, that we may borrow some of your light." But they will be told: "Go back and seek some other light"*[3] shows that the basis of these lights must be provided for in this world and their radiance augmented in the next. As for renewal of light, why, no. To assert anything conjectural on this subject is forbidden; no disclosure has been accorded us, beyond what has been given on trust. We ask that God increase our knowledge and right belief and that the True show us the truth.[4] This level of illumined insight lays bare the nature and the significance of longing.

Proof-texts from Sacred Tradition are beyond enumeration. One of the most famous supplications of God's Messenger (may God bless him and grant him peace) was when he prayed, "O my God, I ask You for contentment following upon Your decree, and true life after death, and the pleasures of contemplating Your august face and of longing to encounter You."[5]

Abū al-Dardā' said to Kaᶜb, "Tell me about the most special verse" (he meant in the Torah) and he replied, "God says, 'The longing of the righteous to meet Me is protracted but I feel the most vehement longing to encounter them.'" Alongside this it is written, "He who seeks Me shall find Me; he who seeks other than Me shall not find Me." Abū al-Dardā' said, "I testify that I heard the Prophet [too] say this."

In the Traditions of David, God is reported to have said, "O David, tell the inhabitants of My earth, 'I am a loving friend to whomever loves Me. I keep company with him who sits with Me. I am close to him who keeps mention of Me close to himself. I am the companion of him who companions Me. I choose him who chooses Me. I am compliant with him who obeys Me. A person does not love Me—and I know this for a certainty from his heart—without My taking him to Myself and I love him with such a love as none of My creation can surpass. He who searches for Me in truth shall find Me, but he who searches for another than Myself will not find Me. O dweller on earth, cast aside the vanities to which you cling and come close to My munificence, My companionship and My converse! Be intimate with Me and I will be so with you and I will rush to love you. I created the clay of My beloved friends from My friend Abraham's own clay and from that of My confidant Moses and from that of My bosom friend Muḥammad, but the hearts of those who yearn I created from My own light and I have given them bliss in My glory.'"

On the authority of one of the pious ancestors, it is reported that God inspired one of the truthful with the following words, "I have certain servants who love Me and I love them. They yearn for Me and I for them. They keep Me in their minds and I them. They gaze on Me and I on them. If you follow their path I will love you but if you swerve from it I will hate you." He asked, "O Lord! What distinguishing marks do these people have?" God said, "They watch over the shadows by day as a tender herdsman watches over his sheep. They long for the sun to set as a bird longs for its nest at dusk. When the night hides them and shadows mingle and dark spreads out its coverings and makes ready the beds and every lover is alone with his beloved, they direct their steps toward Me and raise up their faces before Me, and they whisper confidences to Me in My own speech and cajole Me for My beneficence. So, amid calling out and weeping and moaning and lament, between standing and sitting, between bowing down and prostration, with My own eye I see what they endure for My sake, with My ear I hear what complaint they make about My love. And I shall give them three things: First, I will cast My light into their hearts so that they bear witness to Me, as I to them. Second, if the heavens and the earth and all that is within them were placed in the balances with them, I would account it of little worth compared to them. Third, I shall draw My face close unto them; and to whom I draw near, who will be privy to what I shall give him?"[6]

According to the Traditions of David, God spoke secretly to him saying, "O David, for how long will you mention the Garden but not ask Me about longing for Me?" He answered, "O Lord, who are those who long for You?" God replied, "Those who long for Me are those whom I have cleansed from every impurity and whom I have alerted to watchfulness; they are those whose hearts I have torn open to Me so that they may gaze upon Me. I bear their hearts in My hand and I place them in My firmament. Then I summon the most illustrious of My angels. When they assemble, they prostrate themselves before Me but I say, 'I did not summon you to prostrate yourselves before Me; rather, I summoned you to show you the hearts of those who long for Me. I glory before you in those who long for Me. O David, their hearts shine in My heaven for My angels just as the sun shines for the denizens of earth! Indeed, out of My own good will (*riḍwān*) I created the hearts of those who yearn and I favoured them with the light of My countenance and I have taken them to be My own partners in conversation. Their bodies I made the site of My gaze upon the earth, and from their hearts have I hewn a path by which they can gaze on Me and day after day compound their yearning for Me."

David said, "O Lord, show me the people of Your love!" God replied, "O David, come to Mount Lebanon. Fourteen souls are there, among them youths and old men as well as men in the prime of life. When you come to them give them a greeting from Me and say, 'Your Lord sends you greeting and says to you, "Do you not ask Me for what you need? You are My beloved friends, My chosen ones and My saints. I take delight in your delight and I hasten to your love."'" And so David came to them and found them by a certain spring meditating on the grandeur of God. When they gazed upon David they rose up to scatter before him.[A] Then David said, "I am God's messenger to you. I have come to you to bring you a message from your Lord." They drew near to him and hearkened to him and listened to what he was saying, even though they cast their eyes earthward. And David said, "Truly I am God's messenger to you who brings you His greeting, saying unto you, 'Why do you not ask Me for what you need? If you cry out to Me I will hear your voice and your words. You are My beloved ones, My chosen, My friends. I rejoice in your jubilance and I hurry toward your love. I gaze upon you hourly with the gaze of a tender and pitying mother.'" He continued, "So the tears streamed down their cheeks and their elder spoke, 'Glory to You! Glory to You! We are Your servants and the sons of Your servants. Forgive us for whatever obstructed our hearts from remembering You in years past!' Another said, 'Glory to You! Glory to You! We are Your servants and the sons of Your servants. Bestow upon us true discernment in what is between us and You.' Still another spoke, 'Glory to You! Glory to You! We are Your servants and sons of Your servants! We would be presumptuous to pray when You know already that we have need of nothing in our affairs, but open the way to us to cleave to the path that leads to You, and that brings us through its bounty to perfection.' Yet another spoke, 'We fall short in seeking to please You, so help us to do so through Your generosity!' And another said, 'From a single drop You created us and bestowed upon us contemplation of Your grandeur. And shall one who is absorbed in Your grandeur and contemplative of Your majesty be so bold as to speak? Rather, we seek to draw close to Your light.' There spoke another, 'Our tongues have grown weary from praising You because of Your mighty deeds and Your nearness to Your friends and the profusion of Your bounty to the people of Your love.' Another spoke, 'You guide our hearts to remember You and free us to devote ourselves

[A] According to Zabīdī, they scattered "out of fear of being preoccupied by anything but God" (*Itḥāf*, IX. 606, l. 12).

to You. Even so, forgive us for falling short in thankfulness to You.' Another said, 'You know that we require only to gaze upon Your face.' And another, 'How should the slave presume upon his master? Since You have commanded us to bring supplication through Your generosity, then give us a light by which we may be directed in the darkness of the heavenly levels.' Yet another spoke up, 'We entreat You to turn towards us and to do so perpetually.' Still another said, 'We require nothing of Your creation but grant us to gaze upon the beauty of Your face.' And another, 'We ask You to bring to perfection the felicity which You have bestowed upon us and which You have graciously accorded us.' Yet another spoke, 'From their midst I ask You to blind my eye from looking at this lower world and its inhabitants, and my heart as well from being so preoccupied with the world to come." Still another, 'Blessed and sublime are You for I know that You love Your friends. Grant us a singleness of heart centred on You and nothing other than You.'"

Then God inspired David inwardly, "Say to them, 'I have heard what you say and I respond in accord with what you love. Let each of you separate from his fellow and take a path for himself. I am He who lifts the veil between Me and you so that you may look upon My light and My splendour.'" Then David asked, "O Lord, what has gained them this from You?" God replied, "By thinking well [of Me] (*ḥusn al-ẓann*) and by abstention from this world and its inhabitants and by seeking out solitary retreats with Me and by holding intimate colloquies with Me. He alone reaches this stage who has cast off the world and its denizens, who is not diverted by any recollection of them and who has emptied out his heart for Me and chosen Me over all My creation. Therefore I incline to him and empty him of himself. I lift the veil between Myself and him so that he gazes at Me with the gaze of one who looks at something with his own eye. I show him My wondrous deeds at every hour. I draw him close to the light of My countenance. If he falls sick, I nurse him the way a tender mother nurses her child. If he is thirsty, I give him to drink and I let him taste the savour of mentioning Me. For when I do that for him, O David, I blind his self to the world and all its inhabitants and I make them unlovely to him. He does not slacken in his absorption in Me. He wishes to hasten to meet Me though I am averse to bringing him to die, for he is the locus of the vision of Me among My creatures. He sees no one other than Me while I see no one but him. When I see him, O David, while his soul is melting, his body racked with weariness, his limbs bruised and his heart stripped bare on hearing Me mentioned, I boast of him to My angels and all the inhabitants of My heavens and this redoubles their dread and their worship. Neither My might nor My splendour, O David, would hinder him in paradise nor would they slake his desire to gaze on Me until he attains contentment and all that is beyond contentment."

In the Traditions about David we also find, "Say to My servants who wend their way to My love, 'How does it harm you that I veil Myself from My creation since I lift the veil between Myself and you until you gaze on Me with the eyes of your hearts? How does it harm you that I have cast you out from this world since My religion is spread out before you? How can people's anger harm you when you seek to please Me?'"

And also in the Traditions about David: God whispered secretly to him, "You aver that you love Me. If you love Me, uproot the love of this world from your heart. Truly, love of Me and love of the world are mutually exclusive in a single heart. O David, he who loves Me is whole-hearted while the worldly act from mixed motives. Follow Me unswervingly in your religion; do not make your religion subject to mere men. Cleave to whatever clearly prompts love of Me. As for what is unclear to you, follow Me unswervingly in truth in your religion while I hurry to direct you and set you straight. I will be your leader and your guide. I will give to you without your asking Me and I will help you against obstacles for I have bound Myself with a vow that I will act only for a servant of whom I know that his questing desire will impel him to seek refuge within My hands and that he has no reliance on anyone other than Me. If you are thus, I will strip away lowliness and estrangement from you and detachment will dwell within your heart. Verily, I have laid it as a charge upon Myself: if a person has no peace in his soul, let him consider its actions and if he will not, I abandon him to them. But ascribe matters to Me and what you do will not be hindered; otherwise, you drudge to no avail for yourself or your companions. Of knowledge of Me you will find no end; it is endless. Whenever you seek for more from Me, you will discover no end to what I add unstintingly.

"Therefore teach the Children of Israel that no kinship exists between Me and My creatures. Let them crave and desire mightily from Me and I shall grant to them 'what no eye has seen and no ear heard and what has not entered the mind of man before.'[7] Hold Me before your eyes and look at Me with the vision of your heart. Do not look with the eyes that are in your head at those whose minds I have veiled from Me. They have sullied themselves; they are filthy because My reward has been cut off from them. I have sworn by My might and My glory that I will not grant My reward to a servant who enters into subservience to Me in order to pick and choose and then procrastinate. Be humble to him whom you teach, do not act overbearing with novices. If those favoured with My love knew the rank of novices in My estimation, they would serve as dirt for them to step upon. O David, if you draw a novice from his bewilderment you will save him and I will inscribe you in My presence as one who strives mightily.[8] Whomever I inscribe in My presence as a striver will know neither estrangement nor loss with respect to creatures.

"O David, hold fast to My word and take from yourself for your own self's sake;[9] let your self give you nothing, otherwise, I will veil My love from you. Let My servants not despair of My compassion. Cut off your carnal appetites. For I have allowed appetites only to the weakest among My creatures; how would it be if the strong were to give way to passion? The sweetness of their secret colloquies with Me would be diminished. The punishment of the strongest before Me is precisely at the site of their indulgence; the very least that will befall them is that I shall veil their minds from My presence. I do not find this world good enough for one whom I love. I have raised him high above it.

"O David, do not set between Me and you any scholar who would veil you from My love by his intoxicants.[10] Such people are highway robbers of My novice servants. Seek help to relinquish appetite by protracted fasting but be on guard against temptation when you break your fast. I love fasting best when it is severe. O David, make yourself beloved to Me by treating your carnal self as your enemy. Deny it what it desires. Then will I gaze upon you and you will see veils lifted between you and Me. I will nurture you with My loving friendship so that you may become strong to receive My reward when I confer it upon you; indeed, I am keeping it aside for you while you adhere stubbornly to My precepts."

God whispered secretly to David, "O David, if those who run from Me knew how I wait for them, how much tenderness I have for them and how I long for them to leave off their sins, they would die out of sheer yearning for Me. They would lop off their very limbs out of love for Me! O David, if this is My desire for those who turn from Me, how great must be My desire for those who accept Me?[A] O David, man needs Me most when he thinks to dispense with Me. I am most compassionate when he intrigues against Me, but when he returns to Me he is the most exalted that he can possibly be."

These and similar Traditions, which are beyond counting, demonstrate the existence of love and longing and intimacy; however, their true meanings may be discovered only through what has been discussed earlier.

[A] Note the classic form of argumentation, comparable to the Talmudic *khal va-khomer* "If this, how much the more so that..."

CHAPTER TEN

An Exposition of the Meaning of God's Love for Man

KNOW THAT PROOF-TEXTS from the Qur'ān attest to the fact that God loves man. We must understand what that means. Let us begin then with proof-texts about His love.

God says, *He loves them and they love Him.*[1] He also says, *God loves those who do battle in His way...*[2] He says, *God loves those who repent and He loves the pure.*[3] Yet, God rejects anyone who alleges that he is beloved of God. He says, *Say, "Why does He punish you for your sins?"*[4]

Anas reports of the Prophet (may God bless him and grant him peace) that he said, "When God loves a man, sin cannot harm him; he who repents of sin is like one without sin." And then he recited, *God loves those who repent.*[5] This means that when a man loves God, he turns to Him before he dies and his past sins, however numerous, do not harm him. In the same way, past disbelief does not harm after conversion to Islam.

God may make forgiveness of sins conditional on love for He says, *Say, if you love God, then follow me so that God will love you and forgive you your sins.*[6] And he also said (may God bless him and grant him peace), "God gives the world to those He loves and to those He does not love, but He gives belief only to those He loves."[7] The Messenger of God (may God bless him and grant him peace) said, "Whoever humbles himself to God, God raises on high but whoever glorifies himself, God abases. And God loves him who thinks of Him much."[8] And he said (may God bless him and grant him peace), "God says, 'A servant constantly draws closer to Me through supererogatory prayers until I love him. When I love him I become his hearing by which he hears and his sight by which he sees," etc.[9]

Zayd ibn Aslam said, "God may come to love a man to such an extent that His love for him even reaches the point at which He says 'Do whatever you will, I have forgiven you.'"[10]

Numberless are the sayings handed down about love. We have already stated that man's love for God actually exists; it is no mere metaphor.

By linguistic convention, "love" (*maḥabba*) denotes the soul's inclination for a thing that befits it whereas "passion" (*ᶜishq*) is the term for an overmastering and exuberant inclination.[A] As we have further explained, goodness befits the soul and so, too, does beauty; and beauty and goodness are both perceptible, now to sight, and now to insight. Love is consequent upon both of these but is not distinguished by sight. God's love for man cannot exist in this sense in any way. Quite the opposite: All terms when applied to God and to other-than-God are not to be uttered univocally with reference to either. The term "existence" (*wujūd*), the most universal of terms in univocity, does not include Creator and created under a single rubric. On the contrary, all that is not God has existence derived from God's existence. Such subsidiary existence cannot be equivalent to the existence from which it is

[A] Zabīdī cites Qushayrī concerning the denial of the attribution of passionate love to God by Abū ᶜAlī al-Daqqāq who argued that "passion is an overstepping of limit in love but God may not be characterised as one who oversteps a limit. Therefore, passion [*ᶜishq*] may not be attributed to Him. If all creatures were to be combined in a single individual, that would not come close to meriting the measure of God. So, too, one may not say that man can overstep a limit in loving God. God may not be characterised as having passionate love, nor may man in his ascription to God, for He negates passion. There is no way to attribute this to God, neither on God's part for man, nor on man's part for God." *Itḥāf* IX.610, line 20ff., citing Qushayrī, 615; cf. also the Introduction above for a discussion.

derived. Only in the application of terms may equivalence occur. As a parallel, for instance, both horse and tree share in the term "body" because the sense of corporeality and its very nature are identical in both without either one deserving that term through some intrinsic basis; corporeality does not belong to either of them as something derived from the other. But this is not the case with the term "existence", either with respect to God or to His creation.

This distance becomes more obvious in other terms; for example, knowledge, will, power and the rest. In all these, there can be no likeness between Creator and creature. The Founder of language[A] fixed these terms at first only for the creature; but then the creature quickly availed itself of intellect and understanding as given by its Creator and used such terms with respect to its Creator by way of metaphor, trope and tradition.

In linguistic convention, "love" designates the soul's inclination towards what is fitting and congruent. But this is conceivable only in a deficient soul which lacks whatever is congruent with it. Accordingly, it wishes to perfect itself by attaining that missing thing and delights in attaining it. In God's case, this would be absurd. All beauty, perfection, glory and majesty are possible in the case of divinity, since each is present, actual and necessarily existent for all eternity; neither cessation nor renewal is even thinkable. God has no view of anything other than Himself as being other than Himself. On the contrary, He only sees His own essence and His own acts exclusively since nothing exists except His essence and acts. For this reason, the master Abū Saʿīd al-Mīhanī said, when God's statement *He loves them and they love Him*[II] was recited to him, "In truth He loves them for He loves only Himself," meaning that God is all and that there is nothing in existence other than God. For he who loves only himself, his own actions and his own creations, does not pass beyond his own

[A] Words and their meanings were established (*tawqīf*) by God Himself, the "Founder" of language, and not by human convention (*iṣṭilāḥ*).

essence in his love nor the consequences issuing from his essence, inasmuch as they stand in a nexus with his essence. It is in this way therefore that He loves only Himself.

The interpretation of the utterances transmitted about God's love for His servants refers to the removal of a veil from the heart, so that one sees with his heart, and to God's enabling a person to draw near to Him, and to God's willing that for him from eternity. His love for one whom He does love is everlasting, whether linked with the eternal will which decreed enabling that person to embark on the paths towards divine proximity, or whether linked to His action of stripping the veil from His servant's heart. For this veil is a merely temporal occurrence which comes about through the intervention of a necessary cause,[A] as God Himself says, "My servant shall not stop drawing near to Me through supererogatory prayers until I love him."[12] Through supererogatory prayers his inmost self becomes purified, the veil is removed from his heart, and he attains the level of proximity to his Lord. This is all God's doing as well as His grace. This, then, is the meaning of His love.

This may be understood only by a parable. A king bade his servant approach him. Because he liked him, the king gave him permission to be present at any time on his regal carpet. This may have been so he could help him prevail by his might or in order to refresh himself by looking at him or so that he might consult with him for advice or so that he might prepare various foods and drinks.[B] It is safe to say that the king loved him; this means that he inclined to him since his friend had within him some affinity corresponding to himself. Hence, he drew the servant close to him; he did not forbid him to enter his presence—not because he

[A] The Arabic here displays a formulaic elegance of expression: *fa-huwa ḥādith yaḥduthu bi-ḥudūth al-sabab al-muqtaḍā la-hu*.

[B] For a lively discussion of the "boon companions" (*nudabā'*) with whom a king should surround himself, see Niẓām al-Mulk's *Siyāsat-nāmah*, tr. by Hubert Darke as *The Book of Government or Rules for Kings* (London, 1975), 92-4. Niẓām al-Mulk was the powerful Seljuq vizier who in 484/1091 appointed Ghazālī to the Niẓāmīya *madrasa* in Baghdad.

wished to benefit by him and not because he sought his aid. It was rather because the servant himself was befittingly endowed with pleasing manners and laudable traits that he could approach the monarch's presence; and because of his closeness, he prospered. The king had no designs on him. When the king lifted the veil between himself and the other, it might simply be said that he loved him. If the other acquired those laudable traits to such an extent that the veil ended up being lifted, it could be said that he gained access to the king and made himself lovable to him.

God's love for man exists solely in the second sense, not in the first. The parable holds true in the second sense only on the condition that your mind not anticipate any alteration in God whenever nearness to Him is renewed. The lover is close to God but this closeness is contingent upon a corresponding distance from [the appetites embodied in] the beasts of the field, wild animals, and devils, as also upon modelling one's behaviour on the noblest character traits, which are divine traits. Closeness to God lies in attribute rather than in physical location.

Whoever is not near may become near; he can change. Sometimes this is thought to mean that whenever proximity is renewed, human and divine characteristics undergo alteration in tandem, since he draws near after being far. But, in God's case, this is absurd. For Him alteration is impossible. On the contrary, He ceaselessly remains in those attributes of perfection and of majesty in which He already exists from all eternity.

This may be illumined by parables about individual closeness. Two persons may approach one another by simultaneous impulses; or one may remain immobile while the other moves. In this case, nearness results from an alteration within one of them but without any such alteration on the other's part. Proximity in attributes is similar. The pupil seeks to come close to his teacher's level in perfect and entire knowledge, while the teacher remains unmoving in his perfected knowledge and does not move by stepping down to his pupil's level. Nevertheless, the pupil keeps moving and ascending from the lowland of ignorance to the summit of knowledge. He persists incessantly in changing and advancing until he approaches his teacher who all the while remains fixed and unchanging. In just this way must man's ascent up the levels of nearness be understood. To the degree to which man perfects his godly traits, consummates his knowledge by grasping the true natures of things, and consolidates his strength by subduing Satan, restraining his appetites and purifying himself from vices, to that extent does he draw closer to some perfection. While the utmost perfection belongs to God alone, nearness to God stands in proportion to one's perfection. The pupil may come close to his teacher, may equal or even surpass him, but that is impossible with respect to God Whose perfection is endless. Man's progress along the degrees of perfection is finite and terminates only at a prescribed limit; he has no craving for equality with God. Therefore, the degrees of nearness differ infinitely because of the very endlessness of perfection itself.

So then, God's love for man lies in His drawing him near, and out of himself, by warding off distractions and sins and in purifying his inmost nature from the spots of this world and in lifting the veil from his heart until he eyes Him as though he saw Him with his very heart.

Man's love for God lies in his inclination to seize this absent perfection which he lacks. He yearns for what he lacks; whenever he grasps some part of it, he delights therein. Love in this sense is unthinkable for God.

If you object that God's love for man is an unclear notion—for by what may man know that he is loved by God?—I respond by deducing it from its salient signs. The Prophet (may God bless him and grant him peace) said, "Whenever God loves a servant He visits him with affliction, but if He loves him profoundly He acquires him." Someone asked, "What does 'He acquires him' mean?" The Prophet (may God bless him and grant him peace) replied, "He leaves him neither family nor wealth."[13] The mark of God's love for a man is that He estrange him from all but Him and interpose Himself between him and anyone else.

Jesus was asked, "Why do you not buy a donkey to ride?" He answered, "I am so dear to God that He will not allow me to be distracted from Him by a donkey."

In Sacred Tradition it is reported that whenever God loves a person He afflicts him: If the person endures it in patience, He selects him; but if he accepts it in contentment, God sets him among the elect.[A]

A scholar remarked, "When you manifestly love God while He just as manifestly afflicts you, then know that He means to single you out for preference."[14]

A novice said to his master, "I have been given some slight acquaintance with love." The master said, "O my son, are you tempted by a beloved other than God, one whom you prefer to Him?" "No," he replied. The master exclaimed, "Do not be so eager for love! God gives love to no one unless He afflicts him!"[15]

The Messenger of God (may God bless him and grant him peace) said, "Whenever God loves a person He makes his very self an admonisher and his heart a groaner, commanding and forbidding him."[B16] And he used also to say, "When God wishes to perform good by means of His servant, He makes him see the faults in himself."[17] The most characteristic distinguishing mark of God's love is man's love for God. That proves that God loves him.

Acts too may prove that man is loved. God takes charge of his outer and inner affairs, both private and public; he refers to God as the organiser of his affairs and the improver of his character, the employer of his limbs, the director of his inward self and his outward comportment. He is the one who makes man's various concerns a single concern.[18] He causes him to hate the world in

[A] Cf. Makkī, II.53. The Arabic is succinct: *fa-in ṣabura ijtabāhu fa-in raḍiya iṣṭafāhu*. The difference between *ijtabāhu* ("he selects him") and *iṣṭafāhu* is hard to convey in English; the Prophet is "the elected one" (*al-muṣṭafā*), i.e., chosen for special preference by God Himself.

[B] That is, "to command the good and forbid the evil" (*al-amr bi'l-maʿrūf wa'l-nahy ʿan al-munkar*).

his heart. He estranges him from all but Him. He sets him at ease with the pleasure of whispered colloquies in his seclusion with Him. He raises the veil that lies between him and knowledge of Him. These and their like are salient marks of God's love for His servant.

Let us now mention the signs of man's love for God for these too are marks of God's love for man. It is God who brings success!

CHAPTER ELEVEN

The Distinguishing Marks of Man's Love for God

KNOW THAT EVERYONE makes claims on love. How easy a claim and how glorious in significance![A] Man must not be fooled by Satan's trickery and the swindles of the carnal self (however much it claims to love God) so long as he has not tested that claim in actual practice and demanded conclusive proofs and evidence. Love is a fragrant tree;[B] its root is firmly planted and its branches reach to heaven; its fruits emerge in the heart and in the tongue and in the limbs.[C] These profuse effects of love on the heart and limbs indicate love, just as smoke is indicative of fire or fruits of a tree.[D] The effects are many. One such effect is the love of an encounter with the beloved so as to feast one's eyes in some safe abode. The heart cannot conceivably love another without also loving to see him and encounter him. If he learned that no such encounter were possible without bidding

[A] Zabīdī cites the verse "Everyone claims union with Laylā but Laylā herself does not concede that to them." *Itḥāf* IX. 615.

[B] Allusion to Q. XIV.24 where God's "good word" (*kalima ṭayyiba*) is compared to "a good tree whose root is firm and whose branches are high in the sky." [tr. Abdel Haleem].

[C] Compare the formulation of Aḥmad al-Ghazālī (d. 520/1126), the younger brother of Abū Ḥāmid: "At times the spirit is like the earth for the tree of love to grow from," *Savāniḥ*, 20.

[D] Ghazali here adduces standard examples commonplace in the semiotics of the Kalām and drawn ultimately from Stoic logic; cf. van Ess, *Die Erkenntnislehre des ʿAḍudaddīn al-Īcī* (Wiesbaden, 1966), 359-60 (and, more generally, 20-21).

this world farewell through death, then he would turn to loving death and would not flee it. For a lover it is no burden to travel from his homeland to the beloved's dwelling just to gaze at him. Death is the key to the encounter; it is the entranceway to vision with one's own eyes.

He said (may God bless him and give him peace), "God loves to meet anyone who loves to meet Him."[1]

When he was dying, Ḥudhayfa said, "A destitute lover presents himself with nothing other than remorse."[2]

A pious ancestor said, "After love of encountering God, there is no trait God loves more in a man than frequent prostration."[3] Hence, love of encountering God takes precedence over prostration."

God makes fighting to the death in His way a condition for genuine sincerity in love; when they said, "We love God," He made fighting to the death and the quest for martyrdom distinguishing signs of love. For He says, *God loves those who do battle in His path in ranks.*[4] He says, *They do battle for the path of God, they kill and are killed.*[5]

In the testament of Abū Bakr to ʿUmar (may God be pleased with them both), he says, "Truth is heavy but salubrious despite its heaviness; falsehood is light but pestiferous despite its lightness. If you heed my testament, nothing invisible will be dearer to you than death, for it is overtaking you. But if you neglect my testament, nothing invisible will be more hateful to you than death, for you will never disable it."[6]

It is reported of Isḥāq ibn Saʿd ibn Abī Waqqāṣ that he said, "My father related to me that ʿAbd Allāh ibn Jaḥsh said to him on the day of Uḥud,[A] 'Shall we not pray to God?' So they withdrew to a secluded spot. ʿAbd Allāh ibn Jaḥsh prayed and said, 'O Lord, I vow to You that if I encounter an enemy tomorrow who will cut

[A] Decisive battle on a mountain three miles north of Mecca in the third or fourth year of the *Hijra*. The Muslim army suffered its first defeat there at the hands of Meccan forces. See *EI*², x.782-3.

me in two—a fierce warrior, hot in his wrath—I shall battle him for You as he will battle me. Then let him take me and lop off my nose and ears and rip open my belly. When tomorrow I meet You, You will say, "O ʿAbd Allāh, who has cut off your nose and ears?" I shall reply, "For You, O Lord, and for Your Apostle." Then You will say, "You have spoken the truth!" Saʿd said, 'I saw him at the end of the day and indeed, his nose and both his ears were dangling by a thread [of flesh].'[A] Saʿīd ibn Musayyib said, 'I pray that God will fulfil the last part of his vow as He fulfilled the first!'"[7]

[Sufyān] al-Thawrī and Bishr al-Ḥāfī used to say, "Only a doubter is averse to death."[8] Whatever a lover's state, he isn't averse to meeting his beloved.

Buwayṭī said to a certain ascetic, "Do you love death?" He seemed to waver for he answered, "If I were truly a believer, I would love it" and he recited God's statement *Wish for death if you are truthful.*[9] Then he went on, "The Prophet (may God bless him and grant him peace) said, 'Let no one wish for death' and he explained, "He said that [in the case] a misfortune befalls one, since contentment with God's decree is far more virtuous than seeking to escape from it."[10]

You may object, "For one who does not love death, is it possible for him to love God?" I reply that aversion to death may occur because of a love of this world and a sorrow over parting from one's family, possessions and children, and that this does preclude perfect love of God. Perfect love is one which wholly engages the heart. Even so, it is not impossible that such a man, despite his love for his family and offspring, may possess a tinge of love for God, however weak; people differ from one another in the matter of love. This disparity is indicated by what is related concerning Abū Ḥudhayfa ibn ʿUtba ibn ʿAbd Shams when he gave his sister Fāṭima in marriage to his client Sālim.[B] The Quraysh

[A] In fact, his corpse was mutilated after the battle of Uḥud; see Ṭabarī, *History*, VII.18, 34.

[B] A "client", or *mawlā*, was a non-Arab convert to Islam who had the

censured him for that and said, "You have given the best bride of the Quraysh in marriage to a mere client!" He replied, "By God! I have given her to him in marriage for I know that he is better than she is!" To them, his reply was worse than his deed and so they said, "How can this be? She's your sister while he's your client." He said, "I heard the Messenger of God (may God bless him and grant him peace) say, 'Whoever wants to see a man who loves God with his whole heart should look at Sālim.'"[11] This shows that there are some people who do not love God wholeheartedly; they love Him but they love other things too. A man's bliss upon meeting God when he approaches Him will be in proportion to his love; his distress at separating from this world at death will also be in proportion to his love for it.

The second cause of aversion to death occurs when a person is at the beginning of the station of love. He has no aversion to death as such but rather, to its onrush before he can get ready to meet God. This does not betoken weak love. This is like the lover to whom word comes that his beloved is approaching; he wishes to delay his arrival for an hour to make his house ready and prepare delicacies for him so that he can encounter him as he longs to, with a carefree heart lightened of all burdens. Such an aversion does not at all run counter to perfect love; its telltale mark is unremitting activity and immersion of one's entire aim in making preparations.

Among other distinguishing marks is that he prefers what God loves over what he himself loves, both inwardly and outwardly. So he perseveres in toilsome activity, avoids the promptings of appetite, shuns indolence, practices uninterrupted obedience to God and approaches Him through supererogatory prayers. He searches constantly for higher levels with God the way a lover

protection of a powerful Arab-born Muslim in the early period, especially under the Umayyads and during the expansion of Islam. The clients, or *mawālī*, were, however, considered socially inferior and suffered frequent discrimination; hence, the point of this anecdote.

searches for greater closeness to his beloved's heart. God described those who love by predilection when He said, *They love those who emigrated to them and they do not find in their breasts any need for what they have been given but prefer them to themselves, though they be in need.*[12] Whoever continually[13] pursues his appetite (*hawā*) has the object of his appetite for his beloved.[A] By contrast, the lover abandons the appetites of his carnal soul for the passion of his beloved, as it has been said:

I desire union with him while he wants to flee from me.
I shall renounce what I desire for what he desires.[14]

Love, when it overwhelms, curbs appetite; one has no delight left except for the beloved. So it is related that Zulaykhā, when she became a believer and Joseph (peace be upon him) married her, withdrew herself from him and abandoned herself to worship, devoting herself solely to God. Joseph used to call her to his bed by day but she put him off until night-time. Then, when he summoned her at night, she stalled him until the day. She said, "O Joseph, I loved you alone before I knew Him but now that I know Him, my love for Him cannot be love for anyone else. I wish for none other than Him." He replied, "God has commanded me to do this for He has told me that He will bring forth two sons from you and will make them both prophets." She said, "Since God has commanded you and made of me a way to Him, I obey God."[15] And so she trusted in him.

Whoever loves God does not disobey Him. For this reason Ibn al-Mubārak said:

You disobey God while you proclaim His love.[B]
Upon my life! this is wondrous among acts!
If your love were genuine, you would obey Him.

[A] Zabīdī (*Itḥāf* IX. 619) quotes Q. XXV.43: "Have you seen him who takes his own appetite as his god?"

[B] Zabīdī (IX. 619) reads the first line as "You disobey God and do not manifest love of Him."

The lover is obedient to the one whom he loves.
In this sense it has also been said:
I forgo what I crave for what You have craved.
I am pleased with what pleases You though my soul be vexed.[16]

Sahl said, "A distinguishing mark of love is to prefer Him to yourself."[17] And also, "Not everyone who practices obedience to God becomes a lover. He alone is a lover who avoids forbidden things."[18] And, it is as he said; for man's love for God is a cause of God's love for him; as God said, *He loves them and they love Him.*[19] When God loves a person, He takes him in hand and gives him victory over his enemies; and yet, his enemy is none other than his own self and his own desires. But God does not forsake him nor consign him to his passions and appetites. This is why God says, *God knows your enemies but God suffices as a friend. God suffices as champion.*[20]

You may say, "Is sin then contrary to the very basis of love?" I reply that it is contrary to love's perfection but not to its basis. There is many a man who loves himself and loves health, but when ill still eats harmful things even though he knows they will harm him. This does not indicate lack of love for himself; rather, his knowledge is enfeebled while his appetite is overpowering. He is powerless to give what he truly loves its due. This may be shown by an anecdote. The Messenger of God (may God bless him and grant him peace) had Nuᶜaymān brought before him for every minor infraction and he punished him for every sin he had committed. One day he was brought and, while he was being punished, a man began cursing him, saying, "How many times has the Messenger of God (may God bless him and grant him peace) had to fetch you!" But he (may God bless him and grant him peace) said, "Do not curse him for he loves God and His Messenger."[21] He did not exclude him from love because of his sin; though, to be sure, sin did exclude him from perfect love.

A gnostic said, "When faith is in the outside of the heart, man loves God with a middling love, but when it penetrates the heart's dark interior, he loves Him with an overwhelming love and forsakes his sins."[22]

To lay claim to love is risky. This is why Fuḍayl said, "When someone asks you 'Do you love God?' keep quiet. If you say no, you are guilty of disbelief. If you say yes, you characterise yourself in a way which true lovers would not use. Beware of being hateful!"[23]

A scholar said, "In paradise there is no felicity more sublime than the bliss of those who possess both knowledge and love. Conversely, in hell there is no torment more grievous than the pain of him who claims to possess both knowledge and love but in reality has no part in them."[24]

Another sign of love is that one be so rapt in the litany of God's name that his tongue does not flag nor his heart grow empty. Whoever loves a thing feels compelled to mention it often and to mention anything connected with it. Thus, a mark of love of God is the love of mentioning Him, together with a love of the Qur'ān which is His word, love of His Prophet, and love of all who are related to him. Whoever loves someone loves even the dog in his neighbourhood.

When love is strong, it stretches from the beloved to everything that concerns him and that stands linked with his affairs. This is not to admit partnership in love. He who loves the beloved's messenger because he is his messenger, and his speech because it is his speech, does not mean his love is transferred to another. Quite the opposite—this is an indication of the perfection of his love. He whose heart love of God has overwhelmed loves all God's creation just because they are His creation. Then, how *not* love the Qur'ān and the Messenger and the upright servants of God? We have already mentioned the true nature of this matter in *The Book of Brotherhood and Companionship*. For this reason God says, *If you love God, follow me; God will love you.*[25] He (may God bless him and grant him peace) said, "Love God because He has given you of His blessings and love me for the sake of God."[26] Sufyān said, "One who loves because of God loves only God. One who honours him whom God has honoured, honours God alone."

A novice reportedly said, "I was already discovering the sweetness of interior colloquies with God at the beginning of my novitiate and so I devoted myself assiduously to Qur'ān recitation night and day. Then a kind of indifference came over me, and I ceased to recite the Qur'ān. But in a dream I heard someone say, 'You claim to love Me yet you shun My book. Have you not pondered the graciousness of My reproof that is contained therein?'" The novice went on, "So I was startled awake and my heart was drenched with love of the Qur'ān and I returned to my earlier state."

Ibn Masᶜūd said, "None of you should ask about himself but only about Qur'ān: he who loves the Qur'ān loves God; he who does not love the Qur'ān does not love God."

Sahl said, "One mark of love of God is love of the Qur'ān. A mark of both love of God and love of the Qur'ān is love of the Prophet. A mark of love of the Prophet is love of *sunna*.[A] A mark of love of the *sunna* is love of the Hereafter. A mark of love of the Hereafter is hatred of this world. A mark of hatred of this world is that one take from it nothing more than a provision, just enough for the world-to-come."[27]

Another sign of love is to be on intimate terms with seclusion and with one's inner supplication of God, as well as with recitation of His book. Such a person rises often in the night and avails himself of the night-time quiet, when time is pure and clear of impediments. For the least stage of love brings delight in seclusion with the Beloved and the gladness of conversing with Him in privacy. But how can somebody who finds sleep or idle chat more pleasant than conversation with God be sound in his love? As he was coming down a mountain, Ibrāhīm ibn Adham was asked, "Where are you coming from?" He answered, "From close companionship (*uns*) with God."[28]

In the Traditions of David (peace be upon him), God says, "Do not become intimate with any of My creatures! There are

[A] The *sunna* is the example of the Prophet.

only two types of men I cut off from Me: the man who finds My reward too slow and distances himself; and the man who forgets Me and is pleased with himself. As a sign [of displeasure] I leave him to his own devices and let him remain in perplexity in this world." In whatever way one grows close to beings other than God, to the measure of that closeness is one estranged from God and sinking in the level of his love.

In the tale of Burkh (who was a black servant through whom Moses prayed for rain),[A] God reportedly said to Moses, "Indeed, Burkh is an excellent servant. He belongs to Me but he has one fault." Moses asked, "O Lord, what is his fault?" God answered, "The early morning breezes give him pleasure. He takes his ease in them. He who loves Me takes his ease in nothing."

According to another story, a worshipper long practised his devotions to God in a thicket. He saw a bird nesting in a tree where it had taken refuge and was chirping. He said, "If I moved my place of prayer to that tree I could enjoy the bird's song." No sooner said than done. God sent a revelation to the prophet of that age, saying, "Tell worshipper so-and-so, who is getting on such cosy terms with a creature, 'I will lower you by a degree which you will never attain again, however you may strive.'"[29]

So then, a mark of love is perfect familiarity in conversation with the beloved and perfect delight in solitude with Him, as well as complete estrangement from all that mars solitude and interferes with the pleasure of intimate colloquy. For one of the signs of intimacy is that both the intellect and the understanding become engrossed in the rapture of secret dialogue, like him who addresses one he passionately loves and confides in. With one lover this pleasure may go so far that a fire breaks out in his house while he is praying and he does not even notice it. Another has his leg amputated because of an illness that has befallen him but again, he does not notice because he is at prayer. Whenever love and intimacy overwhelm a man, solitude and secret prayers

[A] For the full story of Moses and Burkh see Chapter Thirteen below.

become his chief delight; they ward off all his cares. Intimacy and love submerge his heart so that he cannot grasp worldly matters unless they are repeated time and again in his hearing, just like a distracted lover. With his tongue he talks to people but his inmost self is absorbed in mention of his beloved.

A lover is someone who is never tranquil except in the presence of his beloved. Qatāda said—with reference to God's words, *Who have believed and whose hearts have rest in the remembrance of God. Verily in the remembrance of God do hearts find rest!*[130]—"[His words] impel them with gladness to Him and with Him they are at ease."

Abū Bakr al-Ṣiddīq said, "Whoever has tasted the pristine love of God will be absorbed by it from any worldly pursuit; it estranges him from all mankind."

Muṭarrif ibn Abī Bakr said, "The lover does not grow weary of the beloved's conversation."

God revealed to David (peace be upon him), "He who claims to love Me is a liar if when night descends upon him, he sleeps and is oblivious of Me. Does not every lover love to meet his beloved? And here I am, present for everyone who seeks Me."

Moses (peace be upon him) said, "O Lord, where are You that I may make my way towards You?" God answered, "If you are making your way you have already arrived."

Yaḥyā ibn Muᶜādh said, "Whoever loves God hates himself." He also said, "Whoever does not have three qualities is no lover: he prefers God's word over that of creatures; the meeting with God over meeting with creatures; and service to God over service to creatures."

Yet another sign of love is not to grieve over anything that one has missed except with regard to God and that one's sorrow intensify over the loss of every single hour empty of mention of God as well as of obedience to Him. After forgetfulness one should return to Him again and again by imploring His kindness, by seeking rebuke from Him and by turning to Him in repentance. An gnostic has said, "To God belong the servants who love Him and are at peace with Him, for grief over what has been lost falls away from them and they are unconcerned about what portion may be theirs. Their King's rule over them is complete. What He wills, is. What they have comes to them without fail; what eludes them does so through His excellent governance over them."

Whenever a lover becomes aware of his own inattention, it behoves him to approach his beloved straightaway, to engage in reproaches and to question Him, saying, "Lord, for which sin of mine have You cut me off from Your blessing and distanced me from Your presence and engrossed my attention solely on myself and on chasing after Satan?" This brings him purified remembrance and a tenderness of heart by which he atones for his earlier indifference. In this way, his very offence becomes an occasion for renewing his remembrance and purifying his heart. As long as the lover sees only the Beloved, sees nothing but as proceeding from Him, he neither grieves nor doubts but accepts all things with contentment. He knows that the beloved determines that alone in which his good resides, and he keeps God's words in mind, *Perhaps you will hate something that is good for you*.[31]

Still another sign is to find joy in obedience to God and not deem it onerous; to allow its burdensomeness to slide away and not even to consider it burdensome. As someone remarked, "For twenty long years I suffered through the night but then I enjoyed it for twenty years." Junayd stated, "It is a mark of love to show unflagging zeal and persistent passion that exhausts the body but not the mind."[32] And another said, "Lassitude does not enter into the work of love." A scholar said, "One who loves God will not set aside [lit. cure himself of] obedience to Him even if he were to come by the most powerful of expedients."[33]

All this, and much that is similar, is present in the vision of God. The fervent lover does not think that striving for the love of his Beloved is burdensome; rather, he takes pleasure in serving Him with his heart, even if it is strenuous for his body. When his body fails, he finds the sensation of returning strength and vanishing incapacity the loveliest of all things for then he can resume his absorption in Him. Such is the love of God. When love overwhelms, it irresistibly conquers all that is not itself. He whose Beloved is dearer to him than indolence casts off indolence to serve Him; he whose Beloved is dearer to him than wealth forsakes wealth for His love.

Someone said to a lover, who had already expended himself and his property until he had nothing left, "What is the reason for this state of love in which you find yourself?" He answered, "One day I heard a lover alone with his beloved who said, 'I love you with all my heart but you turn your face wholly away from me.' The beloved said to him, 'If you do love me, what will you spend for me?' He answered, 'O you who master me, I make yours what is mine and my spirit I shall spend until it perishes!' Then I said, 'This is from creature to creature and slave to slave. But how ought it to be from worshippers to One who is adored?' All of this comes from that reason."[34]

Another sign is to be compassionate and merciful to all the servants of God while remaining harsh to all His enemies and indeed, to everyone who does anything which He hates. This is in accord with God's word: *hard against the disbelievers and merciful among themselves.*[35] He does not fear any reproach,[36] nor does anything turn him aside from anger on God's behalf. God describes His friends thus since He says, "Those who are bent on love of Me the way a boy hankers after something and who take refuge in remembrance of Me like the eagle to its nest, who are wrathful like the leopard who when vexed doesn't care whether people are many or few."[37]

Ponder these examples. When a boy has set his heart on something, he will not let go of it; if it is taken from him, he does nothing but weep and scream until it is given back to him. When he goes to sleep he takes it with him inside his clothes. When he wakes he returns to it and holds it tight. Whenever he has to part with it, he cries; whenever he finds it again, he laughs. Whoever fights him over it, he hates; whoever gives it to him, he loves. As for the leopard, he cannot restrain himself in his fury to such a point that in the very vehemence of his wrath, he destroys himself.

These then are the signs of love. When these signs are completely manifest in someone, his love is perfect and pure. In the hereafter, his wine will be unmixed and his drink sweet. But whoever mingles his love of God with love for other things will find his felicity in the hereafter in proportion to his love, for his drink will be mixed with a portion of the drink of those drawn nigh to God, as He says, with regard to the righteous, *The righteous will be in delight.*[38] He also says, *They are given to drink of a pure wine, sealed, whose seal is musk—for this let all those strive who strive for bliss—and mixed with the waters of Tasnīm, a spring whence those brought near to God drink.*[39] The wine of the righteous (*abrār*) is delicious because the pure wine that belongs to those brought nigh (*muqarrabūn*) to God has been mixed therein.

"Wine" is a term for the totality of bliss in paradise just as "The Book" expresses the totality of acts.[A] God says, *The record of the righteous is in ʿIllīyīn.*[B40] Then He says, *Those who are brought near to God attest it.*[41] The high rank of the Book is indicated by the fact that it has been raised up to where those near to God can see it. Just as the righteous experienced increase in their condition and knowledge by their nearness to those close to God, and by seeing them, so too is their state in the world to come. *Your creation and your resurrection are only as* [the creation and resurrection of] *a single soul.*[42] And again: *As We began the first creation, We shall repeat it.*[43] God also says, *A reward proportioned,*[44] that is, the reward is appropriate to their actions. The pure receive the unmixed wine as drink, those [whose purity is mixed] receive the mixed wine. The mixture in each drink is in the measure of the previous mix of love and actions one has performed. *He who performed an atom's*

[A] Makkī had written (II.57), "The totality of the bliss of paradise is expressed in 'wine' in the same way that all knowledge and action are expressed in 'The Book'."

[B] ʿIllīyūn is the place in the Book where the actions of the righteous are recorded; it is also described as an "inscribed book" (*kitāb marqūm*); cf. Q. LXXXIII.20.

weight of good will see it and he who performed an atom's weight of evil will see it.[45] And *God does not change the condition of a people until they change what is in themselves.*[46] Furthermore: *God does not wrong anyone by as much as even a dust-speck's weight of wrong; and if there is a good deed He will double it.*[47] *Though it be of the weight of a grain of mustard seed, We bring it. And We suffice for reckoners.*[48]

He whose love in this world lies in his hope for the bliss of heaven, for black-eyed virgins and palaces, takes firm hold on paradise so that he may settle down there where he wishes, playing with children and enjoying women. This is what his pleasure in the hereafter comes down to. Each man is granted of love only that which his soul desires and his eye enjoys. But he whose object is the master of the house and the king of the realm and who is dominated solely by his love in sincerity and truth, he is given to dwell *firmly established in the favour of a mighty king.*[49] The righteous revel in the gardens and take pleasure in paradise with the dark-eyed virgins and with slaves, whereas those drawn nigh to God cleave to His presence and hold their gazes fixed upon it, for they reckon the joys of paradise little more than dust in comparison. There are those who[50] are engrossed in fulfilling their passions for food and sex, but there are altogether other people dedicated to keeping company with God.[51] This is why the Messenger of God (may God bless him and grant him peace) said, "Most dwellers in paradise are simple, but ʿIllīyūn belongs to those with understanding."[52] Human minds cannot grasp the meaning of ʿIllīyūn and so God intensifies its import, saying, *What will convey to you what ʿIllīyūn is!*[53] Just as He says, *The calamity! What is the calamity? Ah, what will convey to you what the calamity is!*[54]

Still another sign of love is to be fearful in love and make oneself quite small under the force of dread and awe. Fear is sometimes thought to be contrary to love. This is not so.[A] Just the opposite is

[A] Compare the line of John Donne (1572-1631), from his "Holy Sonnets", where he writes, with reference to the fear and love of God, "Those are my best days when I shake with fear."

true: the perception of grandeur compels awe just as the perception of beauty compels love. The elite among lovers feel fear at the station of love while others feel nothing. Certain of their fears are stronger than others. The first fear is the fear of God's turning away, but the second fear is worse: this is the fear of God's veiling Himself. Even worse is the fear of banishment from God. His understanding of the chapter of Hūd[A] is in fact what turned the hair of the lord of lovers[B] white when he heard God's word, *A far removal for Thamūd!*[55] *A far removal for Madyan, even as Thamūd has been removed afar!*[56] The dread and fear of removal are great only in the heart of someone accustomed to closeness, someone who has tasted and enjoyed it. For this reason any talk of banishment, with reference to those who have been distanced, whitens the hair of those who hear it and who are still near. Someone inured to distance does not pine after nearness. He for whom the carpet of closeness has not been spread does not weep from fear of distance.

The next fear is that of a standstill and of the deprivation of increase. Earlier we explained that the degrees of nearness are infinite. A human being is obliged to strive at each moment to grow in nearness to God. This is why the Messenger of God (may God bless him and grant him peace) said, "When two days are alike for someone he is exposed to harm, but when his today is wickeder than his yesterday, he deserves to be cursed."[C][57] He also said (may God bless him and grant him peace), "Each morning and each evening I find a veil on my heart until I asked God's forgiveness seventy times."[58] He asked forgiveness for the first step only for this was "distance" in comparison to the second step [in nearness to God].

Such stagnation and deprivation are punishments for lassitude along the way and for resorting to things other than the beloved.[D]

[A] Hūd is the eleventh *sūra* of the Qur'ān.

[B] The "lord of lovers" (*Sayyid al-muḥibbīn*) is the Prophet himself.

[C] Remaining at a standstill is dangerous; backsliding is fatal.

[D] This statement is not applicable to the Prophet whose asking for

It is related that God says, "The least that I do to a scholar when he prefers worldly appetites to obedience to Me is to deprive him of the pleasure of intimate conversation with Me." Denial of increase because of indulgence of appetites is punishment for the common folk; but as to the elite, what obstructs increase for them is their making inflated claims for themselves and their satisfaction with the first inklings of divine grace. This is God's secret ruse[59] which those alone who are supremely sure-footed can sidestep.

The next fear is that of losing that which, once lost, can never be recovered. As he was travelling in the mountains, Ibrāhīm ibn Adham heard someone say:

All you have done is forgiven
Except for turning from Us.
We restored to you what you lost by neglect;
Restore to Us then what has been lost to Us.[60]

He was shaken and fell down senseless. For a day and a night he remained that way while mystic states came upon him. Then he exclaimed, "From the mountain I heard a summons: 'O Ibrāhīm! Be a slave!' So I became a slave and I found peace."

Fear of forgetting God comes next. Longing and urgent pursuit cling to the lover; he takes no rest from seeking increase; he finds no delight other than in new instances of grace (for if he should let himself become distracted, it would cause him to arrive at a standstill or even to backslide). Yet, forgetfulness invades him without his noticing it, in just the same way as love once entered into him without his realising it. These fluctuations have hidden spiritual causes beyond human understanding. When God wills a ruse and luringly tempts someone, He hides what has befallen him from him. And so, despite his expectations, he arrives at an impasse.

forgiveness is because one stage of nearness to God is incommensurate with the stage that follows it. For an explanation of this *ḥadīth*, see H. T. Littlejohn's translation of *Kitāb al-ṣabr wa'l-shukr*, *Al-Ghazālī on Patience and Thankfulness* (Cambridge, 2011) p. 87.

His attitude is still good but he grows listless. Heedlessness, or even passion and forgetfulness, may overtake him. But all of these are Satan's troops that prevail over such angelic troops as knowledge, reason, remembrance and articulate discourse.[A]

Just as that which manifests and then necessitates love's agitation—namely, those traits of graciousness, mercy and wisdom—comes from God's very own attributes; so, too, from His attributes comes what flares forth and effects forgetfulness—those traits deriving from coercion, might and self-sufficiency. These, along with deprivation and harsh distress, are the advance guards of God's ruse.[B]

The next fear is that of seeking some substitute for God by allowing the heart to be moved from love of Him to love of another. And that is abomination. Forgetfulness is the precursor of this station just as turning-away and veiling are precursors of forgetfulness. When the breast wearies of righteousness,[61] feels constricted by continual litany and grows bored with the toil of voluntary prayers, then these become the causes of such matters as forgetfulness.

The emergence of these factors betokens a shift from the stage of love to the stage of hatred (we take refuge with God from that!), while the persistence of fear—coupled with the intense effort, by means of single-minded self-scrutiny, to guard against these—betokens authentic love. Whoever loves something must fear to lose it. Hence, love cannot be without fear for the object of love is something that can be lost.

A gnostic said, "Whoever worships God the Exalted purely out of love and without any fear perishes through complacency

[A] The state described here was well known in Christian monastic and ascetic circles under the name "accidie" or "listlessness".

[B] The Qur'ānic notion of *makr,* God's "device" or even "ruse". Cf. Q. III.54 ("God is the best of devisers"). In the Qur'ān, the term is generally used to demonstrate that God is cleverer in His deeds and plans than anything the cleverest human can devise; in Sufi usage, it comes increasingly to be invoked as a check against presumption.

and pride. Whoever worships Him in fear, without any love, is severed from Him by distance and estrangement. But God loves whoever worships Him with both love and fear: He brings him near, He accords him power, He teaches him."[62] Thus, he who loves should not be devoid of fear, nor he who fears devoid of love. Nevertheless, he whom love so overmasters that he expands within it and has but a slight sense of fear is said to be at the stage of love and may be considered one of [God's] lovers.[A] An admixture of fear calms the intoxication of love. If love were to predominate and overwhelm knowledge, human strength could not stand firm. Fear alone gives balance and lightens love's impact on the heart.

In the Traditions it is recounted that one of the righteous (*ṣiddīqūn*) entreated one of the *Abdāl*[B] to ask God to nourish him with a single grain of knowledge of Him. He did this. [As a result, the righteous one] went roaming through the mountains, his reason addled and his mind crazed. For seven days, he remained staring glassily. He could do nothing worthwhile, nor could anything worthwhile be done through him. The *Badal* [sing. of *Abdāl*] prayed to his Lord on the other's behalf, saying, "O Lord, take a bit of this grain away from him!" God revealed to him, "I gave him only one atom of the hundred-thousandth part of a grain of knowledge. When this man asked me, one hundred thousand other servants were asking me simultaneously for a smidgeon of love, but I deferred their request because it was you who interceded on his behalf. When I gave you what you asked for, I gave them too just what I gave to him, apportioning a single grain of knowledge among one hundred thousand servants, and this was his proper share in that." He replied, "Glory be to You!

[A] According to Zabīdī, "Everyone who loves God fears Him, though not everyone who fears, loves; that is, with the love of those 'brought near to God', because he may not have tasted the flavour of love," *Itḥāf* IX. 630, II. 31-32.

[B] The *abdāl* (literally "substitutes"), a secret category in the hierarchy of Sufi saints, uphold the order of the world; cf. *EI*[2] I.94.

Most just of judges![63] Take back some of what you gave him!" So God removed all of it from him, leaving him with a tenth of a thousandth thereof, that is, one part of a ten-thousandth of the hundred-thousandth part of a grain. At this, his fear came into equilibrium with his love and his hope; he was once again tranquil and became like other gnostics.[64]

The following has been said in description of a gnostic's state:

Ahover close to rapture, his wide cast
reaches all people, both free and enslaved.
Strange of aspect he possesses a strange knowledge.
His insights are mighty but he is far too sublime
for glances other than those of the martyr.
Festivals occur in their seasons, but for him
every day ushers in a thousand festivals.
On days of celebration lovers know joy,
but for him there is no pleasure in festivals.[65]

Junayd used to recite verses by which he alluded to the inner states of the gnostics (even though it is impermissible to divulge this). These are the verses:

Their hearts have led men through the hidden realms.
They alighted in the closeness of the Glorious, the Generous,
amid fields[66] of God's nearness, in His sanctity's shade,
where their spirits roved and were wafted away.
There, their watering-holes were tapped from Majesty
and Mind
and their departure thence led to glory that was greater still.
Through a splendour severed from its own epithets
in garments of God's oneness they wandered and strolled.
Later comes that of intricate attributes
which it is better, and more just, to keep secret.
Of my knowledge I will conceal whatever He withholds
and will expend only that which I see God expend.
I give God's servants their due from it.

What it is better to withhold I withhold.
The Merciful possesses a secret which He safeguards
in the inmost hearts of his gnostics. Safeguarding is loveliest!

It is impermissible to share with people such mystical knowledge as is here alluded to; it is equally impermissible for anyone to whom something has been revealed to divulge it to someone to whom it has not been revealed. Quite the opposite, in fact; for if people were to share in it, the world would go to ruin. Wisdom requires that heedlessness exist for the world to thrive. If all people were to eat only permitted food for forty days, the world would fall apart because of their austerity; markets, not to mention livelihoods, would be ruined. Even more, if religious scholars were to eat nothing but permitted foods, they would become occupied only with themselves; their tongues and their feet would grind to a halt and cease from much that they do to spread knowledge abroad.[A] Nevertheless, God has secrets and hidden judgments regarding what is evil in outward appearance, just as He possesses secrets and instances of wisdom in goodness itself. His wisdom is boundless and so is His might.

A further sign is the concealment of love, including avoidance of any amorous declaration and guarding against divulging both ecstasy and love—this, in order to revere the Beloved, to honour His majesty, to demonstrate awe of Him as well as jealousy for His secret. For the lover, love is the supreme and sacred mystery. But because the lover's claims may involve what surpasses or even exceeds the limits of sense, some fabrication may occur, even though this may increase punishment in the next world

[A] Another instance of Ghazālī's practical theodicy: his belief in, and acceptance of, the world as it is. This world represents the elaboration of the divine will in its supremely specifying activity (*takhṣīṣ al-irāda*), i.e., even such mundane matters as the pursuit of a livelihood or the bustle of markets result from God's specifying volition. There is also, of course, another jab at religious scholars here; Ghazālī slyly takes it as given that they do not eat "only permitted food!" See also *Theodicy*, 201-202.

and hasten disaster in this. Furthermore, the lover may experience such intoxication in love that he falls amazed, his "states" are in turmoil, and his love declares itself visibly in his outward aspect. If that occurs, and occurs without any design or volition on his part, he deserves forgiveness, for he is one under compulsion.[A] Still, sometimes the fire of love blazes up with unendurable force and the heart spills over with it so powerfully that its rush is incomprehensible. He who is capable of concealing love says:

> They say 'Near?' and I say, 'What am I doing
> so close to the sun's flames, as though in my very lap?
> What do I have from Him but the memory of a thought
> that stokes the blaze of love and longing in my breast?'
> But he who is incapable of concealing it says:
> He hides, but a tear discloses his secrets.
> His breathing makes his rapture plain to see.
> And he also says:
> How can he be whose heart is with another?
> How can he hide what shows on his own eyelid?

One of the gnostics said, "Those who refer most to God are those who are most distant from Him." He meant that someone who frequently alludes to Him in everything and who always makes himself appear to advantage by mentioning Him, is detested by those who love and know God.

Dhū al-Nūn al-Miṣrī entered the house of a friend who used to talk about love and he found him stricken and afflicted. He said, "He who discovers the pain of His harm does not love Him!" But the friend replied, "I say, however, that he does not love Him who takes no delight in His harm!" Dhū al-Nūn countered with "I say that he does not love Him who makes himself famous for loving Him!" The friend replied, "I ask God's forgiveness. I repent before Him."[67]

[A] Perhaps a veiled allusion to Ḥallāj who was initially exculpated of blasphemy by the jurist Ibn Surayj because he was out of control of his utterances and so legally blameless.

Suppose you object that love is the highest station (*maqām*); to display it makes known what is good: why then must divulging it be disparaged? Know: love is laudable; so is its outward display. What is reprehensible is to parade it like a sham into which presumptuous claims and self-important swaggering intrude. The lover's true duty is to allow his actions and his inner states, rather than his words, to bring his hidden love to perfection.[68] His actions should make his love evident without any wish on his part to display either his love or any act betokening love. On the contrary, the lover's intent must always be to get to know the beloved and nobody else. The desire to get to know anyone else is polytheism in love and deserves rebuke. This is exactly as related in the Gospel: "When you give alms, give so that your left hand does not know what your right hand does, for He who sees hidden things will reward you openly. And when you fast, wash your face and anoint your head, so that no one other than your Lord may know of it."[69]

To make a show of love in word or in deed is reprehensible, except when love so overmasters one that the tongue is loosed and the limbs are in tumult. Someone in this state should not be censured.[A]

It is recounted that a man saw a lover[70] doing something for which he deemed him witless. When he reported that to Maʿrūf al-Karkhī, the latter smiled and said, "O my brother, God has lovers who are little and lovers who are big, lovers who are reasonable and lovers who are crazy. The man you have seen is one of the crazies."[71]

Making a show of love is to be eschewed. If the lover is a gnostic—one who knows the angels' states in their lasting love and persistent longing in which they give glory night and day without tiring and who obey God in whatever He commands and who carry out what they have been ordered to do[72]—he will despise his own self and any show of his love. He knows that in God's realm

[A] Another probable allusion to Ḥallāj.

he is the least of those who love and that his love is more flawed than that of any of God's lovers. A lover, one of the illuminated, said, "I worshipped God for thirty years by works of the heart and of the limbs to the utmost of my effort and the exhaustion of my strength until I considered myself to have attained some tiny portion of God's regard."[73] In a lengthy account he related matters pertaining to the illuminations of the signs of heaven. At the end, he said, "I reached a row of angels as abundant as all that God had created and I asked, 'Who are you?' and they replied, 'We are those who love God the Exalted. We have worshipped Him here for three hundred thousand years during which time no thought of anything other than Him ever entered our minds in any way, nor have we mentioned anyone other than Him.' He went on to say, 'At that I felt shame for my deeds and I offered them to those for whom the Warning (*al-waʿīd*) was due in order to lighten their lot in hell.'"

When one knows himself and knows his Lord and is genuinely ashamed of himself, his tongue turns dumb to all ostentation and inflated claims.[A] He bears witness to his love in his movements and in his stillness, in his advances and in his withdrawals, as well as in his very waverings. Of Junayd it is related that he said, "Our master Sarī was sick and we could neither find a remedy for his illness, nor could we discover its cause. We were told of a clever doctor and so we took a vial of Sarī's urine to him. The doctor looked at it again and again for a long time and then he said, 'I see that this is the urine of a man in love.'" And Junayd went on: "I was stunned. I fell into a faint and the vial dropped from my hand. I went back to Sarī and told him what had happened. He smiled and said, 'What a sharp-eyed son-of-a-bitch!'[74] I said, 'O Master, does love show even in the urine?' He replied, 'Yes.'"[75]

[A] On concealment (*kitmān*) of love in an erotic context, on which Ghazālī draws, see Ibn Ḥazm, *Ṭawq al-ḥamāma*, in *Rasāʾil*, 1.144: "One of the characteristics of love is concealment in speech and the lover's 'veiling' himself if he is questioned."

Sarī said once, "If I wanted to, I could tell what has dried my skin out over my bones. Love alone has eaten away my body."[76] At that he fainted dead away. His fainting made plain that he expressed himself on the onset of rapture and at the very outset of his swoon.

These then are the four signs and fruits of love. Intimacy and contentment are also among them, as will be shown.

In short, all the merits of religion as well as the virtues of human character are the fruits of love. Love does not occasion mere adherence to appetite (which belongs among the character defects). Of course, a person may love God because of His goodness to him. He may love Him because of His majesty and beauty, even when He has not been kind to him. Lovers belong to these two classes alone. For this reason, Junayd said, "In love of God people are either ordinary or elite. The ordinary acquire love through knowing God's ceaseless benevolence and the profusion of His bounties and do not refrain from striving to please Him; however, their love decreases or increases in proportion to His beneficence and favour. By contrast, the elite attain love through the greatness of God's decree, through His power and knowledge and wisdom, and through His uniqueness in sovereignty. Since they know His perfect attributes and His most beautiful names they are unrestrained in loving Him. In their view He deserves love because He is worthy of it, even if He were to take away all favours from them."

Of course, there are people who are in love with their own passion and with Iblīs, God's enemy. Nevertheless, they are deceived about themselves because of their own ignorance and delusion. They think that they love God—but in them the signs of God's love are nowhere to be found—or they garb themselves in these signs out of hypocrisy and dissimulation or for the sake of reputation. Their goal is a fleeting portion of this world even though they exhibit the very opposite of this; such are wicked divines[77] and wicked Qur'ān-readers.[A] These are the people God

[A] Yet another scornful swipe at the *ʿulamāʾ*!

hates on His earth. Whenever Sahl would speak with people he would say, "*Yā dūst*! That is, 'dear one.'"[A] Someone objected to him, "He may not be dear, so why do you say this?" Sahl whispered in the questioner's ear, "There are two alternatives: either he is a believer or a hypocrite. If he is a believer he is dear to God; if he is a hypocrite he is dear to Iblīs."

Abū Turāb al-Nakhshabī composed some verses on the signs of love which follow:

Do not be deceived, for the lover has signs
and from the Beloved's gifts he possesses means.
He has enjoyment in the midst of bitter distress
and pleasure in all that his beloved may do.
Refusal is a gift to be accepted at his hand.
Poverty is benevolence and a kindness in this world.
One sign is that he is manifestly resolved
to obey his lover though a scolder harass him.[B]
Another sign is that he is seen all in smiles
though his heart is troubled for his beloved's sake.
A further sign is that he is always seen toiling to know
the discourse of one who has found grace with him.
And it is a sign that you observe him living
abstemious and circumspect in all that he says.

And Yaḥyā ibn Muʿādh said:

It is a sign that you glimpse him tucking up his robes
in twin tatters on the shores of the stream.
His sadness is a sign, as is his lamentation,
amid deepest darkness where no one can censure him.
It is a sign that you witness him journeying
to spiritual combat and to every noble deed.

[A] *Yā dūst*: Persian for "O Friend!" (Arabic *ḥabīb*).

[B] For the traditional figure of the "scolder," see Ibn Ḥazm, *Ṭawq al-ḥamāma* in *Rasā'il*, 1.161-62.

His renunciation of all that he sees is a sign
in a lowly abode or in transient bliss.
If you see him in tears, that too is a sign
that he has caught himself in some evil he has done.
It is a sign that you see him surrender
all things to the just king.
His visible satisfaction is also a sign
in every judgment that comes down from his king.
His laughter in the midst of people forms a sign
though his heart be grieving like a mourner's heart.

CHAPTER TWELVE

An Exposition of the Meaning of Intimacy with God

AS WE HAVE already mentioned, intimacy, fear and longing are among the effects of love. These effects are various. They vary for a lover in accord with his viewpoint and the degree to which he is overcome by love at a particular moment. When the thirst to know what lies behind the veil of the unseen, even unto the utmost beauty, grips him and he perceives his own inability to know the inmost essence of that beauty, his mind, roused and stirred, is driven to seek. This state of excitation, which occurs with regard to things unseen, is termed "longing". When the happiness of being near God seizes him as he gazes on the divine presence and on the actual content of revelation (although his gaze falls short of knowing that beauty in the immanence of disclosure), his heart, though there is much he cannot yet grasp, exults in what he does glimpse. This exultation is termed "intimacy."

But if his gaze is directed to the divine attributes of might, self-sufficiency and needlessness (along with the concomitant perils of non-existence and distance [from God]), then his heart wrenches him in this perception.[1] This agony is termed "fear". Such states result from these perceptions; and the perceptions themselves result from necessitating causes too numerous to list.

Intimacy denotes the mind's jubilance and gladness in the contemplation of beauty. This continues until the mind is overwhelmed, freed from consideration of what remains hidden, as well as from whatever danger of extinction impinges upon it; then its bliss and delight grow great. Hence the view of one gnostic who, when asked whether he yearned, answered, "No, longing occurs only for someone who is absent. But since the absent one is present, for whom should I yearn?" This is the remark of someone immersed in the joy of what he already possesses without any regard for what further graces may remain in the realm of possibility.[A] The man overcome by intimacy desires nothing but isolation and seclusion. In this vein, it is related that Ibrāhīm ibn Adham was coming down from a mountain when he was asked, "Where are you coming from?" He replied, "From the tender clasp of God."

Intimacy with God forces upon the gnostic an estrangement from all that is not God. In fact, anything that constitutes an impediment to seclusion turns into a terrible heaviness on the heart. It is said that Moses (peace be upon him), after his Lord had spoken to him, remained for a long time incapable of listening to anyone else's words without being gripped by nausea. Love transforms the speech of the beloved to a compelling sweetness—sweetness in recollecting him—and this drives the sweetness of anything else out of the heart. For this reason, a sage at prayer declared, "O Thou Who hast brought me close to Thee in thought and estranged me from Thy creatures!" And God said to David (peace be upon him), "Be thou to Me a tender intimate but be alien from all else but Me." When asked how she had attained her spiritual rank, Rābiʿa replied, "By forsaking what did not concern me and by cleaving fast to what never ceases."

ʿAbd al-Wāḥid ibn Zayd remarked, "I passed by an anchorite and asked, 'O anchorite, do you like solitude?' He answered, 'O you, whoever you are, if you had tasted the sweetness of solitude, you would turn to it and seek to estrange your carnal self. Solitude is the beginning of worship.' I pursued the subject, 'O anchorite, what is the least thing you have discovered in your solitude?' And

[A] Aḥmad al-Ghazālī, Abū Ḥāmid's younger brother, seems to reject such notions of intimacy as contrary to the true nature of love, for he writes, "Love in its true nature is but an affliction, and intimacy and ease are something alien to it." Cf. his *Savāniḥ*, 17 (tr. Pourjavady, 36).

he, 'Relief from people's fawning and safety from their wickedness.' I continued, 'O anchorite, when can a person taste the sweetness of close contact with God?' And he, 'When his love becomes pure and his worship sincere.' And I questioned him further, 'When does love become pure?' He answered, 'When it merges with sorrow and turns into a single concern over obedience to God.'"

A gnostic said, "How wondrous-strange creatures are! How can they want any substitute for You? How wondrous-strange hearts are! How can they find ease apart from You and in anyone other than You?"

Perhaps you will ask what the signs of intimacy are. Know then that its specific sign is a constriction of the breast provoked by associating with other people and a sense of dissatisfaction with them coupled with a passion for the sweetness of litany.[A] If one does mingle with people, he is like a solitary in society, a social being in seclusion, a stranger in a settled place, a sedentary *en voyage*, one present in absence and absent in presence, mixed in body, isolated in mind, immersed in the sweetness of remembrance of God.[B]

This is as ʿAlī (may God ennoble his visage) said in describing such folk, "They are people whose knowledge causes them to pounce on the very essence of a matter. They touch the spirit of certainty. They find soft what the pampered[2] find rough. They are at ease with what the ignorant deem strange. They befriend the world with their bodies while their spirits are linked to the supreme site on high. These are God's deputies on His earth and the summoners to His religion."

[A] "Litany", that is, *dhikr*.

[B] Such estrangement is a classic Sufi trait; cf. the remark of the Spanish philosopher and mystic Ibn Bājja (d.c. 553/1139), a younger contemporary of Ghazālī: "These are those whom the Sufis mean in speaking of 'strangers' because although they are in their native lands and among their companions and neighbours, they are strangers in their views and they journey in their thoughts into other levels which are their true native lands." *Tadbīr al-mutawaḥḥid* (ed. Asín-Palacios; Madrid, 1946), 11.

This is the meaning of intimacy with God. These are its signs. These are its proof-texts.

Certain theologians tend to reject intimacy, longing, contentment, and love, espousing the view that these betoken anthropomorphism.[A] They are ignorant of the fact that the beauty of inner perceptions is more perfect than that grasped by the eyes of sense; they are unaware that the pleasure of knowing these inner perceptions holds sway in those endowed with hearts. One of these was Aḥmad ibn Ghālib, known as Ghulām al-Khalīl, who rebuked Junayd, Abū al-Ḥusayn al-Nūrī and their colleagues for speaking of love, longing and passion; to such an extent did he do this that some of them even rejected the stage of contentment on the ground that endurance (*ṣabr*) alone exists while contentment is inconceivable.[B] This, however, is the doctrine of a flawed and limited person who knows nothing but mere husks of the stages of contentment and so fancies that nothing but husks exists. But in fact, sense perception and all that enters into the imagination with regard to religion is mere husk. Beyond this, however, lies the long-sought pith. He who stops at the shell of the walnut fancies that the nut is all wood and of necessity thinks it impossible that oil might be extracted from it.[C] This is pardonable and yet, his excuse is unacceptable. It is said:

[A] The doctrine known as *tashbīh*, or "likening", i.e., interpreting the Qur'ānic verses in which God is described with physical attributes (e.g., God's "hand" in Q. III.73, or His "face" in Q. LV.26) in a literal sense—a doctrine associated especially with such sects as the Karrāmīya; cf. Wensinck, *Muslim Creed*, 207-10, and van Ess, *The Flowering of Muslim Theology*, 51.

[B] On this conflict, see the Introduction to the present translation (p. XVI).

[C] This is an echo of the famous passage in Book XXXV of the *Iḥyā'* (IV.262) in which Ghazālī explicates God's unity by the analogy of a nut (again using his cherished fourfold approach): those who are content with the shell profess God's oneness with their tongues, but not their hearts; those who reach the inner husk are conventional believers; those who approach the kernel have attained illumination; but those who pierce to the innermost oil "see only unity when they regard existence." On this, see also H. Landolt, "Ghazālī and 'Religionswissenschaft'" in *Recherches en spiritualité iranienne* (Tehran, 2005), 71.

No idle swaggerer enjoys close friendship with God.
No trickster gains it by sharp-sightedness.
God's confidants are men all of whom are noble,
All of them elected, all toilers for God.[3]

CHAPTER THIRTEEN

An Exposition of the Meaning of the Uninhibitedness and Forwardness which Overmastering Intimacy Produces

KNOW THAT WHEN intimacy persists and dominates and becomes firmly established, and when neither the stirrings of longing confuse it nor the fear of change and hindrance trouble it, then it engenders a kind of freedom from inhibition in one's words, deeds and secret communications with God.[A] In its outward form, there may be something reprehensible in this as a certain audacity and a lessening of dread reside therein. Even so, for those elevated to this stage of intimacy, this may be permissible. But one who has not been lifted to this stage and yet who in his actions imitates those who have, verges on unbelief and perishes.

An example of this may be found in the prayers of Burkh al-Aswad. God commanded His confidant Moses to ask him to pray for rain for the children of Israel after they had suffered a seven-year drought. Moses went out and prayed for rain amid 70,000 persons.[1] But God revealed to him, "How shall I answer their prayer when their sins are dark upon them and their inmost hearts are wicked, when they call out to Me without any certainty and feel secure against My ruse? Go to My servant named Burkh

[A] "Uninhibitedness" (*inbisāṭ*) means to act boldly and without reserve, and so denotes openness to the beloved. "Forwardness" (*idlāl*) signifies boldness also or, in the definition of Lane (901), "coquettish boldness". Both terms are drawn from the lexicon of erotic love.

and tell him that he should go out so that I may hear his prayer. Moses asked after Burkh but could learn nothing of him. Now one day while Moses was walking on the road, lo, he came upon a black slave with dust between his eyes from his prostrations and wearing a cloak which he had knotted about his neck. Through God's light Moses recognised him. He greeted him, saying, "What is your name?" The man answered, "My name is Burkh." Moses said, "We have been searching for you for a long time. Go out and pray for rain for us." Then Burkh went out and spoke in his own words and said, "What's this that You are doing? Is this what You call mildness? Whatever are You thinking? Are You short on springs of water? Or have the winds resisted obeying You? Are Your supplies exhausted? Or has Your wrath against sinners grown so fierce? Were You not already a pardoner before sinners were even created? You created compassion and commanded kindness. Will You show us that You are hindered or that You are afraid of some evasion that You hurry so to punish?"[A] Burkh spoke without pause until the Israelites were drenched with rain. In half a day God made the grass grow until it reached up to the knees. Then Burkh returned [another day] and Moses met up with him. Burkh said, "What do you think? I contended with My Lord and He treated me fairly!" Moses was irritated with Burkh but God revealed to him, "Burkh makes Me laugh three times a day!"[2]

Of al-Ḥasan al-Baṣrī it is related that he said, "In Basra huts burned to the ground, but in the very midst of them there remained one hut that was not burnt. Abū Mūsā [al-Ashʿarī] was governor of Basra at that time. When he was informed of this, he sent for the owner of the hut. They brought an old man and the governor said, 'O elder! How is it that your hut did not burn?' The old man answered, 'I adjured my Lord not to burn it.'[B]

[A] For this kind of wrangling with God, characteristic of certain early Sufis, and Burkh specifically, see H. Ritter, *The Ocean of the Soul*, 584.

[B] For another similar anecdote, see Ritter, *op.cit.*, 580.

Abū Mūsā said, 'I heard the Messenger of God (may God bless him and grant him peace) say, "In my community there are people with dishevelled heads and filthy clothes for whom God, if they adjured Him, would fulfil their vows."'"[3] And he went on, "A fire broke out in Basra. Abū ʿUbayda al-Khawwāṣ came and strode through the fire. The governor of Basra said to him, 'I see that you are not burned by the fire!' And he replied, 'I adjured my Lord not to burn me with the fire.' The governor countered, 'Then order the fire to go out.' So he commanded the fire and it went out."

Abū Ḥafṣ went walking on a certain day and a crazed villager[4] came up to him. Abū Ḥafṣ said to him, "What's happened to you?" The man answered, "My donkey has strayed and I have no other." Abū Ḥafṣ stopped and said, "By Your might! I will not budge a single step until You return his donkey to him!" At once the donkey appeared and Abū Ḥafṣ continued on his way.

Such happenings are commonplace among those granted intimacy with God. Others should not mimic them. Junayd said, "Those admitted to God's intimacy in their affection and prayer and seclusion say things which would be unbelief in the mouths of common folk." Another time he said, "If ordinary people were to hear these things, they would accuse them of unbelief; and yet, they discover an enhancement of their states therein." From intimates with God this is allowable and indeed, quite proper. A poet alludes to this when he says:

People whom pride in their Lord pervades
—a slave takes pride in the stature of his lord—
boast at the sight of Him over everything else.
How lovely to see them swagger in that glory!

They do not deem it improbable that God may be pleased with one servant for what would anger Him in another, so long as their rank differs. In the Qur'ān there are directives in this sense for those who discern and comprehend. All the tales of the Qur'ān are directives for those endowed with both insight and eyesight, so that they regard them with an explicative eye.[A] Only for the deluded are these mere bedtime stories.[5]

First among these tales is that of Adam and Iblīs. Don't you see how both of them shared and shared alike in the name of sin and opposition, and then differed from each other in election and protection? But Iblīs despaired of God's mercy. Hence it is said that he is among those removed far from God. Of Adam, by contrast, it is said that he disobeyed and went astray, but that later his Lord selected him and so he turned to Him in repentance and was guided aright.

God rebuked His Prophet (may God bless him and grant him peace) for turning away from one worshipper and going toward another; both were equal in their worship and yet, they differed in their manner of worship. God said, *But as for him who comes to you with earnest purpose and is afraid, from him are you distracted.*[6] And regarding the other He said, *As for him who thinks himself independent, to him do you pay regard.*[7] So, too, He ordered him to sit with a certain group and said, *And when those who believe in Our revelations come to you, say 'Peace be upon you.'*[8] But He commanded him to turn away from others, for He said, *And when you see those who tamper with Our revelations, turn away from them*, and He went on, *Do not sit with the assembly of wrong-doers after the remembrance.*[9] Again He says, *Restrain yourself together with those who cry out to their Lord both at morning and at evening.*[10]

Therefore, forwardness and freedom from inhibition are allowable from some of God's servants but not from others. A saying of Moses (peace be upon him) aptly addresses the unrestrained nature of intimacy: *That is only Your way of testing by which You lead astray whom You will and guide rightly whom You will.*[11] And this statement of his is extenuation and excuse for himself when he was told, *Go to Pharaoh*[12] for he said, *And they have charged me*

[A] Arabic *ʿayn al-iʿtibār*. The phrase designates the faculty of drawing spiritual inferences from the contemplation of phenomena; cf. Q. LIX.2: "Draw an inference [*faʿtabirū*], you who have eyes!"

with a crime[13] as well as *I am afraid that they will deny me and I will be constricted and tongue-tied,*[14] along with Moses' further statement *We fear that he may gravely harm us or that he may play the tyrant.*[15] Anything even similar to this, from anyone but Moses, would be bad conduct, but he who has been uplifted to the stage of intimacy is treated with gracious indulgence.

Jonah (peace be upon him), however, though what he did was less, was not so indulged. He was lifted to the stage of constriction[A] and awe but then punished by imprisonment in the belly of the whale *in a triple darkness.*[B16] Indeed, until the Day of Resurrection it is cried out over Jonah: *Had it not been that favour from his Lord reached him he would surely have been cast into a bare place while he was still blameworthy.*[17] On this al-Ḥasan [al-Baṣrī] commented that "the bare place" is resurrection. Our Prophet was forbidden from imitating Jonah; instead, it was said to him, *Be patient for the judgment of your Lord and do not be like him of the fish who called out when he was confined.*[18]

Some of these differences are due to differences in states (*aḥwāl*) and stations (*maqāmāt*); others are due to God's prior and eternally decreed allotment of preference and distinction among people. God says, *We preferred some of the prophets to others.*[19] And also: *Among them are some with whom God spoke and others He exalted in degrees.*[20] Jesus was one of God's preferred ones. It was because of his very boldness that he wished himself peace and said, *Peace be upon me the day I was born and the day on which I die and the day on which I will be raised alive.*[21] This was uninhibitedness on his part; it was based on the graciousness he had witnessed in the stage of intimacy. As for John, son of Zachariah, he was raised to the level of awe and shame. He did not speak until his Creator praised him saying, *Peace be upon him!*[22]

[A] "Constriction" (Arabic *qabḍ*), a Sufi technical term, the antithesis of "expansion" (*basṭ*); cf. Zaehner, *Hindu and Muslim Mysticism*, 118-119.

[B] Zabīdī explains this triple darkness as that of the whale's belly, the ocean, and the night; *Itḥāf*, IX.643.

Consider how what Joseph's brothers did to him was tolerated! Indeed, one scholar noted, "I have counted, from his first word *When they said, "Joseph and his brother are more beloved by our father than we are"*[23] to the beginning of verse twenty where God relates [his brothers'] disavowal of him, some forty sins, some of which are worse than others; in a single utterance there may even be three or four at once. Even so, God forgave them and pardoned them."

In the case of ᶜUzayr[A] even the single question he posed on predestination was not tolerated from him; hence, of him it came to be said that he has been effaced from the register of the prophets.[24] So too with Balᶜām ibn Bāᶜūrā', one of the greatest of scholars, a man who prospered through religion and yet, from whom such behaviour was not tolerated. Again, Āṣaf was one of the dissolute; he sinned through his limbs but God forgave him.[25]

It is related that God said to Solomon (peace be upon him), "O Chief of Worshippers! O Son of the Ascetics' Pilgrim Goal! For how long will your nephew Āṣaf sin against Me while I treat him with mildness time and time again? By My Glory and Majesty, if I take back a single token of My loving-kindness towards him, I shall certainly leave him behind as an example to those now living and as a warning to those who will come after him." When Āṣaf came to Solomon he told him what God had confided to him. Āṣaf went out and climbed upon a sand-dune. He raised his head and both his hands towards heaven and said, "O my God and my Lord, You are You and I am I. How can I repent if You do not turn to me as well? How can I resist temptation if You do not preserve me? Surely I will backslide!" Then God replied to him, "You have spoken truthfully, O Āṣaf! You are you and I am I. Turn towards repentance for I have already turned towards you in repentance. *I am the Ever-Forgiving and Merciful.*"[26] This is the discourse of a man who is bold towards God through Him, who flees from Him towards Him, who looks at Him through Him.[27]

[A] The Biblical prophet Ezra.

In Tradition it is related that to a man whom He had set aright after he had been on the very brink of destruction God revealed the following words, "With how many sins have you come before Me and yet, I have forgiven you. I have destroyed whole peoples for less!"[28]

Indeed, this is God's custom towards His servants: to prefer and advance and hold them back in accord with what His primordial will has foreordained. In the Qur'ān, these tales occur so that through them you may know God's custom toward His servants who lived in former ages. In the Qur'ān, there is nothing other than right guidance, light and providential disclosure from God to His creatures. At times, He makes Himself known to them through affirmation of His sanctity, as He says: *Say, He is God, the One, God the Eternal, He neither begets nor is begotten, and there is no one comparable to Him.*[29] At other times, He discloses Himself through attributes of majesty, as when He says: *The sovereign Lord, the Holy One, Peace, Keeper of the Faith, the Guardian, the Majestic, the Compeller, the Superb.*[30] Yet again, at other times, He makes himself known to them through His actions that inspire fear and hope; He recites to them His custom regarding His foes and His prophets, for He says: *Have you not seen how your Lord dealt with ʿĀd, with Iram the many-pillared?*[31] And also: *Have you not seen how your Lord dealt with the people of the Elephant?*[32] Beyond these three, the Qur'ān does not go, namely: guidance to knowledge of God's nature and holiness; knowledge of His attributes and names; and knowledge of His actions and His custom with regard to His servants.

Sūrat al-Ikhlāṣ[A] contains one of these three types, to wit, affirmation of holiness. The Messenger of God (may God bless him and grant him peace) likened this chapter to a third of the Qur'ān, saying, "Whoever reads the *Sūrat al-Ikhlāṣ* has read one-third of the Qur'ān."[B] This is because supreme sanctity resides in God being One according to three matters, and that what issues from

[A] That is, *Sūra* 112.

[B] There are only four verses in this *sūra*, hence the force of the Tradition.

Him can never be like Him or comparable to Him. His statement shows this: *He does not beget.*[33] Nor does He come forth from anyone else who is like Him or comparable to Him, and His further words show this: *He is not begotten.*[34] And finally, nothing, be it substance or accident, is on His level. His words again show this: *There is no one comparable to Him.*[35] Indeed, the whole is a detailed exposition on the words "There is no God but God."

These are the secrets of the Qur'ān which has infinite such secrets. *Nothing of wet or dry but it is in a clear Book.*[36] For this reason Ibn Masᶜūd said, "Study the Qur'ān and seek out its wonders. Indeed, the knowledge of the first and of the last is contained therein."[37] It is as he said, but he alone knows this who has pored over its individual words thoughtfully and has purified his understanding until very word in it bears witness to him that it is the speech of a mighty Compeller, an omnipotent King, and that it transcends human capacity. Most of the Qur'ān's secrets lie hidden in tales and reports. Therefore, be avid to extract them so that such marvels may be disclosed to you that you will despise all gaudy sciences outside its purview.

This, then, is what we intended to say on the significance of intimacy and freedom from constraint, as well as to explain the disparity among people on this score.

[PROLOGUE]

The Meaning of Contentment with God's Decree: Its True Nature and What Tradition Reports of Its Merit

CONTENTMENT IS ONE of the fruits of paradise and one of the supreme stages of those brought near to God. To the multitude its true nature remains obscure. Whatever ambiguity and misleading supposition may enter into it remain unclear except to him whom God has instructed in mystical explication and granted religious comprehension. To be sure, there are some who deny the notion that contentment can exist in opposition to the passions. They argue that contentment with everything because it is the creation of God means that one must be content with unbelief and sin. People are misled by this; they see contentment with immorality and iniquity and they abandon resistance and rejection of them [sins] on the pretext of surrendering to God's decree. If these mysteries [of contentment] had been divulged to those who limit themselves to hearkening to the outward aspects of Revelation, the Messenger of God (may God bless him and grant him peace) would not have prayed for Ibn ʿAbbās, as when he said, "O God, give him discernment in religion and teach him mystical interpretation (*ta'wīl*)!"[1]

Let us begin then by explaining the merit of contentment. After that we shall move on to anecdotes about the states of the contented. We shall then discuss the true nature of contentment and how to conceive of it as something counter to passion. Finally, we shall mention what is deemed to be perfected contentment and yet is nothing of the sort, such as abandoning prayer and quiescence in the face of sin.

CHAPTER FOURTEEN

An Exposition of the Merit of Contentment

TO BEGIN WITH Qur'ānic verses: God says, *God is content with them and they with Him.*[2] He says further, *Is the reward of goodness anything but goodness?*[3] The aim of goodness is God's contentment with His servant. This is the reward for the servant's contentment with God. God states, *blessed dwellings in Gardens of Eden, though God's contentment is a far greater thing.*[4] God exalts contentment above the Gardens of Eden just as He has elevated remembrance of Him above ritual prayer, as He says, *Prayer preserves from lewdness and iniquity and yet, remembrance of God is greater.*[5] Just as seeing the one remembered in worship is greater than prayer alone, so, too, the contentment of the Lord of Paradise is more sublime than paradise itself. Indeed, it is the goal sought by all the inhabitants of paradise. In Sacred Tradition [it is related] that God reveals Himself to believers and says "Pray to Me," and that they reply, "Your contentment!"[6] Their request for contentment after gazing upon Him indicates the utmost preference.

We shall discuss the true nature of human contentment later; but God's good pleasure with man partakes of another signification that comes close to something we discussed earlier concerning God's love for man. Since human nature cannot grasp it, its inmost nature cannot possibly be divulged. If someone were strong enough to grasp it, his grasp would be independent of his own self. Beyond the vision of God there is no further level; the blessed ask for contentment solely because it is the reason that that vision endures. When they attain the bliss of vision it is as if they glimpsed the utmost of all goals and the ultimate of all wishes; hence, when they were commanded to ask, they asked only for its continuance for they knew that God's contentment was the reason for the continual lifting of the veil. God says, *And there is more with Us.*[7] A commentator remarks, "At the moment of increase the inhabitants of paradise receive three gifts from the Lord of the Worlds. First, a gift from God the like of which the inhabitants of paradise do not possess. This is His word, *No soul knows what delight has been concealed for them!*[8] Second, the 'peace be upon them!' from their Lord. This goes beyond the gift in worthiness and consists of His saying, *'Peace!' the word from a merciful Lord.*[9] Third, God says, 'I am pleased with you,' for this is more excellent than both the gift and the greeting, as when He says, *and greater is God's contentment*[10], that is, than any bliss in which they exist." This then is the merit of God's satisfaction which is a fruit of human satisfaction.

With regard to Sacred Tradition, it is reported that the Prophet (may God bless him and grant him peace) asked a group of his companions, "What are you?" They answered, "Believers." He asked, "What is the mark of your belief?" They replied, "We endure patiently in affliction and we give thanks in well-being and we are content in whatever God decrees." He exclaimed, "Believers, by the Lord of the Kaʿba!"[11] According to another Sacred Tradition he said, "Wise men, learned men, are very nearly prophets because of their insight."[12] Again in Sacred Tradition it is said, "Blessed is he who is guided to Islam and whose livelihood suffices and who is content with it."[13] He (may God bless him and grant him peace) said, "Whoever is content with even a little sustenance from God, God is pleased with even a little good work from him."[14] He also said, "When God loves a person He afflicts him and if he endures patiently, He selects him and if he is content, He singles him out."[15] Then too he said, "At the Day of Judgement God will cause a group of my community to sprout wings and then they will fly up from their graves to heaven where they will roam freely and take pleasure in whatever they wish. The angels will say to them, 'Have you seen the Final Accounting?' And they will reply, 'We have not seen any accounting.' Again the angels will ask, 'Have you crossed the Bridge of Ṣirāṭ?' And they will answer, 'We have not seen Ṣirāṭ.' Then the angels will ask, 'Have you seen hell?' And they will reply, 'We have not seen a thing!' The angels will ask, 'From whose community do you come?' And they will answer, 'From the community of Muḥammad.' The angels will exclaim, 'By God, we beseech you, tell us what your deeds were in the world!' And they will reply, 'Two traits we had and for these God allowed us by His gracious mercy to attain to this rank.' 'And what are these two?' the angels ask further. And they will reply, 'Whenever we were alone we were ashamed that we had sinned against Him and were contented with the little which He had apportioned for us.' At this the angels will cry out, 'Truly you are worthy!'"[16]

He (may God bless him and grant him peace) said, "O community of the poor! Give God your contented hearts and so win the reward for your poverty; otherwise, nothing."[17]

In the Traditions of Moses (peace be upon him), it is recorded that the Children of Israel said to him, "Ask your Lord on our behalf what we may do to please Him." Moses said, "My God! You have heard what they said!" God replied, "O Moses, say to them that they should be pleased with Me and then I will be pleased with them."[18]

In further witness to this is what has been reported on the authority of our Prophet (may God bless him and grant him peace) when he said, "Whoever would like to know where he stands with God should consider how God stands with him. Indeed, God places a person at the level at which he himself has placed God."[19]

In the Traditions of David (peace be upon him), God says, "Why should My friends have any concern for this world? Such concern takes the sweetness of silent colloquy with Me away from their hearts. O David, My love for My friends is that they be spiritual and not riven by anxiety."[20]

And it is related that Moses (peace be upon him) said, "O Lord, show me what pleases You so that I may perform it!" God confided to him, "My contentment lies in what you loathe but even so, you do not bear up steadfastly against what you loathe." Moses replied, "Show me [what pleases You]." God said, "My contentment resides in your contentment with My decree."[21]

When Moses prayed he said, "O Lord, which of Your creatures is dearest to You?" God replied, "He who is at peace with Me even when I take away what he loves." Moses again asked, "Which of Your creatures are You angry with?" And God answered, "He who asks Me for guidance in a matter and then, when I choose for him, is angry with My decree."[22] Something even harsher than that is recorded, namely, that God says, "I am God. There is no God but I. He who does not endure against My trial of him nor show gratitude for My beneficence to him and is not content with My decree—let him take a lord other than Myself!"[23]

Equally disastrous, according to what our Prophet (may God bless him and grant him peace) has related, is that God say, "I have ordained the measures. I have set the arrangement of things in order. I have strengthened My handiwork. He who is content shall find contentment with Me until he meet Me. He who is disgruntled shall find anger with Me until he meet Me."[24]

In a well-known Tradition God says, "I created good and evil. Blessed is he whom I created for good and at whose hands I have effected good. Woe to him whom I have created for evil and at whose hands I have made evil occur. And woe upon woe to him who says 'why?' and 'how?'"[25]

According to early Traditions, a prophet complained to God of hunger, poverty and lice for ten years but God did not respond to his wishes. Finally, God spoke to him, "Why do you complain like this? Your beginning was with Me in the Mother of the Book before I created the heavens and the earth. Thus was it established for you by Me from before; thus did I ordain for you before I created the world. Do you want Me to redo the world for your sake or change what I have decreed for you? Is what you prefer to be set above what I prefer? Or what you wish above what I wish? By My glory and majesty, stammer this even once more in your breast and I will rub you out of the registry of prophecy."[26]

Of Adam (peace be upon him) it is related that some of his young sons were climbing up and down on his body and that one of them placed his foot on his ribs as if they were steps and then clambered onto his head and descended again. All this while Adam kept bowing silently toward the ground, nor did he even raise his head. One of his other sons said to him, "Father, do not you see what this one is doing to you? You should forbid him from doing that." Adam answered, "My son, I see what you do not see. I know what you do not know. Once I did move and at that I dropped from the abode of bliss to the habitation of misery. I am afraid that if I move yet again I shall be struck by what I do not know."[27]

Anas ibn Mālik (may God be pleased with him) said, "I served the Messenger of God (may God bless him and grant him peace) for ten years. He never said to me of anything I did, 'Why did you do this?' Nor about anything I did not do, 'Why did you not do this?' He said of nothing, 'Would that it were not!' Nor of anything that didn't exist, 'Would that it were!' And when anyone among his people disputed with me he used to say, 'Leave him be. If something has been ordained, it will be.'"[28]

It is related that God said to David (peace be upon him), "O David, you wish and I wish, but only what I wish, is."[29]

As for the early Traditions, Ibn ᶜAbbās (may God be pleased with him) said, "The first who will be summoned to paradise on the Day of Resurrection will be those who praise God under every circumstance."

ᶜUmar ibn ᶜAbd al-ᶜAzīz said, "No joys remain for me apart from the workings of divine predestination."[30] Someone questioned him, "What do you desire?" He answered, "What God has decreed."

And Maymūn ibn Mihrān said, "Whoever is discontented with the divine decree has no remedy for his stupidity."

Fuḍayl declared, "If you are not at peace[31] with what God has ordained, neither will you be content with what your own self decrees."

And ʿAbd al-ʿAzīz ibn Abī Rawwād said, "What is important is not to eat barley bread and vinegar, or to put on clothing of hair and wool. What is important is to be content with God."

ʿAbd Allāh ibn Masʿūd declared, "To lick a hot coal—burn what it may, leave what it may!—is preferable than that I should say about anything that exists 'Would that it were not!' or of something that is not, 'Would that it were!'"[32]

A man was looking at an abscess on the leg of Muḥammad ibn Wāsiʿ and remarked, "I pity you because of this abscess." But he replied, "Ever since it emerged, I have been thankful for it because it did not break out in my eye."[33]

In the accounts of the Israelites, it is related that a worshipper who worshipped God for a long time was shown in a dream that such-and-such a shepherdess would be his consort in paradise. He began to ask about her until he found her. He invited her to be his guest for three days so that he might see how she acted. He kept vigil all night while she slept and he fasted while she ate. At last he said, "Do you do anything other than what I have seen?" She answered, "By God, nothing but what you have seen! I know nothing else." But he kept after her to search her memory until she said, "There is one trait. If I am suffering hardship I do not wish to be at ease. If I am sick I do not wish to be well. If I am in the sun I do not wish to be in the shade." The worshipper set his hand upon his head and exclaimed, "This is the trait to have! By God, this is a mighty quality of which most of God's servants are incapable!"[34]

One of the pious ancestors said, "Whenever God hands down a decree from heaven He likes people to be pleased with His decree."

Abū al-Dardāʾ said, "The summit of belief is patience with God's decision and contentment with His decree."[35]

ʿUmar (may God be pleased with him) said, "Whatever condition of need or of ease in which I find myself is all the same to me, whether at morning or at evening."[36]

[Sufyān] al-Thawrī stated, "One day I was with Rābiʿa and I said, 'O God, be pleased with us!' She remarked, 'Are you not ashamed before God to ask Him to be pleased when you yourself are not pleased?' Thawrī exclaimed, 'I ask God's forgiveness!'"[37]

Jaʿfar ibn Sulaymān al-Ḍabuʿī asked her, "When is a person pleased with God?" She replied, "Whenever his pleasure in distress is equal to his pleasure in delight."[38]

Fuḍayl used to say, "A man is pleased with God whenever it is equal in his eyes whether he receives largesse or does not receive it."[39]

Aḥmad ibn Abī al-Ḥawārī remarked, "Abū Sulaymān al-Dārānī used to say, 'In His generosity God is pleased with a person for the same thing that a servant may be pleased with in his masters.' I asked him, 'How so?' And he told me, 'Is it not the wish of a servant in the human sphere that his master be satisfied with him?' 'Yes,' I replied. And he went on, 'Indeed, God loves it in His servants that they be pleased with Him.'"[40]

Sahl said, "People's share of certitude is in proportion to their share of satisfaction; their share of satisfaction is in proportion to their life with God."

The Prophet (may God bless him and grant him peace) said, "God in His judgement and majesty has placed vitality and gladness in contentment and in certitude, but in doubt and discontent He has set sorrow and sadness."[41]

CHAPTER FIFTEEN

An Exposition of the Essence of Contentment (and How It Can be Conceived as a Check to Appetite)

KNOW THAT ANYONE who asserts that only patient endurance will suffice to counter appetite and the array of our tribulations—and that mere contentment cannot conceivably do so—does all but repudiate love itself. Nevertheless, if it be affirmed that love for God and immersion of one's purpose within Him are in fact conceivable, then there is no alternative but to concede that love engenders contentment with the actions of the lover. This falls under two aspects.

First, sensitivity to pain is abolished: one can run up against a painful thing and not feel it, or one can be wounded without feeling pain. For example, in war a man in a state of fury or of fear may be wounded and not feel it until he spots blood and then infers that he is wounded. Even more, someone absorbed in an urgent task may step on a thorn and not perceive the pain because his mind is so taken up. Then, too, someone undergoing cupping or having his head shaved with a dull razor feels pain but if his mind is absorbed in some weighty concern, the barber and the cupper do their jobs without his noticing it. This is all because the mind, when plunged in its own affairs and dealing with them, apprehends nothing else.

The lover is like this. His whole concern is to be submerged in contemplation of his beloved. He does not perceive what would normally cause him pain or distress because of the overwhelming force of love upon his mind.[A] This can occur when he is afflicted by something other than the beloved; how much the more so when it is the beloved in person who afflicts him and seizes his mind with love? For amorous passion is one of the mightiest distractions. Since this is conceivable when the pain is small and the love is light, it is easily conceivable in a great pain when love is intense. Love too can be conceived as doubling in force just as pain redoubles in its strength. In the same way that the love of beautiful forms increases when perceived by the eye, so does love of beautiful inner forms intensify when seized by the light of insight, even though the beauty of the divine presence and majesty are incommensurate with both "beauty" and "majesty". Anyone to whom the merest jot of this is disclosed is dazzled and dumbfounded. He faints and grows insensible to what has overcome him.

It is related that Fatḥ al-Mawṣilī's wife stumbled and tore off her toenail. She laughed. Someone asked, "Don't you feel the pain?" She answered, "The pleasure of the reward removes the bitterness of the pain from my mind." Sahl had an illness of which he cured others but not himself. When asked about this he said, "O friend! A blow from the beloved does not hurt."[1]

The second aspect involves feeling and perceiving the pain—desiring it and even willing it—while remaining content with it; that is, willing it with one's own mind, although it is repugnant to nature. This is like the person who asks for a blood-letter for blood-letting or for cupping: he feels the pain but he is content with it; indeed, he craves it and even feels a certain friendliness towards the blood-letter for his action.

This is the condition of someone who is content with whatever pain befalls him. So too, anyone who travels in search of profit experiences the hardships of the road. And yet, his love for the outcome of his journey makes the toil of travel seem good to him and renders him content. Whenever some trial from God befalls a

[A] In his *K. al-Arbaʿīn* (Cairo, 1344; 267), Ghazālī remarks, "One who is absorbed in love does not feel even the pain of a sword-blow."

person, as long as he possesses the certainty that there is a reward stored up for him that is over and above what he has lost, he is contented with it; he desires it and loves it and thanks God for it.

The man who glimpses the reward and the benevolence with which he will be requited for his travails is in a similar situation; however, love may overwhelm him to such an extent that his share as a lover rests in whatever the beloved wants and finds satisfaction in, and he can conceive of nothing beyond this. The will and the pleasure of the lover become that which is to be loved and sought after.

All of this takes place in human love concerning those things that can be [physically] seen; lovers depict it for one another in both verse and prose. It has no meaning except as a physical vision of the beauty of external form. But if we consider this [physical] beauty, it is nothing but skin, flesh and blood crammed full of filth and reeking impurities, the beginning of which is a putrid drop and the end of which is a foul cadaver while in the intervening time, it lugs its own excrement about. If we consider that which perceives beauty—that is, the eye—it is a wretched organ, which is so often muddled in what it sees, falsifies the little as big and the big as little, the far as near, the ugly as beautiful!

Thus, if dominion by this sort of love be conceivable, how can the notion arise that love of eternal and everlasting beauty is impossible: beauty of endless perfection, perceived by the inward sight which error cannot assail and death does not set spinning! Quite the contrary: at death it remains living in God's presence, gladdened by God's sustenance and growing through death into ever greater wakefulness and discovery. The matter is obvious; viewed by the discerning eye it presents no puzzling riddles. Existence itself, together with the tales and states and utterances of spiritual lovers, bears witness of it to you.

Shaqīq al-Balkhī said, "He who considers the reward for suffering has no desire to escape from it."[2]

Junayd said, "I asked Sarī al-Saqaṭī, 'Does the lover feel the pain of his affliction?' He replied, 'No.' I persisted, 'Even if he is struck with a sword?' He replied, 'Yes, even if he is struck seventy times in succession with a sword!'"[3]

Another said, "I love everything that He loves such that if He were to love hellfire, I would love to enter it."

Bishr ibn al-Ḥārith said, "I passed a man in the eastern section of Baghdad who had been given a thousand lashes and had not uttered a word. He was carried off to prison and I followed. I asked him, 'Why were you whipped?' And he replied, 'Because I am in love.' I continued, 'And why were you silent?' He replied, 'Because my beloved was face to face with me and looking right at me.' I went on, 'What if you were looking into the face of the Supremely Beloved?' At that he gave a loud shriek and dropped to the ground dead."[4]

Yaḥyā ibn Muᶜādh al-Rāzī said, "When the blessed in heaven gaze on God their eyes meld into their hearts from the sheer pleasure of gazing upon Him for eight hundred years without returning to their place. What then do you think happens to hearts in this world when they fall between His beauty and His majesty? When they glimpse His majesty they are awestruck and when they catch sight of His beauty they are lost in wonder."

Bishr said, "I was going toward ᶜAbbādān[A] at the start of my spiritual life. I met a man who was blind and leprous and who had had a seizure; the ants were feasting on his flesh. I lifted up his head and placed it on my lap and all the while I kept talking to him. When he came to he said, 'Who is this busybody who comes between me and my Lord? If He tore me limb from limb I would only grow in love for Him!'" And Bishr remarked, "Afterwards, whenever I have witnessed a trial of affliction between a servant and his Lord I've refused to intervene."

Abū ᶜAmr Muḥammad ibn al-Ashᶜath said, "The Egyptians went for four months without any food other than gazing upon

[A] In Abbasid times, this city—the present-day Ābādān in Iran—on the left bank of the Shaṭṭ al-ᶜArab, near the mouth of the Persian Gulf, was famed as a centre for pious ascetics; cf. *EI*^{2}, 1.5; Hugh Kennedy, *An Historical Atlas of Islam*, 21.

the face of Joseph the Truthful. When they felt hungry they gazed upon his face so that his beauty might distract them from feeling the pain of hunger." In fact, in the Qur'ān there is an even more vivid example than that. This is when the women cut their hands out of giddiness at the sight of Joseph's beauty and felt nothing at all.[A]

Saʿīd ibn Yaḥyā said, "In Basra in the *khān* of ʿAṭā' ibn Muslim, I saw a young man with a knife in his hand. While people crowded all about him, he cried out at the top of his voice, saying,

> The day of leave-taking is longer than Judgement Day.
> Death is better than the agony of parting.
> They say, 'Set out!' But I answer, 'I am not travelling.
> It is my own heart's blood that is setting out.'

At this he ripped his belly open with the knife and fell down dead. I inquired about him and his story. I learned that he was in love with a boy belonging to one of the rulers who had been barred from him for a day."

Reportedly Jonah said to Gabriel (peace be upon him), "Show me the most worshipful person on earth." He pointed out a man whose hands and feet and eyes leprosy had destroyed. Jonah overheard him saying, "My God, You let me enjoy what You willed through them and You took away from me what You had willed but, O Righteous and Bountiful One, You have left me hope in You."

Of ʿAbd Allāh ibn ʿUmar it is reported that one of his sons suffered from an illness. ʿUmar's pain on his behalf was so fierce that some people remarked, "We fear for this old man if something should happen to the boy." The boy died. When Ibn ʿUmar went out for his funeral procession, no one was happier than he. When questioned he replied, "My sadness came from pity for him but when God's command came, we were content with it."

Masrūq said, "A man in the desert had a dog, a donkey and a rooster. The rooster woke his people up for prayer. The donkey

[A] See Q. XII.30-31.

served to carry water for them along with their tent. The dog stood on guard for them. There came a fox and made off with the rooster. The people were distressed but this righteous man exclaimed, "Perhaps it is good." Not long after a jackal came and ripped the donkey's belly open and killed him. The people mourned but the man said again, "Maybe it is good." Still later the dog was struck down and yet the man still said, "Maybe it is good." On that very day they awoke and saw that round about them everyone had been taken prisoner while they alone remained. The righteous man remarked, "They took these people captive because of the racket made by their dogs, donkeys and roosters, whereas for us there was some good in the loss of our animals, just as God had ordained." Therefore, he who recognises the hidden grace of God is content with whatever He does under any circumstance.[A]

It is reported that Jesus (peace be upon him) passed by a man who was blind and leprous, crippled and afflicted with paralysis on both sides;[5] his flesh was crumbling away from leprosy. Even so he said, "Praise be to God for saving me from that with which He has afflicted so many of His creatures!" Jesus exclaimed, "O, what affliction might I see that you have been spared!" The man answered, "O Spirit of God, I am better off than those in whose hearts God has not placed what He has placed in mine; by that I mean, knowledge of Him." Jesus declared, "You have spoken the truth! Give me your hand!" He gave him his hand and suddenly he had the handsomest face and the finest form of any man. God had removed his affliction. He followed Jesus and served God with him.[6]

ᶜUrwa ibn Zubayr had his leg amputated at the knee because of a gangrenous sore which had erupted there. Afterwards he exclaimed, "Praise God Who took only one of my legs! I swear by You—even if You have taken away, You have also let remain and even if You have afflicted, You have safeguarded as well!" And all that night he prayed without ceasing.[7]

[A] Ghazālī tells the same story in his *Kitāb al-arbaᶜīn*, 268; see *Theodicy*, 255-6, for further references.

Ibn Masʿūd said, "Poverty and wealth are two mounts. To me it is the same which of them I ride. If poverty, then there is opportunity for patient endurance. If wealth, then there is occasion for generous giving."[8]

Abū Sulaymān al-Dārānī remarked, "From every [spiritual] station, except for the station of contentment, I have gained a state. But from it I have only the semblance of its breeze. Even so, were God to bring all creatures into paradise and thrust me into hellfire, I would be content."[9]

Someone said to a gnostic, "Have you attained the utmost in contentment with God?" He answered, "The utmost? No. But I have attained the station of contentment. If God were to make of me a bridge over hell by which creatures could cross to paradise, and then had filled hell with me alone, in order to fulfil His vow and to have a substitute for His creatures, I would be pleased with His judgement and I would be content with His decree."[10] These are the words of a man who knows that love can possess the mind so fully that it blocks him from feeling the pain of hellfire. If sensation does remain, the fullest possible pleasure floods his mind for he is aware that by meeting him in hell, he obtains his beloved's satisfaction. This state of mind is conceivable, even if remote from our usual insipid states of mind. A weak person, who is excluded from such knowledge, ought not deny the states of the powerful by assuming that what he cannot attain lies beyond the capability of God's friends.

Rūdhabārī said, "I asked Abū ʿAbd Allāh Ibn al-Jallāʾ al-Dimashqī the meaning of a certain person's remark: 'I would like my body cut into pieces with scissors if only so that people might obey God.' He explained, 'I say to you, if this comes from compassion and good counsel to humanity then I approve it; but if it proceeds from self-glorification[11] then I do not acknowledge it.'" He went on to say, "At this I passed out."[12]

ʿImrān ibn al-Ḥusayn had dropsy of the abdomen and had to lie flat on his back for thirty years; he could neither stand nor sit. A hole had been pierced in his bed of stripped palm-fronds where he lay so that he could answer the call of nature. Muṭarrif and his brother al-ʿAlāʾ[13] came into his room. Muṭarrif began to weep when he observed his condition. But ʿImrān said, "Why are you crying?" To which he replied, "Because I see you in this atrocious state." But the other enjoined him, "Do not cry. If this is what pleases God most, it pleases me too." Later he added, "I will tell you something. Maybe God will give you some benefit from it. But keep quiet about it until I am dead. Angels visit me and I am friends with them. They greet me and I hear their salutation. From that I know that this affliction is no punishment. In fact, it is the cause of tremendous favour. How could someone who witnesses this in the midst of his suffering not be content with Him?"[14]

Muṭarrif also said, "We came to pay Suwayd ibn Mathʿaba[15] a visit. We saw a garment that had been flung down but we did not think anything was under it until someone picked it up.[A] His wife said to him, 'May my family be your ransom! What shall we give you to eat and what to drink?' He replied, 'Long have I lain here and my hipbones are covered with bedsores. I have turned into a tattered garment. I do not relish food and I cannot stomach drink since such-and-such a time' (he mentioned the days). 'Still it would not give me pleasure to have even the thinnest fingernail-paring less of this misery.'"[16]

When Saʿd ibn Abī Waqqāṣ came to Mecca after he had lost his sight, people came rushing up to him and each one asked him to pray for him. So he prayed for this one and he prayed for that one since he was someone whose prayers were answered. ʿAbd Allāh ibn al-Sāʾib recounted, "I came to him while still a boy and I made myself known to him. He acknowledged me for he said, 'Are you Qurʾān-reciter for the Meccans?' I answered, 'Yes.' Sāʾib then told a story at the end of which he said, "O Uncle, you pray for other people but if you would pray for yourself, God might

[A] Mathʿaba has become so emaciated that he looks to his visitors like nothing more than a ragged cloth.

restore your sight." Saᶜd smiled and said, "O my son, God's decree is more excellent to me than my own eyesight!"[17]

A Sufi lost his small boy for three days and had no news of him. Someone remarked to him that if he asked God, He would restore the child to him. But the Sufi rejoined, "For me to take issue with what God has ordained would be worse than the loss of my son."[18]

Of a certain worshipper it is related that he said, "I committed a great sin and for sixty years now I have been weeping over it." He exerted himself in worship to repent of that sin. When somebody asked him what his sin was, he answered, "On one occasion I said of something that had come to pass 'Would that it had not happened!'" One of the pious ancestors declared, "I would rather have my body slashed with scissors than to say about anything which God has ordained 'Would that He had not ordained it!'"[19]

Once someone said to ᶜAbd al-Wāḥid ibn Zayd, "Here is a man who has served God for fifty years." Upon which he went to him and inquired, "Dear fellow, tell me about yourself. Are you content with God?" "No," he replied. "Are you on good terms with Him?" Again he answered no. "Are you content with Him?" Again he said no. "So then the only increase you have from Him is in fasting and in prayer?" "Yes," he conceded. So he said to that man, "If I were not ashamed in your presence, I would tell you that your practice of fifty years has been diseased."[20] The meaning of this is: The door of your heart has not opened so that you might rise to the level of nearness to God by works of the heart. Rather, you are classed only in the category of those on the right hand since the increase God has granted you consists solely in activities of the limbs. But these are increase only for common folk.

Several people came to see Shiblī in the lunatic asylum where he was confined. He had collected a pile of stones in front of him. When he asked, "Who are you?" his visitors answered, "Those who love you." He advanced hurling stones at them and they ran away. He cried out, "What's the matter with you? You claim to love me. If you speak the truth, then be patient when I put you to the test!"[21] The following verse is by Shiblī:

Love for the Merciful has made me drunk.
Have you ever seen a lover who was not drunk?[22]

A Syrian servant of God declared, "You will all encounter God and find Him truthful and yet in the past you may have deemed Him untruthful. This is because if one of you were to have a finger made out of gold he would keep on showing it off but if he were to have a crippled finger he would try to hide it."[23] By this he meant that gold is reprehensible in God's sight though people brag to have it. Affliction is embellishment to people in the world-to-come even though people here look down on it with loathing.

Once there was a fire in the market. When Sarī was told that the market had burned but that his own shop had not, he exclaimed, "Praise God!" A bit later he reflected, "How could I say 'Praise God!' for my own well-being instead of that of other Muslims?" And so he turned from commerce and abandoned his shop for the remainder of his days, repenting and asking forgiveness for having said 'Praise God!'[24]

When you ponder these stories, you surely recognise that satisfaction with what runs counter to our desires is not impossible. Rather, it is a tremendous station among religious people. Just as in whatever way love and its various outcomes may be possible for people [in this world], so too the love of God and the shares of the world-to-come are certainly possible too. In fact, this is possible in two ways.

One lies in contentment with pain when one anticipates a benefit to occur, as in satisfaction with blood-letting or cupping or ingesting medicaments in expectation of a cure. Another lies in contentment with pain, not because of something beyond it but rather because it is what a beloved person wishes and is pleased with. Indeed, love may overmaster to such an extent that the lover's will becomes submerged in that of the beloved. Then the heart's delight of the beloved is the most pleasurable of all things to the lover, along with giving the beloved satisfaction and carrying out his will, even if that results in the destruction of the lover's own spirit, as it is said:

When pain brings pleasure, what is a wound?

Even when the pain is perceptible this is possible, for love may so forcefully dominate one that he is too stunned to feel the pain. Analogy, experience and direct observation indicate that such does occur. No one who has not experienced it for himself ought to deny it. He has not experienced it only because he has not known its cause, which is the overwhelming exuberance of love. Whoever has not tasted the savour of love knows nothing of its wonders. Those who do know love know marvels more prodigious than any we could describe here.

ʿAmr ibn al-Ḥārith al-Rāfiqī is reported to have said, "I was at a gathering in al-Raqqah at the house of a friend of mine. There was a young man with us who had fallen passionately in love with a singing slave-girl, and she was there too. She struck her lute and began to sing:

> The mark of love's abasement on lovers is weeping,
> Especially on a lover who finds no way to complain.

The young man said to her, "By God, how beautifully you have sung, O lady! Will you give me permission to die?" She replied, "Die at once!" He placed his head on a cushion, closed his mouth, and shut his eyes. We shook him but lo, he was dead.[25]

Junayd said, "I saw a man hanging on the sleeve of a boy, wheedling him obsequiously and parading his love for him. The boy turned to him and said, 'How long will you keep up this sham of yours?' The man answered, 'God knows that I am sincere in what I say, so much so that if you said to me "Die!" I would die.' The boy shot back, 'Die then, if you are sincere!' The man turned aside, closed his eyes, and died."[26]

Sumnūn al-Muḥibb remarked, "Among our neighbours was a man who owned a slave-girl whom he loved utterly. The girl fell ill. The man sat beside her to make a sweet-meat[A] for her. While he was stirring the pot the girl cried out 'Oh!' He was startled and

[A] Arabic *ḥays*, or date-meal mixed with butter and curds.

the spoon dropped from his hand. He began stirring the pot with his hand until his fingers fell off. 'What is this?' the girl asked, and he replied, 'This is the result of your crying out 'Oh!'"

Muḥammad ibn ʿAbd Allāh al-Baghdādī is reported to have said, "In Basra I saw a young man on a steep roof. High above the people he was reciting:

Whoever dies of love let him die thus!
In love without death there is nothing good!

Then he hurled himself to the ground and they bore him away, a dead man.

This story and others like it are given credence when human love is involved. But to believe in the Creator's love is far more appropriate since insight is more veracious than eyesight. The beauty of God's presence is fuller than any other beauty; indeed, all the beauty of this world is merely a lovely benefaction of that beauty. One who has lost his sight denies the beauty of forms; one who has lost his hearing denies the delight of melodies and songs in measured tones; one who has lost his heart has no recourse but to deny as well those ecstasies that have no locus but the heart.

CHAPTER SIXTEEN

An Exposition that Supplication is not in Conflict with Contentment

He who supplicates does not relinquish the stage of contentment. Similarly, a repugnance for sin and a hatred of sinners and the occasions of sin, coupled with the zeal to eliminate them by "commanding the good and prohibiting the forbidden," do not stand in opposition to supplication (*duʿāʾ*). Some deluded good-for-nothings have erred in this, declaring that sin, iniquity and unbelief come about through God's predestination and so one must be content with them. This is ignorance of true interpretation and obtuseness to the mysteries of divine revelation.

By supplication we worship. Many supplications of God's Messenger (may God bless him and grant him peace) indicate this, as do those of the other prophets (we have transmitted them in the *Book of Invocations*).[A] Even so, the Messenger of God (may God bless him and grant him peace) stood at the supreme station of contentment. God praised certain servants of His by saying, *They called to Us in longing and in fear.*[1] As for rejecting sin, as well as repugnance and dissatisfaction with it, this is in fact the way His servants show God reverence. Indeed, God rebukes them when they are content with sin, for He says, *They are pleased with the life of the world and feel tranquil in it.*[2] He also says, *They are content that they should be with the useless and their hearts are sealed.*[3]

[A] See *Al-Ghazālī on Invocations and Supplications*, tr. K. Nakamura (Cambridge, 1990).

In Sacred Tradition this is well attested, "Whoever witnesses a misdeed and is content with it is as though he had committed it himself." And again: "He who guides to evil is equal to him who commits it."[4] On the authority of Ibn Masᶜūd it is stated, "A man may not be present when a sin is committed and yet he may be as guilty as he who carried it out." "How can that be?" he was asked, and replied, "If, when he learns about it, he is pleased." In Sacred Tradition it is also said, "If a man be killed in the east and another man in the west be pleased with it, he becomes an accomplice to that murder."

God has commanded us to be envious as well as competitive in the good and to be on our guard against evils, for He has said, *For this let all strive who strive for bliss.*[5] The Prophet (may God bless him and grant him peace) said, "Only two things are worthy of envy: A man whom God has granted wisdom and who propagates it among people and instructs them; and a man to whom God has given wealth and to whom He has given the power to expend it rightly." (In another version it reads, "A man whom God has given the Qur'ān and who is immersed in it day and night to such an extent that another says, 'Had God given me what He has given him, I would do as he has done!'")

There are innumerable proof-texts about hatred of unbelievers and evildoers, as well as about rejection and detestation of them, in both the Qur'ān and Sacred Tradition. Thus, God says, *Let not believers take unbelievers for their friends in preference to believers.*[6] God says as well, *O you who believe! Take not the Jews and Christians for friends.*[7] And He says, *Thus We made some of the wrongdoers friends with others.*[8] In Sacred Tradition it says, "God has made a covenant binding upon every believer to hate every hypocrite, and upon every hypocrite to hate every believer." The Prophet (may God bless him and grant him peace) said, "A man is one with those whom he loves." He also said, "Whoever loves a people and is their friend will rise up with them on Judgement Day." And he said (may God bless him and grant him peace), "The firmest bonds of faith are love in God and hate in God." We have already mentioned the proofs for these statements in the Exposition of love and hate in God in *The Book of Manners in Society* as well as in *The Book of Commanding the Good and Forbidding the Bad* and so we will not reiterate them here.[A]

If you object that Qur'ānic verses and Sacred Traditions adduce contentment with whatever God decrees and yet, sins are not decreed by God, thus this is absurd, for it is an offence against God's oneness. But if sins do occur through God's foreordainment, then aversion and hatred of them are also aversion to God's decree. What then is the way to reconcile these positions, since in some way they are contradictory? How can there be reconciliation between satisfaction and dissatisfaction in one and the self-same thing?

Know that this is perplexing only to the weak-minded who are incapable of grasping the arcana of knowledge. It so confuses people that they even consider silence about forbidden acts to be a station of contentment, and they term it "good character" (*ḥusn al-khuluq*), but this is sheerest ignorance. Indeed, we claim quite the opposite. Satisfaction and aversion are in opposition whenever they coincide in a single thing from a single aspect and in one and the same way; however, they are not in opposition in one thing if it is found repellent from one perspective and satisfactory from another. Thus, your enemy may die, an enemy who is also an enemy of one of your other enemies and actively striving to destroy the latter. His death displeases you inasmuch as your enemy's enemy has died, but it pleases you inasmuch as one of your enemies is dead. Sin too has two aspects. One aspect pertains to God, in that He performed it, He chose it and He willed it; hence, one is content with it under this aspect, yielding sovereignty to the *Owner of Sovereignty*[9] and finding contentment in whatever He may do.[B] The other aspect regards man inasmuch as

[A] These are, respectively, Books II.1 and II.9 of the *Iḥyā'*.

[B] This does not mean that God "performs, chooses and wills" individual sins, but that sin as such is integral to all that is created as opposed to the supreme perfection of the Uncreated.

he acquires[A] [the sinful act], since he may be described and singled out as hateful to God and detestable in His sight because he surrendered himself to the causes of estrangement from God and hatred by Him. From this perspective he is to be rejected and censured.

This will become clear to you only by means of parable. Let us suppose that a man who is loved says in the company of those who love him, "I wish to distinguish between him who loves me and him who hates me. Therefore I have set up a truthful criterion and a reasonable scale; namely, I will go towards someone and vex him and strike him with a blow that will force him to revile me. When he reviles me, I will hate him and deem him my enemy. Then, everyone whom he loves I shall also know to be my enemy, and everyone whom he hates I shall know to be my friend and lover." He did this and there came to pass both the vilification which he had intended (and which is a cause of hatred), and the hatred (which is a cause of enmity). All those who genuinely loved him and were cognizant of love's conditions felt obliged to exclaim, "Your plan to vex and strike and distance this person, and your exposure of him to hatred and enmity, I love and approve, for this is your view, your plan, your act and your will. However, his vilification of you is hostility on his part; rather, he should have borne up patiently and not reviled you. Still, this was your intention for him; by striking him you meant to make him utter the abuse that obliges hate. Therefore, inasmuch as this occurred in accord with your intent and plan, which you yourself set in motion, we are content with it. Had it not occurred, this would have been a flaw in your plan and an obstacle to your intention; and yet, we are averse to any lapse in your intention. Nevertheless, insofar as this is an apt description of the person, together with his acquisition [of the sinful act], and there has been enmity and an

[A] This reflects the Ashʿarite doctrine of "acquisition" (*kasb* or *iktisāb*) which seeks to reconcile the apparent disparity between God's role in willing all action and man's responsibility for his own deeds. God wills all that happens but humans "acquire" the moral "fruits" of their deeds. See *EI*², IV.692–694.

attack against you on his part, quite contrary to what your beauty demands—indeed, this demands that he bear your blow and not return abuse—we are averse to it, for the wrongful act is quite rightly ascribed to him and is his very characteristic, and not insofar as it was your intention and the inevitable result of your plan. We are also pleased with your hatred for him because of his abuse; indeed, we even love it because it is what you have wished. In fact, being in perfect congruence with you, we too detest him. It is one of the conditions of being a lover that the beloved's friend be his friend too, and his enemy his enemy. We are also content with his hatred of you inasmuch as you have willed him to hate you by distancing him from you so that all the stirrings of hatred possessed him. Even so, I hate his hatred inasmuch as it is the very characteristic of that hater as well as his "acquisition" and action, and we loathe him for that. In our view, he merits hatred because of his hatred for you. His hatred and loathing of you are abhorrent to us inasmuch as they are his traits. And yet, insofar as all this is your wish, it is to be accepted with contentment."

Contradiction arises only when one says that something is pleasing when it is your wish and abhorrent when it is your wish; however, when it is abhorrent not inasmuch as it is his will and deed but rather inasmuch as it is a description of somebody else, and that somebody's "acquisition", this is not contradictory. Everything that is abhorrent from one aspect and pleasing from another bears witness to this. Parallel instances are countless.

Therefore, when God gives the promptings of appetite and of sin power over a man until that drives him into a love of sin, and that love draws him to commit sinful acts, it is comparable to the blow that the beloved inflicts on the person in our parable: the blow drives him to anger and anger drives him to abuse.

God's hatred of anyone who sins against Him—even though that person's sin occurs through His plan—is like the loathing felt by someone reviled towards the one who reviles him, even though the abuse comes about solely through his plan and his choice of means. God does this with all of His servants. I mean by this that the domination of temptations over a person stands as an indication that divine volition to distance him—along with divine hate—have already come to pass. For this reason it is incumbent on everyone who loves God to hate whomever God hates and to detest whomever God detests and to be at enmity with whomever God has banished from His presence, even if God compelled him to that enmity and opposition through His might and power. For in fact, such a person is far-removed, cursed and driven out from the Presence, even though he be already far-removed by God's banishment, vanquished and outcast by His expulsion—and involuntarily so—and an exile from the degrees of closeness—even so, he must be loathsome and hateful to all lovers who, out of affinity for the Beloved, manifest their wrath against anyone whom the Beloved has felt wrathful enough to banish. Everything that Sacred Traditions adduce confirms hatred in God and love in God, including harsh treatment and severity towards unbelievers, as well as going to extremes in hatred of them alongside contentment with whatever God has ordained, insofar as it is His decree. He is mighty and glorious!

All this derives from the mystery of predestination which is impermissible to divulge.[A] Both evil and good fall under the aegis of divine will and volition: evil is willed but abhorrent, good is willed but agreeable. Anyone who claims that no evil comes from God is an ignoramus. And he too is flawed who claims that both are from God without any divergence in acceptability or unacceptability. On this subject, the veil may not be raised. Here silence and that tact prescribed by Revelation[10] are most fitting. He (may God bless him and grant him peace) said, "Predestination is God's secret; do not disclose it." This secret is linked with the knowledge that comes from illumination.[B]

[A] On the mystery or "secret" of predestination (*sirr al-qadar*), which is "God's secret," see *Theodicy*, 69ff. and *passim*.

[B] That is, the *ʿilm al-mukāshafa* which Ghazālī declines to discuss throughout.

Now, however, we propose to explain that in human worship of God it is possible to reconcile contentment with His decree and with hatred of sins, despite the fact that these latter do occur through God's decree. Our purpose is sufficiently clear so that there will be no need to infringe upon any mystery in the process.

Through this one may know also that supplication for forgiveness and for protection from sin, along with all other means that assist religion, are not contradictory to contentment with God's decree. God brings people to worship Him through supplication in order that such prayer might draw forth purity of remembrance, quiescence of mind and tenderness of entreaty and that it may burnish the mind to clarity; it is a key to disclosure and a means to the continual augmentation of grace. In just the same way to carry a clay jug and to drink water are not contradictory with respect to thirst; drinking the water is an attempt to eliminate thirst right away, using that very means which the Causer of causes[A] set in order. The same is true of supplication: It is a cause which God set in order and commanded. As we have already noted, adherence to such means as are in conformity with God's *sunna* does not contradict contentment for the very reason that contentment is a stage that borders on trust in God and is continuous with it. To parade one's misery in an outburst of complaint and to reproach God in one's heart does contradict contentment, whereas to manifest one's misery through thanks and as a disclosure of God's power does not contradict it.

One of the pious ancestors remarked, "An example of excellent contentment with God's decree is not to say, 'This day is hot'—that is, as a kind of complaint—when one is in the midst of summer; in winter, by contrast, it becomes an expression of

[A] An epithet for God drawn from the terminology of the philosophers (*Musabbib al-asbāb*) who influenced Ghazālī profoundly despite his repudiation of several of their doctrines; it is striking that here he links supplication with the secondary causality he had seemed so firmly to reject in such earlier works as the *Tahāfut al-falāsifa* (*The Incoherence of the Philosophers*).

gratitude." Complaint is contrary to contentment. To disparage or find fault with food runs counter to contentment with God's decree: disparagement of the work is disparagement of the workman. And yet, all is the work of God. When someone says that poverty is affliction and trial and that family is a burdensome concern and that earning a living is toil and trouble, that offends against contentment. Instead, one ought to submit to the order of things because of Him who so ordered them, one ought to concede the realm to Him who owns it and declare, like ʿUmar, "It is the same to me whether I start the day rich or poor, for I do not know which of the two is better for me."

CHAPTER SEVENTEEN

An Exposition that Fleeing and Censuring a Country Reputed Sinful Is not Contrary to Contentment

KNOW THAT THE feeble-minded fancy that the prohibition of God's Messenger (may God bless him and grant him peace) against leaving a place where plague has appeared implies a prohibition against leaving a place where sin is openly prevalent, since each of these cases represents evasion from God's foreordainment. This is ridiculous. The prohibition against leaving a place where plague has broken out is because if this door were to be opened, the healthy would depart and the sick would remain behind; neglected and without anyone to care for them, they would perish from deprivation and lack of food. For this reason God's Messenger (may God bless him and grant him peace), in some reports, compares it to deserting from an army. But if this were part and parcel of a flight from predestination, he would not have permitted anyone approaching the city to depart. We have already mentioned this case in the *Book of Trust in God*.[A] If the sense of this be grasped, to escape from a country which is a hotbed of sin is obviously no escape from God's decree. On the contrary, God's decree is to escape from that which should be escaped from.

Therefore, it is not reprehensible to denounce places which tempt one to sin together with the occasions of sin they present so

[A] Book xxxv of the *Iḥyā'*; translated as *Faith in Divine Unity and Trust in Divine Providence* by David B. Burrell (Louisville, 2001).

as to warn against evil. The pious ancestors did this unceasingly. In fact, some of them gathered together to condemn Baghdad and to proclaim their censure of it publicly and to flee from it.[A] Ibn al-Mubārak said, "I've roamed in both East and West but never have I beheld a city more evil than Baghdad!" When he was asked why, he answered, "This is a city in which God's bounty is exposed to scorn while sinning against God is considered trivial." When he reached Khorasan he was asked again, "What is your opinion of Baghdad?" and he answered, "There I saw only raging police and anxious businessmen and baffled reciters of the Qur'ān."[1] You must not assume that this is mere slander; it is not meant to injure any specific individual. By this he means simply to warn people. Once en route to Mecca, when he had a stopover in Baghdad and had to wait sixteen days for the caravan to be made ready, he disbursed sixteen *dīnār*s, one *dīnār* for each day, as charity to expiate for his staying there.

But many people have condemned Iraq; among them: ʿUmar ibn ʿAbd al-ʿAzīz and Kaʿb al-Akhbār. Ibn ʿUmar[B] (may God be pleased with them both) said to one of his clients, "Where do you live?" The man replied, "Iraq." He asked further, "What do you do there? For I have heard that no one dwells in Iraq without God foreordaining misery as his companion."[2] And Kaʿb al-Akhbār mentioned Iraq one day, saying, "There are nine-tenths evil there as well as incurable disease." Sometimes it is said, "The good is divisible into ten parts: nine-tenths are in Syria but only one-tenth in Iraq. Evil too is divisible into ten parts but the situation is the reverse."[3]

A specialist in Sacred Tradition remarked, "One day we were with Fuḍayl ibn ʿIyāḍ when a Sufi came to him clad in a woollen

[A] This passage may reflect Ghazālī's reaction to the opposition that swirled around him in Iraq during his lifetime, especially among the learned; it may also constitute an oblique, and retrospective, justification for his departure from Baghdad in 488/1095 to embark on the Sufi way; cf. *Munqidh* (ed. Jabre), 38-9; tr. McCarthy, *Freedom and Fulfillment*, 92-3.

[B] According to Zabīdī (*Itḥāf* IX.671, line 10), this is an error in the original text and should refer to ʿUmar ibn ʿAbd al-ʿAzīz himself.

cloak. Fuḍayl sat him beside him, then brought his face up close to him and asked, "Where do you live?" The Sufi answered, "Baghdad." Fuḍayl averted his face and said, "Someone comes to us clad in monk's apparel. When we ask him where he dwells, he answers, 'In the nest of darkness.'"

Bishr ibn al-Ḥārith used to say, "Someone who worships God in Baghdad is like one who worships Him in the privy."[4] He also used to say, "Do not follow my example in living there! Let him who wants to leave, leave."

And Aḥmad ibn Ḥanbal would say, "Were it not for the ties that bind me to these young men, I would prefer to quit this city." When he was asked, "Where would you choose to live?" he replied, "At the border posts!"

Another said, "Of the inhabitants of Baghdad it may be said that the ascetic among them is truly ascetic while those among them who are evil are really evil."

This shows that whoever is destined [to live in] a city in which sins abound and the good is scant has no excuse for remaining there. Quite the opposite: He must emigrate. God says, *Is not God's earth spacious enough that you might emigrate within it?*[5] Nevertheless, if family or blood-ties prevent one from leaving he must not be satisfied with his circumstances or at ease within himself; rather, he must remain troubled in mind and say repeatedly, *Lord, bring us out of this village whose inhabitants are wicked.*[6] Whenever injustice is general, misfortune strikes and destroys all, encompassing even the righteous. God says, *Be strong against temptation; not only those who are evildoers among you will be singled out for smiting.*[7] Therefore, there can be absolutely no acceptance of anything that causes a weakening of religion except inasmuch as it stands in relation to God's doing; in itself, however, it can never be acceptable.

Scholars disagree as to who is superior among those who have reached the following three states: The man who loves death out of longing to meet God; the man who loves abiding to serve his Lord; or the man who says, "I choose nothing; rather, I am content with whatever God chooses." This question was raised before one of the gnostics and he declared, "The man who possesses contentment is superior to the others because he is the least meddlesome of them all."[8]

One day Wahīb ibn al-Ward, Sufyān al-Thawrī, and Yūsuf ibn Asbāṭ met. Thawrī said, "Before today I used to feel aversion for sudden death but today I would love to be dead." Yūsuf asked him why and he replied, "Because of the temptation I feel." Yūsuf said, "I, however, am not averse to continuing to live for a long time." When Sufyān asked why he answered, "Maybe I will encounter a single day on which I may repent and do good." Wahīb then was asked, "Well, what do you say?"[9] He answered, "I choose nothing. What is most desirable to me is what is most desirable to God—praise Him!" Thawrī kissed him between the eyes and exclaimed, "What lofty spirituality, by the Lord of the Kaʿba!"[10]

CHAPTER EIGHTEEN

A Compilation of Anecdotes about Lovers, Together with their Sayings and Innermost Illuminations

IT WAS SAID to a gnostic, "You truly are a lover," but he replied, "I am no lover, I am only a beloved, for the lover is worn out with toil."[1] It was also said to him, "People say that you are one of the Seven," and he answered, "I am all Seven."[A] He also used to say, "When you see me you see forty *Abdāl*," and when they asked, "How can this be since you are only one person?" he explained, "Because I see forty *Abdāl* and take one trait from each." They said to the same gnostic also, "We have heard that you see Khiḍr."[B] He smiled and said, "To see Khiḍr is no cause for wonderment but to be someone whom Khiḍr would like to see and yet, to conceal oneself from him, is cause for astonishment."[2]

And of Khiḍr (peace be upon him) it is reported that he said, "There has never been a day on which I said to myself that none of God's friends remains whom I do not already know when on that very day I did not see one of His friends whom I did not know."

[A] One of the seven *Abrār* ("pious") who are above the forty *Abdāl* in the hierarchy of Sufi saints. The gnostic here is Abū Yazīd al-Bisṭāmī; see Gramlich, 753. Zabīdī (*Itḥāf* IX.673, line 11) glosses, "It is as if whoever sees me sees the Seven."

[B] In Muslim tradition, Khiḍr is recognised as a prophet who never dies but mysteriously appears to guide people. He is believed to be the companion of Moses in the Qur'ān (Q. XVIII.65-82). See *EI*², IV.902-5.

It was once said to Abū Yazīd al-Bisṭāmī, "Tell us about the beatific visions that have come to you from God." He cried out and said, "Woe upon you! It would not be right for you to know that!" They said, "Then tell us of your most strenuous struggle with your own soul for God." He replied, "This too is not permitted for me to tell you." Again he was asked, "Then tell us of the spiritual exercises you used against your carnal self at the very outset." He conceded, "All right. I summoned my self to God but my self rose up stubbornly against me. So I steeled my resolve against it neither to drink water nor to taste sleep for a year. In that way it grew loyal to me."[3]

Of Yaḥyā ibn Muʿādh it is related that during one of his visionary trances, lasting from the evening prayer until daybreak, he saw Abū Yazīd in a state of alert tension, standing on the balls of his feet and lifting his soles. With his heels raised from the ground and striking his breast with his chin he stared fixedly and unblinkingly with both eyes. Yaḥyā went on to say, "Then, at dawn, he prostrated himself and remained a long time like that, after which he sat down and said, 'O God, some people seek You and You give them the power to walk on water or to walk on the air, and they are happy with that. But I take refuge with You from all of that. Other people seek You and You allow the distant places of the earth to be near to them, so they too are content. But I take shelter with You from all of that. Another group seeks You and You give them all the treasures of earth and they are satisfied. But I take refuge with you from all of that!' He enumerated some twenty instances of the wonders of the saints, then he turned and saw me and exclaimed, 'Yaḥyā!' I said, 'Yes, my master.' He asked how long I had been there and I replied, 'For a while.' He fell silent. 'O my master,' I said, 'tell me a little about this.' He said, 'I will tell you something that will do you good. God made me enter the lowest sphere, then He let me wander within the lowest of His realms. He showed me the worlds of what is beneath them down to the earth itself. He then let me enter the higher sphere and let me circumambulate the heavens. He showed me what is within them from the Gardens to the Throne. He brought me into His presence and He said, "Ask Me for anything you have seen and I will give it to you." I replied, "O my Lord, I have seen nothing that I deem beautiful enough to ask You for it." He answered, "You are truly My servant, you who worship Me in truth for My own sake. I will do this and this for you." He mentioned several things.' Yaḥyā said, 'This terrified me and filled my mind and I was amazed and said, "O master, why did you not ask Him for knowledge? For the King of Kings did say to you, 'Ask of Me what you wish?'" But Abū Yazīd shrieked at me loudly, 'Silence! Woe upon you! I am jealous of my own self for His sake and I do not like anyone other than Him knowing Him!'"[A4]

Abū Turāb al-Nakhshabī, it is reported, had great admiration for one of his novices. He used to draw him close and ply him with all sorts of good things. The novice, however, remained absorbed in his worship and mystical fervour. One day Abū Turāb said to him, "What if you were to see Abū Yazīd?" The novice replied, "I would be too absorbed to notice him." But when Abū Turāb kept on saying again and again, "If you were to see Abū Yazīd…!" the novice became agitated and cried out, "Shame on you! What do I want with Abū Yazīd when I am seeing God Himself and He has made Abū Yazīd superfluous to me?" Abū Turāb remarked, "I was so stirred up with emotion that I could barely contain myself but I said, 'Woe to you! You have been bedazzled by God! Were you to see Abū Yazīd only once it would be more beneficial to you than to see God seventy times!' The lad was too flabbergasted even to speak and disapproved of his master but finally he did ask, "How could that be?" Abū Turāb replied, "Silly you! Do you not see

[A] Zabīdī comments that jealousy is one of the results of love. The passage seems to mean that Abū Yazīd is jealous of his own self for the knowledge of God it possesses; only God, the beloved, should know Himself. Cf. *Itḥāf* IX.674, line 11; also Ritter, *The Ocean of the Soul*, 394-98, esp. 395, citing Aḥmad al-Ghazālī, "It can reach the point that the lover harbours jealousy toward himself and is jealous of his own eye."

God before you in such a way that He appears in your own measure, while you would see Abū Yazīd before God Who appears to him in His true measure?" Then he understood what I was saying and exclaimed, "Bring me to him!" Continuing the story he said at last, "We stopped at a hill where we could wait for Abū Yazīd to come to us out of a thicket. He used to repair to the thicket where wild beasts were. He passed by us, a pelt slung over his back. I said to the young man, 'This is Abū Yazīd, look at him!' The young man looked at him and passed out. We hurried over to him but he was dead. As we worked together to bury him I said to Abū Yazīd, "O master, glancing at you killed him;" but he replied, "No, and yet, your pupil was truthful. There was a secret hidden in his heart that had not revealed itself to him. When he saw us, his heart's secret was revealed to him and he could not bear it because he was still at the beginner's stage. It was this that killed him."[5]

When the Zanj[A] entered Basra they slaughtered and pillaged. His brothers gathered around Sahl and said, "If you were to ask God, He would ward them off." Sahl remained silent and then said, "If God's faithful in this land were to call down evil upon these wicked men, not one unjust man would remain on the face of the earth but would die in a single night; even so, they do not do this." They asked him why and he said, "Because they do not love whatever He does not love," and he mentioned things which God had granted (but which may not be mentioned here). Finally, he said, "If you were to entreat Him not to bring the Day of Judgement, He would not bring it."[6] These are things possible in themselves; whoever has no share therein must not withhold credence and belief in their possibility: God's power is vast and His goodness universal and the wonders of His rule in this world and the next are innumerable. Indeed, the objects of His power are infinite and His goodness to His faithful, whom He has chosen, knows no end. For this reason, Abū Yazīd used to say, "If He

[A] For the Zanj revolts in Iraq, the first of which began in 70/689, see *EI*[2], XI.444-6; also, al-Ṭabarī, *History* (trans. D. Waines), vol. 36.

grants you the whispered colloquies of Moses and the spiritual depth of Jesus and the friendship of Abraham, even so, seek what is beyond all that. God possesses incalculably redoubled graces above and beyond all those. If you stop at those, He causes them to be a veil for you; and this is an affliction for the likes of these [gnostics], and of those who are like them, because they are as alike as like can be."[7]

One mystic said, "In vision forty houris were revealed to me whom I beheld running upon the air. They wore golden and silver garments and jewels that clinked and swirled with them as they moved. I gazed upon them and was punished for forty days. Afterwards eighty houris were revealed to me, far more beautiful, far lovelier, than the first. I was told to gaze upon them but I prostrated myself and covered my eyes in order not to see them. I said, 'I take refuge with You from all that is not You. I have no need of this.' And thus I implored God without stopping until He removed them from my sight."[8]

The believer should not deny these and similar illuminations just because he himself has been deprived of them. If everybody believed nothing but what he himself had witnessed with his own murky self and stubborn heart, faith's domain would be severely narrowed. Rather, these states appear after one has crossed beyond obstacles and attained several stages—the lowest of which is purity of heart—and dispelled the cravings of the self as well as others' good opinion of one's inner and outer acts. Later one conceals all that from other people by veiling one's inner state until he remains immured in the stronghold of his own obscurity.[9] These are the precepts of their path and the least of their stations, although among those who fear God, it is also the most glorious thing in existence. After cleansing the heart and mind of the turbidity that comes from regard for creatures, the light of certitude pours over one and the axioms of the real are made known to him. To deny this without having experienced it or having trod the mystic path, is like the denial of a man who rejects the possibility of an image appearing in a piece of iron after it has been shaped, scoured and burnished until it takes the form of a mirror. The denier looks at what is in his hand: a chunk of iron, dim and covered with rust and filth; it resembles no form at all, so he denies the possibility of anything appearing reflected in it when its true nature does shine through. Such denial is error and supreme ignorance.

This is the verdict of all who deny the miracles of the saints; however, this has no basis except for their own inability, and the inability of those whom they see, to perform such miracles. What a sorry basis this is for denying the power of God! On the contrary, only he who has trod the path, however briefly, can smell the fragrance of illumination, even at its very beginning. To Bishr it was said, "By what means did you attain this level?" He replied, "By hiding my inmost state with God."[10] What this means is that "I ask Him to hide and conceal my situation from me."[A] Reportedly Bishr saw Khiḍr and said to him, "Pray to God for me!" Khiḍr replied, "May God make your devotion to Him a pleasure!" I said, "Add to this prayer for me," and he answered, "May He conceal it even from you!"[11] This means: "Conceal it from other people." But it might also mean: "May He hide it from you so that you give it no regard."

On the authority of another he is reported as saying, "A yearning for Khiḍr kept me in turmoil. On one occasion I asked God to show him to me so that he could teach me what might be the most important thing for me. Thus I did see him but only one thing dominated both my intention and my resolve: To say to him, 'O Abū ʿAbbās,[B] teach me something such that when I speak it out I become hidden from the hearts of others and have no standing with them and no one knows me to be devout and righteous.' Khiḍr replied, 'Say, "O Lord, drape Your thickest veil over me and set the canopies of Your concealment upon me. Put me in the hiddenness of Your invisibility and camouflage me from

[A] Zabīdī comments (*Itḥāf*, IX.676, line 7): "that he hide (my state)...so that others do not know it."

[B] This is the *kunya* of Khiḍr.

the hearts of others!'" At this he vanished and I could no longer see him but after that I no longer yearned for him. Every day I persisted in saying these words."[12] It is related that he came in this way to be despised and derided so that even non-Muslims[13] mocked him and put him to work in the streets carrying their belongings for them, so low did he fall in their estimation. Even young boys made fun of him. His solace lay in the stillness of his own heart since the upright sincerity of his inmost state lay in abasement and obscurity.[14]

Such is the inner state of the saints of God. One must search among such people as these; however, the bedazzled seek only beneath tattered rags and woollen shawls those celebrated for their knowledge, piety and leadership among men. God, however, is jealous on behalf of His saints and disdains anything other than concealing them, as He says, "My saints are under My tent. Only I know who they are."[15] He (may God bless him and grant him peace) said, "Lord, many a dishevelled, dusty man in a pair of tattered rags to whom no one gives any mind may find his oath granted when he swears by God."[16]

In summary, the hearts farthest from the fragrance of these notions are swaggering hearts, full of pride in themselves and blithely pleased with their own works and their own knowledge. Hearts closest to those scents, however, are those that have been pulverised and who are so conscious of their own lowliness that they do not perceive it as abasement when they suffer injustice and oppression, just as a slave feels no humiliation however loftily his master may look down at him. Quite the opposite: In his own estimation he is at too contemptible a level to see all forms of humiliation combined in relation to his own; rather, he sees himself as beneath even that, and so his humility becomes an essential characteristic of his very self. A heart such as this, it may be hoped, can catch the scent of the first wafts of these fragrances. But if we are deprived of such a heart and denied such a spirit, we must not abandon belief in its possibility for those so endowed. Whoever is unable to become a saint may still be one who loves God's saints and believes in them; perhaps then he too will be raised up with those he loves.

What has been reported about Jesus (peace be upon him) is attested in this way; namely, that he said to the Israelites, "Where does a seed grow?" They answered, "In the dust." He said, "Truly I say unto you, wisdom grows only in a heart that is like dust."[17] Those who aspire to sainthood come at last to meet its preconditions by self-abasement in the most extreme humility and self-contempt.

Of Ibn al-Karanbī, the teacher of Junayd, it is related that a man invited him three times to a meal but then turned him away. He sent to invite him once again; he returned and on the fourth attempt was allowed to enter. When asked about this he said, "For twenty years my soul was content in lowliness until it finally sank to the level of a dog that has been driven away and runs off; but when it is called back and a bone is slung to it, it comes home to stay. If you had turned me away fifty times and then invited me back again, I would have come."[18] It is also reported of him that he said, "I arrived at a certain place where I had a reputation for righteousness. My heart became distracted. I entered the bath-house and went over to some sumptuous clothing which I then stole and put on. I put my own rags on over the fine garments and left the bath-house. I began walking away very slowly. Some people confronted me, took off my rags and seized the garments. They struck me and injured me with their blows. After that I came to be known as a bath-house thief and my soul was at rest within me."[19]

This is how they tame and break their carnal selves until God delivers them from directing their gaze towards creatures and then towards themselves. Someone who is forever gazing at his own soul is blocked from God; self-preoccupation is his veil. Between the heart and God there is no estranging distance or intervening obstacle; the heart's distance comes about only from its being absorbed in things other than Him or in itself. In fact, the mightiest of all obstructions is self-absorption.

To this effect we are told that a very worthy authority, one of the most esteemed men of Bisṭām, was inseparable from Abū

Yazīd's circle. One day he said to the saint, "For thirty years I have fasted without interruption and I have stood all night without sleep but in my heart I find nothing of the knowledge which you mention although I both believe in it and love it." Abū Yazīd replied, "If you were to fast for three hundred years and stand in prayer for as many nights, you would still not find a single speck of such knowledge!" When he asked why, Abū Yazīd said, "Because you are obstructed by your own self." And when he asked whether there was a remedy for that Abū Yazīd remarked, "You won't accept it." The other insisted, "Tell it to me so I may use it!" Abū Yazīd replied, "Go right away to the barber and have your head and beard shaved. Take off those clothes and put on a woollen cloak. Hang a feedbag filled with walnuts from your neck, gather some boys around you and say to them, 'Whoever hits me will get a walnut.' Then go into the market-place and wander around all the markets in the sight of all and where there are people who know you, while you are in this state." The man exclaimed, "Glory be to God! What on earth are you saying?" Abū Yazīd answered, "Your saying 'Glory be to God' is polytheism." "How?" he asked and the saint replied, "Because you exalt yourself and give glory to your self and do not give glory to your Lord." But he replied, "I cannot do this but please, show me some other way!" Abū Yazīd said, "Begin with this before anything else." The man said, "I cannot do it," and Abū Yazīd remarked, "Did I not say to you that you would not accept it?"[20]

This then is what Abū Yazīd reported. It is a remedy for somebody ill with self-regard and sickened by the regard that others may have for him. No other remedy can save one from this sickness but this or a similar remedy. He who cannot take the medicine ought not to impugn the possibility of healing with respect to someone who has cured himself after sickness or who has not been sick at all.[A] The lowest rung to health is belief in its possibility. Woe to him who denies even this meagre measure!

[A] Perhaps a veiled reference to Ghazālī's own sickness, as described in *Munqidh*, 37; tr. McCarthy, 92.

These are exalted matters that are yet clear enough in revelation; nevertheless, in the opinion of those who count themselves among 'scholars of revelation' they are deemed trivial. The Messenger of God (may God bless him and grant him peace) said, "The worshipper has not perfected his belief until scarcity is more precious to him than abundance and not-being-known is more precious than being known."[21] He also said (may God bless him and grant him peace), "Three things there are and he who possesses them perfects his belief: he fears no rebuke in God; in whatever he performs there is no hypocrisy; and when two things are presented to him, one of which belongs to this world and one to the next world, he chooses what belongs to the next world over this one."[22] The Messenger of God (may God bless him and grant him peace) said as well, "A believer cannot perfect his faith until he possesses three traits: when he grows angry he does not allow his anger to exceed what is right; when he is content, he does not let his contentment lead him into triviality; and even when he can he does not permit himself to take what does not belong to him."[23] In yet another Sacred Tradition it says, "Three things: he to whom they befall enjoys what the family of David enjoyed, namely, justice in both contentment and in wrath; moderation in wealth as in poverty; the fear of God in private and in public."[24] These are conditions God's Messenger (may God bless him and grant him peace) mentioned to the faithful. The only person to be wondered at[25] is he who claims religious knowledge when within him not a speck of these three conditions exists. His share of knowledge and of reason induces him to disavow what does exist after one has crossed the tremendous stages that lie beyond belief. In the Traditions it is said that God revealed to one of His prophets, "I take as My friend only him who is not tepid in remembrance of Me, one who has no grave concern other than Me, and one who prefers nothing in My creation over Me, one who feels no pain when he is scorched by fire, one who even if he is slashed to death by a saw feels no pain at the touch of the iron."[26]

Whoever does not go so far as to be overwhelmed by love to this extent—how will he know what wonders and what illuminations lie beyond love? All of that lies on the other side of love. Love is beyond perfected faith while the stages of belief and their fluctuations—now more, now less—are boundless. This is why he (may God bless him and grant him peace) said to [Abū Bakr] al-Ṣiddīq (may God be pleased with him), "God gave you belief equal to that of every believing member of my community, whereas to me He gave belief equal to that of all the believing children of Adam."[27] In another Sacred Tradition it says, "God has three hundred attributes (*khuluq*). When He encounters somebody with even one of them, together with belief in His unity, that person enters paradise."[28] Abū Bakr said, "O Messenger of God, is there even one of these attributes in me?" He answered, "All of them are in you, O Abū Bakr, and the attribute God loves most is generosity."[29] He said (peace be upon him), "I saw a scale dangling from heaven. I was placed on one pan and my community on the other. I weighed more than they. Then Abū Bakr was placed on a scale and my community was brought and placed there too, and he outweighed them all."[30] Nevertheless, the Messenger of God (may God bless him and grant him peace) was so immersed in God that his heart was simply not commodious enough for friendship with anyone else. Thus he said, "Were I to take a friend from among people I would take Abū Bakr as my friend; however, your companion is God's friend."[31] By this he meant himself.

CHAPTER NINETEEN

Conclusion: Various Useful Sayings Regarding Love

SUFYĀN SAID, "Love means to follow God's Messenger (may God bless him and grant him peace)."[1] Another said, "Love means to keep God continuously in mind." Still another remarked, "Love means to prefer the Beloved." Yet another said, "Love is an aversion to remaining in this world." All this refers to the fruits of love; and yet, such sayings do not adequately deal with love itself.

Someone has said, "Love is a notion[2] coming from the beloved that overwhelms hearts from understanding it and blocks tongues from expressing it."

Junayd said, "God has proscribed love for anyone who has attachments."[3] He also said, "Every love that is based on some reciprocal benefit vanishes when the benefit does."[4]

Dhū al-Nūn said, "Tell anyone who manifests love of God to be careful not to abase himself before anyone other than Him."

And to Shiblī (may God show him mercy) it was said, "Describe the gnostic and the lover for us," and he replied, "The gnostic is someone who perishes when he speaks while the lover perishes when he keeps quiet."[5] Shiblī said,

O Noble Lord,
My love for You is in my entrails.
O You who lift the sleep from my eyelids,
You know what has passed me by.[6]

Another wrote:

I am amazed at someone who says, 'I keep my Lord in mind.'
How can I forget and then think of what I forgot?
I die when I think of You, then I am revived.
Were it not for my good opinion of You I would not live.
I live with desire but I die of longing.
How often will I live through You, how often die?
In cup upon cup I drink love.
The wine is not depleted nor am I slaked.
Would that his phantom were raised up for my eye!
If I falter in my gaze may I go blind![7]

Rābiʿa al-ʿAdawīya said one day, "Who will guide us to our lover?" Her maid-servant responded, "Our lover is already with us but the world has severed us from Him."

Ibn al-Jallā' (may God show him mercy) said, "God revealed to Jesus (peace be upon him), 'When I search out a man's innermost heart and find no love either for this world or the next, I fill him full of love for Me and shelter him with My protection.'"[8]

Sumnūn was speaking one day on love when a bird alighted before him; he kept pecking with his beak on the ground until blood flowed out and he died.[9]

Ibrāhīm ibn Adham said, "O my God, You know that paradise weighs less than a gnat's wing in my estimation alongside the love with which You have honoured me, the remembrance of You with which You have made me Your intimate, and the meditation on Your might and splendour for which You have emptied me out."[10]

Sarī (may God show him mercy) said, "The man who loves God lives; the man who inclines to the world is empty-headed. The smart man searches out his failings; the fool goes out in the morning and returns at evening in nothingness."

Rābiʿa was asked how it stood with her love for the Messenger (may God bless him and grant him peace) and she answered, "By God, I love him fiercely and yet, love for the Creator possesses me to the exclusion of love for created things."[11]

Moses[12] (peace be upon him) was asked what the best deed might be and he replied, "Contentment with God and love for Him." Abū Yazīd said, "The lover loves neither this world nor the next. Of his master he loves only his Master."[13]

Shiblī stated, "Love is astonishment in pleasure and bewilderment in exaltation."

It has been said that love means that you wipe away every trace of yourself until nothing remains within you that might refer back to yourself. Also: "Love is the heart's nearness to the beloved through happiness and joy."

Khawwāṣ said, "Love means to wipe away impulses of the will, to cast one's personal characteristics and needs into the fire."[14]

Sahl was asked about love and said, "God inclines His servant's heart to see Him after he understands what is wanted from him."

It is also said, "The lover's transactions are on four levels: love, awe, shame and exaltation. The noblest of these are exaltation and love because these two stages continue in the inhabitants of paradise whereas the other two are removed from them."

Harim ibn Ḥayyān remarked, "When a believer knows his Lord, he loves Him. When he loves Him, he turns towards Him. When he discovers the sweetness of his turning towards Him he no longer looks on this world with a craving eye, nor does he regard the next world with an indifferent eye, for [craving] pains him in this world while the other revives him for the world to come."

ʿAbd Allāh ibn Muḥammad said, "I heard a pious woman declare, while tears were streaming down her face, 'I am so fed up with life that if I found death for sale I would buy it out of yearning for God and love to meet Him.' I asked her, 'Do you have confidence in your deeds?' She replied, 'No, but given my love for Him and my good opinion of Him, can you imagine Him tormenting me—I who love Him?'"

God inspired David (peace be upon him) by saying, "If those who turn from Me knew how I wait for them and how tenderly I treat them and how I long for them to desist from their sins, they would die out of sheer longing for Me and their limbs would be hacked into pieces for love of Me.[15] O David, this is My will for those who turn away from Me. How then would My will be for those who come towards Me? O David, man needs Me most when he thinks to dispense with Me. I am most compassionate of My servant when he turns from Me but man is most sublime when he comes back to Me."

Abū Khālid al-Ṣaffār said, "One of the prophets met a man and said to him, 'You believers act on a basis that we prophets do not act upon: You act out of fear and hope while we act out of love and longing.'"

Shiblī (may God show him mercy) stated, "God revealed to David (peace be upon him), 'O David, mindfulness of Me belongs to those who are mindful[A] while paradise belongs to those who are obedient; visiting Me belongs to those who yearn; but I belong exclusively to those who love.'"

God revealed to Adam (peace be upon him), "O Adam, he who loves his friend believes what he says. He who is familiar with his friend is content with whatever he does. He who yearns for him quickens his footstep after him."

Khawwāṣ struck his breast and said, "O alas, that my longing is for One who sees me while I see Him not!"[16]

Junayd said, "Jonah[B] wept until he went blind, he stood until he bent crooked, he prayed until he went lame. He said, 'By Your Glory and Might! Were there an ocean of fire between us, I would plunge into it out of my longing for You.'"

ʿAlī ibn Abī Ṭālib said, "I asked the Messenger of God (may God bless him and grant him peace) about his *sunna* and he replied, 'Knowledge (*maʿrifa*) is my capital, intellect (*ʿaql*) is the root of my religion, love (*ḥubb*) is my foundation, longing (*shawq*) is my mount, remembrance of God (*dhikr Allāh*) my bosom-friend, trust

[A] *Dhikrī li'l-dhākirīn*: "Remembrance of Me belongs to those who remember."

[B] The prophet Yūnus in Arabic.

(*thiqa*) my treasure and sadness (*ḥuzn*) my companion, knowledge (*ᶜilm*) is my weapon, endurance (*ṣabr*) my cloak, contentment (*riḍā*) my booty, weakness (*ᶜajz*) my boast, renunciation (*zuhd*) my trade, certainty (*yaqīn*) my food, truthfulness (*ṣidq*) my intercessor, obedience (*ṭāᶜa*) my sufficiency, holy war (*jihād*) my moral nature, but prayer (*ṣalāh*) is the delight of my eyes.'"

Dhū al-Nūn said, "Glory be to Him who set the souls 'in serried ranks.'[17] The souls of gnostics are holy and exalted and so they yearn after God. The souls of believers are spiritual and so they long for paradise. The souls of the heedless are insubstantial as puffs of air and so they incline to this world."

A certain elder said, "I saw a man on Mt. Lukkām.[A] He was dark-skinned and emaciated; he sprang from one stone to another and sang out:

Fierce longing has turned me to what you see."[18]

Longing, it has been said, is the fire which God ignites in the hearts of His saints so that they may burn up stray thoughts, wilful deeds, hindrances and needs, by that fire in their hearts.

This now suffices for comment on love, intimacy, longing and contentment. Let us then curtail our discussion. And God gives success for what is right.

Here ends the Book of Love, Longing and Intimacy. The Book on Intention, Sincerity and Truthfulness follows.

[A] Sometimes transliterated as Mt. Lukām (cf. Gramlich, 766); part of a mountain chain in northern Syria; cf. *EI*[2], v.810.

NOTES

Chapter 1

1 Q. v.54.

2 Q. II.165.

3 Ibn Ḥanbal, IV.11; Makkī, II. 50, 26–27.

4 Muslim, I.66 (*imān* 67); Ibn Ḥanbal, III.103; Bukhārī, *imān* 9 & 14; Nasā'ī, VIII.86–87 (*imān* 3–4); Ibn Māja, II.1338, no. 4033 (*fitan* 23); Makkī, II.50.

5 Muslim, I.67, no. 69; Bukhārī, īmān 8; Ibn Ḥanbal, III.207, 275, 278; Nasā'ī, VIII.100–101; cf. also Makkī, *loc.cit.*

6 Q. IX.24 (not V.24, as in Gramlich, p. 633).

7 Makkī, II.50, 35–36.

8 Abū Nuᶜaym, I.108.

9 Abū Nuᶜaym, x.9; Ritter, *The Ocean of Soul*, 552.

10 Abū Nuᶜaym, I.226–227.

11 Wensinck, *Concordances*. I.406a; Qushayrī, 148; Bukhārī, Adab, 96; Ibn Ḥajar, *Fatḥ*, XIII.179.

12 Ibn Ḥanbal, III.104.

13 Makkī, II.56; III.82; cf. Gramlich, 635.

14 Qushayrī, 146, 32–33.

15 Qushayrī, 147.

Chapter 2

1 Ibn Ḥanbal, III.128, 199, 285; Nasā'ī, VII.58; Munāwī, *Fayḍ*, III.370, no. 3669. For an extended commentary on this celebrated tradition, cf. Ibn al-ᶜArabī, *Fuṣūs al-ḥikam*, trans. R. W. J. Austin, 272ff.

2 Q. L.37.

3 Q. XXXIII.62; XLVIII.23.

4 Munāwī, *Fayḍ*, III.344–45.

5 Gramlich cites ᶜAlī al-Qārī, *Al-Asrār al-marfūᶜa*, 171, for this Tradition; cf. Zabīdī, IX.554.

6 Muslim, I.93, *īmān* 147; Ibn Ḥanbal, IV.133–34, 151; Bukhārī, I, 93, *imān*; Munāwī, *Fayḍ*, II.224–26.

7 Ibn Ḥanbal, II.295; XV.77–78; Bukhārī, 231–232, *al-adab al-mufrad*, no. 900–901; Muslim, IV.2031–2032, *birr* 159–60; Abū Dāūd, IV.359, no. 4834 (for further references, see Gramlich, 643).

Chapter 3

1 Q. XIV.34.

2 Q. XXXIV.3.

3 Q. XVII.85.

4 Q. II.255.

5 Q. XVIII.84.

6 Q. II.255.

7 Allusion to Q. XXXIX.67.

8 Allusion to Q. XLVI.33 and L.38.

9 Q. LIX.23.

10 Q. LV.27.

11 Q. XXXIV.3.

12 Tradition found in all the

canonical sources; cf. Wensinck, IV.286a; Munāwī, *Fayḍ*, II.139, no. 1521; Nabhānī, *Fatḥ*, I.239.

13 Q. XXX.7.

14 Q. XVI.75.

15 Makkī, II.56.

16 *Ibid.*

17 *Ibid.*

18 *Ibid.*

19 *Ibid*; Abū Nuʿaym, III.242.

20 Reading *najjār* with M and B, rather than *tujjār* with Z (*Itḥāf*, IX.567, *paen.*).

21 Ibn Ḥanbal, II.295; Bukhārī, *anbiyā'* 2; *al-adab al-mufrad* 231–232; Muslim, IV.2031–2032, *birr* 159–60; Abū Dāūd, IV.359, no. 4834 (for further references, see Gramlich, 643).

22 Q. XVII.85.

23 Q. XV.29; XXXVIII.72.

24 Q. XXXVIII.26.

25 Ibn Ḥanbal (ed. Shākir) XIII.152–53; (ed. Ḥalabī) II.251, 315, 323, 434, 519; Bukhārī, *isti'dhān*, 1; Muslim, *birr*, 115; *janna*, 28. See also Ghazālī, *Imlā'*, 193–99; *Iljām*, I.6–7.

26 Q. XVII.43.

27 Attributed to Abū Hurayra, ultimately deriving from *Matthew* 25:31–46; Muslim, IV.1990, *birr* 43.

28 Ibn Ḥanbal, VI.256; Bukhārī, *riqāq*, 38.

Chapter 4

1 Q. XXXIX.22.

2 Q. XXXII.17.

3 Wensinck, *Concordances*, II.48a; Bukhārī, *tawḥīd*, 35, *bad' al-khalq*, 8, *tafsīr Sūra* 32; Muslim, 312, *janna*, 2–5; Tirmidhī, *janna*, 15, *tafsīr Sūrat* 32/2, 56; Ibn Māja, *zuhd*, 39; Dārimī, *riqāq*, 98; cf. Gramlich, 658.

4 Q. X.24.

5 Q. III.169–70.

6 Ibn Ḥanbal [ed. Ḥalabī], III.173, 276; Bukhārī, *jihād*, 21; Muslim, III.1498, *imāra* 109.

7 Unattested tradition given in Subkī, *Ṭabaqāt al-Shāfiʿīya*, IV.177; VI.375 (Gramlich, 659).

8 Q. III.133.

9 See above, p. 7.

10 Another reading has "a young man burning with zeal" (*al-fatā mashghūf*); cf. Gramlich, 660.

11 Makkī, II.56; III.83.

12 Makkī, II.57; III.83.

13 *Ibid.*

14 Arabic *ḥubb al-hawā*.

15 See note 3 above for references.

16 Q. XXXII.17.

17 Q. LVII.20.

18 Allusion to Q. XI.38.

Chapter 5

1 Q. VII.143.

2 Q. VI.103.

3 Q. XIX.71–72 (Dawood, 309).

4 *wa-balagha al-kitāb ajlahu*; see also Gramlich, 665.

5 Q. LXVI.8 (Dawood, 560).

6 Dhahabī, *Mīzān al-iʿtidāl* (Cairo, 1325), II.221–222; ʿAlī al-Qārī, *al-Asrār al-marfūʿa fī al-akhbār al-mawḍūʿa*, 476 (cited in Gramlich, 666).

7 Q. XXXVII.8.

8 Q. XCV.5.

9 Q. XXIX.64.

10 For this *hadith*, see Ibn Ḥanbal (ed. Ḥalabi), v.40; see also Wensinck, *Concordances*, IV.359a. For a variant, see *Itḥāf*, IX.90.

Chapter 6

1 Q. XXXIII.4.

2 Q. VI.91.

3 Q. XLI.30 and XLVI.13

4 Q. XXV.43

5 A tradition with a weak chain of transmission, according to Zabīdī (*Itḥāf*, IX.586, l. 12, who gives Ṭabarānī as his source.

6 Munāwī, *Fayḍ*, VI.189; ʿAzīzī, *al-Sirāj al-munīr*, III.376; Nabhānī, *al-Fatḥ al-kabīr*, III.220 (Gramlich, 671).

7 *Itḥāf*, IX.587 gives as authorities Muslim and Tirmidhī as sources for this Tradition; Gramlich, 141, lists several other sources, including Aḥmad Ibn Ḥanbal.

8 Q. XIV.24.

9 Q. XXXV.10.

10 *Itḥāf* IX.587, line 18, has *ka'l-jammāli*. I read *ka'l-ḥammāli* with Gramlich, 672.

11 Q. XLI.53.

12 Q. III.18.

13 Q. XLI.53.

14 Q. VII.185.

15 Q. X.101.

16 Q. LXVII.3–4.

17 Q. XVIII.109.

18 Zabīdī finds no source for this tradition, but see Gramlich, 674.

19 Ibn Ḥanbal, I.390; V.261–3, no. 3704; for variants, see Gramlich, 228.

20 Q. XVI.68.

21 Allusion to Q. XVI.69.

Chapter 7

1 Q. LVI.88–89.

2 Q. XVII.21

Chapter 9

1 Makkī, II.61; III.89.

2 Q. LXVI.8.

3 Q. LVII.13.

4 Arabic: *wa-yurīyanā al-Ḥaqq ḥaqqan*.

5 Nasā'ī, III.46–7; Ibn Ḥanbal (ed. Ḥalabī), IV.264; V.191.

6 Drawn from Makkī, II.60.

7 A reference to the well-known Tradition; see above, p. 47.

8 Reading *jahīd* ("striver") rather than *jihbidh* ("erudite"); Gramlich, 689, chooses the latter reading, though with some reluctance.

9 Arabic *khudh min nafsik li-nafsik*.

10 Reading *bi-sukrihi* with M rather than *bi-shukrihi* with Z (IX.608, l. 17).

Chapter 10

1 Q. V.54.

2 Q. LXI.4.

3 Q. II.222.

4 Q. V.18.

5 Q. II.222. Cf. Makkī, II.50, 14–16; III.73.

6 Q. III.31.

7 Makkī, II.50; III.74.

8 Makkī, II.51; III.74; Ibn Māja, II.1398, no. 4176; Muslim, IV.2001, *birr* 69.

9 Bukhārī, riqāq 38; Ibn Ḥanbal, VI.256; Tirmidhī, *Khatm al-awliyā'* 332; 406; Qushayrī, 42, 11–13.

10 Makkī, II.50; III.73.

11 Q. V.54.

12 For this tradition, see above, p.100.

13 Makkī, II.53; III.77.

14 *Ibid.*

15 *Ibid.*

16 ʿIrāqī, *Mughnī*, IV.320; Munāwī, *Fayḍ*, I.256, no. 378.

17 ʿIrāqī, *loc.cit.*

18 Allusion to a *ḥadīth* frequently referred to by Ghazālī. Cf. Wensinck, *Concordances*, VII.107.

Chapter II

1 Makkī, II.44; III.65; Wensinck, *Concordances*, VI.139b–140b.

2 Makkī, II.51; III.75

3 *Ibid.*

4 Q. LXI.4.

5 Q. IX.111.

6 Makkī, II.51; III.75.

7 Abū Nuʿaym, I.108–9.

8 Makkī, II.51; III.75.

9 Q. II.94.

10 The remark is based on a Tradition; cf. Bukhārī, IV.2064, dhikr 10; also Ibn Ḥanbal, III.101; III.104, 195; Ibn Māja, II.1425, no. 4265, zuhd 31.

11 Makkī, II.51; III.75.

12 Q. LIX.9.

13 Reading *mustamirran* with Z (*Itḥāf* IX.619), instead of *mustaqirran* with B.

14 As Gramlich notes (699), the same verse occurs in Persian in Ḥāfiẓ, *Dīvān* (ed. Ghanī), 44.

15 Makkī, II.52; III.76.

16 Makkī, II.54; III.79.

17 Makkī, II.54; III.80.

18 *Ibid.*

19 Q. V.54.

20 Q. IV.45.

21 Makkī, II.51; III.75.

22 *Ibid.*

23 Makkī, II.52; III.76.

24 *Ibid.*

25 Q. III.31.

26 Munāwī, *Fayḍ*, I.177–8, no. 224; ʿAzīzī, *al-Sirāj al-munīr*, I.57; Nabhānī, I.49.

27 Makkī, II.53; III.78.

28 *Ibid.* II.64; III.94; Abū Nuʿaym, VIII.20.

29 Makkī, II.54; III.79.

30 Q. XIII.28.

31 Q. II.216.

32 Makkī, II.55; III.81.

33 *Ibid.*

34 *Ibid.*

35 Q. XLVIII.29.

36 Allusion to Q. V.54.

37 Abū Nuʿaym, I.13.

38 Q. LXXXII.13; LXXXIII.22.

39 Q. LXXXIII.25–28.

40 Q. LXXXIII.18.

41 Q. LXXXIII.21.

42 Q. XXXI.28.

43 Q. XXI.104.

44 Q. LXXVIII.26.

45 Q. XCIX.7–8.

46 Q. XIII.11.

47 Q. IV.40.

48 Q. XXI.47.

49 Q. LIV.55.

50 Reading *fa-qawm* with M, instead of *fa-hum* with Z.

51 I translate *mujālasa* here as "keeping company [with God]." Gramlich (70–8) renders this "Beisammensein [mit Gott]," which is correct, whereas Siauve (188) translates the term as "la société des autres," which is clearly wrong.

52 Cited in Makki, II.68.

53 Q. LXXXIII.19.

54 Q. CI.1–3.

55 Q. XI.68.

56 Q. XI.95.

57 ʿIrāqī, IV.326; ʿAlī al-Qārī, *al-Maṣnūʿ*, 174–175, no. 311.

58 Wensinck, *Concordances*, V.38b; Munāwī, *Fayḍ*, III.11, no. 2621.

59 The Arabic is *makr khafī*.

60 Reading *fa-hab la-nā* with B and M; Z has *baqiya*, i.e., "what is lost to us remains [missing]."

61 Reading *birr* with B and M, rather than *bard*, as in Z.

62 Makkī, II.59; III.87.

63 Q. XI.45; Q. XCV.8.

64 For this anecdote, see Makkī, II.60.

65 The poet remains unidentified. The metre is *wāfir*.

66 Reading *ʿirāṣ* ("fields") with Gramlich ("Gefilden"), 712.

67 Makkī, II.67; III.98.

68 Read *yutimma* with Z and M, rather than *yanumma* ("reveal") with B.

69 Matthew 6:3–4, 17–18.

70 Gramlich (715) reads this *muḥibbīna* (["one of] the lovers"], instead of *majānīna* (["one of] the madmen") in the Arabic originals.

71 Makkī, II.67; III.98–9.

72 Allusion to Q. LXVI.6.

73 The Arabic reads: *ḥatta ẓannatu anna lī ʿinda Allāhi shay'an*.

74 Arabic *qātalahu Allāh mā abṣarahu*, more literally rendered as "Damn him! How sharp-sighted he is!" I have preferred a more colloquial translation to convey the force of the remark.

75 Anon., *Mukāshafāt al-qulūb*, 32; Munāwī, *al-Kawākib al-durrīya*, I.233.

76 A variant in ʿAṭṭār, *Tadhkirat al-awliyā'*, I.277.

77 Arabic: *ʿulamā'*.

Chapter 12

1 Reading *istishʿār* with B, instead of *istibshār* with Z.

2 Reading *mutrafūn* with B, instead of *mutafarriqūn* with Z.

3 Makkī, II.64; III.94.

Chapter 13

1 Siauve translates (216): "Moïse...était sorti pour puiser lui-même de l'eau, pour eux, soixante-dix mille fois... » whereas Gramlich (720) translates this correctly as : « ...und Mose ausgezogen war, um inmitten von siebzig tausend Personen für sie um Regen zu beten... » (for : *kharaja Mūsā li-yastasqiya la-hum fī sabʿīna alf...*).

2 Makkī, II.54; III.79.

3 Munawī, *Fayḍ*, no. 4401, cited in Ritter, *The Ocean of the Soul*, 583.

4 Arabic *rastāqī madhūsh* (from Persian *rūstā* ["village"].

5 *Fa-innamā hīya ʿinda dhawī al-ightirār min al-asmār.* Reading *asmār* with Z.(IX.643, l. 2); B and margin read *asmā'* [but see Gramlich, 722]. Note the rhyme *ightirār/asmār*; Ghazālī frequently resorts to rhyme to clinch a point.

6 Q. LXXX.8–10.

7 Q. LXXX.5–6.

8 Q. VI.54.

9 Q. VI.68.

10 Q. XVIII.28.

11 Q. VII.155.

12 Q. XX.24.

13 Q. XXVI.14.

14 Q. XXVI.12–13.

15 Q. XX.45.

16 Q. XXXIX.6.

17 Q. LXVIII.49.

18 Q. LXVIII.48.

19 Q. XVII.55.

20 Q. II.253.

21 Q. XIX.33.

22 Q. XIX.15.

23 Q. XII.8.

24 For the only reference to ʿUzayr in the Qur'ān, see Q. IX.30.

25 Makkī, II.65; III.95.

26 Q. II.160.

27 Makkī, II.65; III.96.

28 *Ibid.* II. 66; III. 96.

29 Q. CXII.1–4.

30 Q. LIX.23.

31 Q. LXXXIX.6–7.

32 Q. CV.1.

33 Q. CXII.3.

34 *Ibid.*

35 Q. CXII.4.

36 Q. VI.59.

37 Sarrāj, *Lumaʿ*, 72.

Chapter 14

1 Ibn Ḥanbal, I.266; IV.127, no. 2397; I.314; IV.315–16, no. 2881; I.328; V.15, no. 3033; Bukhārī, wuḍū' 10; Muslim, IV.1927, faḍā'il al-ṣaḥāba.

2 Q. V.119; IX.100.

3 Q. LV.60.

4 Q. IX.72.

5 Q. XXIX.45.

6 Qushayrī, 88–89.

7 Q. L.35.

8 Q. XXXII.7.

9 Q. XXXVI.58.

10 Q. IX.72.

11 Makkī, II.39; III.57.

12 *Ibid.*

13 Makkī, II.39; III.58; Ibn Ḥanbal, VI.19.

14 Makkī, *loc.cit.*

15 *Ibid.*

16 Makkī, II.39–40; III.58.

17 *Ibid.*

18 *Ibid.*

19 *Ibid.*; cf. Munāwī, *Fayḍ*, VI.49, no. 8386.

20 Makkī, II.40; III.59.

21 *Ibid.*, II.41; III.60; Qushayrī, 89.

22 Makkī, *loc.cit.*

23 *Ibid.*

24 *Ibid.*

25 *Ibid.*, II.41; III.50; cited also in *Kitāb al-arbaʿīn*, 265.

26 Makkī, II.41; III.60.

27 *Ibid.*

28 *Ibid.*, II.42; III.61.

29 In M and in B (though not in Z), the following sentence is added: "If you submit to what I will, I will requite you with what you will but if you do not submit to what I will, I will make you wear yourself out in what you do will. Only that which I will can come to be." *Itḥāf*, IX.653.

30 Makkī, II.40; III.59.

31 M and B read *taṣbir* instead of *taṣluḥ*.

32 Abū Nuʿaym, I.137; also, Makkī, II.43; III.63.

33 Abū Nuʿaym, II.352.

34 Makkī, II. 39; III.57; Abū Nuʿaym, VIII.193.

35 Makkī, *loc.cit.*; Abū Nuʿaym, I.216.

36 Makkī, II.40; III.59.

37 *Ibid.*; Kalābādhī, *Al-Taʿarruf*, 73; Arberry, *The Doctrine of the Sufis*, 93.

38 Makkī, II.40; III.59; Qushayrī, 89.

39 Makkī, *loc.cit.*

40 *Ibid.*

41 Makkī, II.41; III.61.

Chapter 15

1 Makkī, II.67; III.99. "O friend!" is in Persian in the original (*yā dūst*).

2 Ibn al-Dabbāgh, *Mashāriq anwār al-qulūb*, 75; ʿAṭṭār, *Tadhkirat al-awliyā'*, I.277–78.

3 Ghazālī uses this example also in his *Kitāb al-arbaʿīn*, 267.

4 Ibn al-Dabbāgh, *loc.cit.*

5 Reading *bi-fālij* with B and M instead of *yuʿālij* with Z.

6 On this tale, see *Theodicy*, 254.

7 Abū Nuʿaym, II.179.

8 *Ibid.*, I.132.

9 Makkī, II.42; III.62.

10 *Ibid.*

11 The order of words is reversed in M and in B. "Self-glorification" seems to be the implication of the words *taʿẓīm* and *ijlāl.*

12 *Ibid.*

13 Ghazālī here copies an error from Makkī; the correct name, as Gramlich notes (740), is Abū al-ʿAlā' Yazīd ibn ʿAbd Allāh ibn al-Shikhkhīr al-ʿĀmirī al-Baṣrī (d. 111/729–30).

14 Makkī, II.43; III.62–3.

15 *Mathʿaba* in Z (IX.660, l. 19), according to whom the correct name is Suwayd ibn Shuʿba; *Matʿaba* in M and B.

16 Makkī, II.43; III.63.

17 *Ibid.*

18 *Ibid.*

19 *Ibid.*

20 *Ibid.*

21 Sarrāj, *Lumaʿ*, 50; Qushayrī, 86; ʿAṭṭār, II.163.

22 *Dīwān Abī Bakr al-Shiblī*, 129, no. 67.

23 Makkī, II.43–4; III.64.

24 Makkī, II.46; III.68.

25 Ibn al-Dabbāgh, *Mashāriq anwār al-qulūb*, 75–6.

26 See Ritter, *The Ocean of the Soul*, 406.

Chapter 16

1 Q. xxi.90.

2 Q. x.7.

3 Q. ix.87.

4 Reading, with M and B, *al-dāll ʿalā al-sharr* instead of *ʿalā al-khayr* with Z.

5 Q. lxxxiii.26.

6 Q. iii.28.

7 Q. v.51.

8 Q. vi.129.

9 Q. iii.26.

10 Arabic *al-taʾaddub bi-ādāb al-sharʿ*.

Chapter 17

1 Makkī, ii.49; iii.72.

2 *Ibid.*

3 *Ibid.*

4 For *ḥishsh* ("privy"), see Lane, p. 573.

5 Q. iv.97.

6 Q. iv.75.

7 Q. viii.25.

8 Makkī, ii.44; iii.64.

9 The dialogue here has a colloquial ring: *īsh taqūl anta?*

10 Makkī, ii.44–45; iii.65.

Chapter 18

1 Makkī, ii.69; iii.101–102.

2 *Ibid.*

3 Makkī ii.70; iii.102–103.

4 Makkī, ii.70; iii.70.

5 Makkī, ii.70; iii.103; also, Ghazālī, *al-Imlāʾ*, 200.

6 Makkī, ii.71; iii.104.

7 Makkī, ii.72; iii.106.

8 Makkī, ii.73; iii.107.

9 *Ibid.*

10 *Ibid.*

11 *Ibid.*

12 *Ibid.*

13 In Arabic, *dhimmī*.

14 Makkī, ii.73; iii.107–8.

15 For this *hadīth qudsī*, reading *khibāʾī* with Z (ix.676, line 20), not *qabābī* as in *Iḥyāʾ* iv.377, line 1.

16 Cf. above, p. 140.

17 Makkī, ii.74; iii.108.

18 Makkī, ii.74; iii.109.

19 *Ibid.* In this passage, Makkī attributes this anecdote to "another *shaykh*," not to Ibn al-Karanbī.

20 Makkī, ii.74–5; iii.109–10.

21 *Ibid.*

22 Makkī, ii.75; iii.110; also Munāwī, *Fayḍ*, iii.320, and ʿAzīzī, *al-Sirāj al-munīr*, ii.197.

23 Makkī, *loc.cit.*; Munāwī, *Fayḍ*, iii.292, no. 3432; Nabhānī, *al-Fatḥ al-kabīr*, ii.45.

24 Makkī, *loc.cit.*; Munāwī, *loc. cit.*; Nabhānī, *al-Fatḥ al-kabīr*, ii.46.

25 Reading *ʿajab* with Z (IX.678, l. 21), instead of *ḥajab* with *Iḥyāʾ*, iv.378, l. 8.

26 Makkī, ii.77; iii.113 (who attributes it, however, to al-Ḥasan al-Baṣrī).

27 Makkī, ii.78; iii.115.

28 Munāwī, *Fayḍ* ii.482, no. 2364; Nabhānī, *al-Fatḥ al-kabīr*, i.409.

29 Makkī, ii.78; iii.115.

30 Makkī, *loc.cit.*; Ibn Ḥanbal, iv.63, 376; v.44, 50; Abū Dāūd, iv.289, *kitāb al-sunna, bāb fī al-khulafāʾ*.

31 Makkī, *loc.cit.*; cf. also Muslim, IV.1855, *faḍā'il al-ṣaḥāba* 3; Bukhārī, *ṣalāt* 80, and *faḍā'il al-ṣaḥāba* 3 and 5; Ibn Ḥanbal (ed. Ḥalabī), III.18; IV.4, 5; Ibn Māja, I.36, *muqaddima* 11, no. 93.

Chapter 19

1 Qushayrī, 145; also, Kalabādhī, *al-Taʿarruf* 79.

2 In the Arabic, *maʿnā*.

3 Abū Nuʿaym, x.274.

4 Qushayrī, 146.

5 *Ibid.*

6 *Ibid.*

7 *Ibid* (omits the final verse).

8 *Ibid.*

9 *Ibid.*; cf. also ʿAṭṭār, *Tadhkirat al-awliyā'*, II.83; Ibn al-ʿArabī, *al-Futūḥāt al-makkīya*, II.346.

10 Based on a Sacred Tradition; cf. Ibn Māja, II.1376–77, *zuhd* 3, no. 4110; for a variant, see Abū Nuʿaym, VIII.36.

11 A version in ʿAṭṭār, *Tadhkirat al-awliyā'*, I.67.

12 In other versions, it is Jesus, not Moses, who is asked; cf. Gramlich, 765.

13 In Arabic, *innamā yuḥibbu min mawlāhu mawlāhu*.

14 Sarrāj, *Lumaʿ*, 59.

15 Qushayrī, 149–50 (*bāb al-shawq*).

16 For the construction *wā-shawqāh*, see Wright, *A Grammar of the Arabic Language*, II.93C.

17 An allusion to the well-known Tradition; cf. *supra*, 38.

18 Reading *shiddat al-shawq* with Gramlich, 767; for a variant of the verse, see Sarrāj, *Maṣāriʿ al-ʿushshāq*, II.89.

APPENDIX

PERSONS CITED IN TEXT — EXCLUDING PROPHETS

ʿABD ALLĀH IBN JAḤSH, b. Riʾāb b. Yaʿmar al-Asadī (d. 3 [625]). A Companion of the Prophet, and the son of Muḥammad's maternal aunt, he was sent on the expedition to Nakhla in 623; he was killed at the Battle of Uḥud and his body was mutilated. (Ṭabarī, *History*, VII.18, 34; Gramlich, 786.)

ʿABD ALLĀH IBN MUḤAMMAD. He is perhaps to be identified as ABŪ ʿABD ALLĀH ibn Muḥammad ibn Salīm al-Baṣrī (d. 297 [909]), the life-long disciple and assistant of the Sufi master Sahl al-Tustarī. (*EI*[2] VIII.840.)

ʿABD ALLĀH IBN AL-SĀʾIB, ibn Abī al-Sāʾib Ṣayfī b. ʿĀbid al-Makhzūmī (d. ca.73 [692]). A Companion and Qurʾān reciter, to whom many important traditions are due. (Juynboll, 218, 661.)

ʿABD AL-ʿAZĪZ IBN ABĪ RAWWĀD (d. ca. 159 [775–6]). An early Meccan *mawlā* and transmitter of traditions, especially on the authority of Mālik ibn Anas. (Abū Nuʿaym, VIII.164–75; Juynboll, 402.)

ʿABD AL-WAHHĀB AL-WARRĀQ, b. ʿAbd al-Ḥakam b. Nāfiʿ al-Baghdādī (d. 250 or 51 [864 or 66]). A figure of immense piety and discipline, he was a reliable transmitter of *ḥadīth*, as well as a teacher of such traditionists as Abū Dāwūd, Tirmidhī, and Nasāʾī, and a close associate of Aḥmad ibn Ḥanbal. He was renowned for his asceticism. Among his students were Ibn Abī al-Dunyā, Ḥākim al-Tirmidhī, Abū al-Qāsim al-Baghawī, and others. (Mizzī, *Tahdhīb al-kamāl*, XVIII.497–501; Dhahabī, *Siyar aʿlām al-nubalāʾ*, XII.323–4; ʿAsqalānī, *Tahdhīb al-tahdhīb*, VI.391; Gramlich,787.)

ʿABD AL-WĀḤID IBN ZAYD (d. 177 [793]). An ascetic of Basra, and a companion of Ḥasan al-Baṣrī and Dārānī chiefly cited for the importance which he attached to solitude. He was held up as a model in Sufi literature and given the honorific title "Master of the Ascetics". According to Abū Nuʿaym, he was partially paralysed, from which affliction he was released only at the time of prayer. (Abū Nuʿaym, VI.155–65; Makkī, II.137; *Bidāya*, X.171; Massignon, *Essai*, 214–5; Vadet, 209; F. Meier, *Abū Saʿīd*, 3, 303.)

ABŪ ʿABD ALLĀH IBN AL-JALLĀʾ al-Dimashqī. Perhaps a mistake for Abū ʿAbd Allāh Aḥmad b. Yaḥyā al-Jallāʾ, a celebrated Sufi, and associate of Junayd and Nūrī, who died in 306 [918]. (Sulamī, 166–9; Hujwīrī, 134–5; cf. T. J. Winter (tr.), *Al-Ghazālī on Disciplining the Soul*, 210.)

ABŪ ʿALĪ AL-RŪDHABĀRĪ (d. 322 [933 or 4]). A well-known Sufi of Baghdad, who also spent time in Egypt. He was associated with the circle of Junayd and Nūrī. He was also a *ḥadīth* scholar and jurist who studied under Ibrāhīm al-Ḥarbī. His name is sometimes given as al-Rūdhbārī. (Sulamī, 362–9; Qushayrī, I.162; *Lumaʿ*, xviii–xix.)

ABŪ ʿAMR MUḤAMMAD IBN AL-ASHʿATH [IBN QAYS AL-KINDĪ, ABŪ AL-QĀSIM AL-KŪFĪ] (d. 67 [686]). A senior Follower, born to Umm Farwa, the niece of Abū Bakr. He transmitted from his father, al-Ashʿath ibn Qays, ʿĀʾisha, Ibn Masʿūd, ʿUmar ibn al-Khaṭṭāb, and ʿUthmān ibn ʿAffān. His most notable students were Zuhrī, Mujāhid ibn Jabr, the exegete, ʿĀmir al-Shaʿbī, Bakr ibn Qays and his son Qays. (Mizzī, XXIV.495–98; ʿAsqalānī, IX.52–53.)

ABŪ BAKR AL-ṢIDDĪQ ibn Abī Quḥāfa al-Taymī (d. 13 [634]). A small businessman of Mecca who personally accompanied the Prophet on his emigration to Medina, Abū Bakr became the Prophet's closest advisor, and after his death became the first caliph. (*EI²*, I.109–11.)

ABŪ AL-DARDĀʾ, ʿUwaymir al-Khazrajī (d. 32 [652/3]). A celebrated Companion of the Prophet who joined Islam sometime after the battle of Badr, whereupon he is said to have given up commerce in order to occupy himself with worship with the *ahl al-Ṣuffa*. He died in Damascus, where he was buried, and is venerated in particular by Sufis. (*EI²*, I. 113–4; Abū Nuʿaym, I.208–27.)

ABŪ ḤAFṢ al-Nīsābūrī (d. 265 [878 or 9]). A renowned mystic who said, "Man has nothing to do with repentance: it comes to him, not from him." He was known for his love of nature and used to take his novices out in spring on nature walks. (Sulamī, 105–113; Qushayrī, II.114; F. Meier, *Abū Saʿīd*, 2, 6, 8, 107, 203, 297.)

ABŪ ḤANĪFA al-Nuʿmān ibn Thābit ibn Zūṭā (d. 150 [767]). The eponymous founder of the Ḥanafī school of law, he was born in Kufa, the grandson of a Persian slave, and devoted himself at an early age to the study of law and Sacred Traditions. In theology, he was a Murjiʿite, i.e., one who believed in the suspension of judgment as to the fate of sinners. The authenticity of the books ascribed to him seems doubtful but his influence was vast. (*GAS* I.409–19; *EI²*, I.123–4.)

ABŪ ḤĀZIM, Salama ibn Dīnār al-Makhzūmī al-Madanī al-Aʿraj (d. 140 [757/8]). An ascetic who became an important figure for the early Sufis. "Everything which does not bring you to God," he said, "can only bring you to destruction." (*GAS*, I.634–5; Makkī, II.56; Abū Nuʿaym, III.229–59.)

ABŪ ḤUDHAYFA ibn ʿUtba ibn Rabīʿa b. ʿAbd Shams (d. 12 [633]). An early Companion of the Prophet, he joined the emigration to Abyssinia shortly before the Hijra. (Ṭabarī, *History*, VI.99–100.)

ABŪ JAHL, Abū al-Ḥakam ʿAmr ibn Hishām ibn al-Mughīra (d. 17 [624]). One of the chief opponents of Muḥammad, and who reportedly conspired to have the Prophet murdered, he died at the battle of Badr. (*EI*² I.115.)

ABŪ KHĀLID AL-ṢAFFĀR is perhaps to be identified as Abū ʿAbd Allāh Muḥammad b. ʿAbd Allāh b. Aḥmad al-Iṣfahānī al-Ṣaffār (d. 339 [951]). (Gramlich, 788.)

ABŪ MŪSĀ AL-ASHʿARĪ, ʿAbd Allāh b. Qays (d. ca. 42 [662]). He converted to Islam during the Khaybar campaign. During the caliphate of ʿUmar he was responsible for the conquest of Khūzistān, and was made governor of Basra. Later he became ʿAlī's representative at the arbitration following the battle of Ṣiffīn (37/657), after which he took no further part in public life. (*EI*², I.695–6; Abū Nuʿaym, I.236–43.)

ABŪ NAṢR AL-TAMMĀR, ʿAbd al-Malik b. ʿAbd al-ʿAzīz al-Qushayrī (d. 228 [842]). An expert traditionist who was known for his voluntary poverty, he was considered to be among the forty *abdāl* of his time. (Mizzī, XVIII.354–58; ʿAsqalānī, VI.355–6; Ibn Saʿd, *al-Ṭabaqāt al-kubrā,* VII.340.)

ABŪ RĀZIN AL-ʿUQAYLĪ, Laqīṭ ibn ʿĀmir b. Ṣabra b. ʿAbd Allāh b. al-Muntafiq, (fl. 1st c. [7th c.]). A Companion, sometimes confused with Laqīṭ b. Ṣabra, another transmitter (though some sources—such as Ibn ʿAbd al-Barr below—consider them variant names of the same individual). He came from al-Ṭāʾif. He asked the Prophet about performing the pilgrimage on behalf of others. (Mizzī, XXIV.248–9; ʿAṣqalānī, VIII.398–9; Ibn ʿAbd al-Barr, *al-Istīʿāb fī maʿrifat al-Aṣḥāb*, III.397; Gramlich, 809.)

ABŪ SAʿĪD AL-MĪHANĪ is better known as ABŪ SAʿĪD IBN ABĪ AL-KHAYR (d. 440 [1049]). Born in Mīhāna (or Māyhana), he was one of the best-loved of the saints of Khorasan. He studied Shāfiʿī jurisprudence before his conversion to Sufism and was a class-mate of the father of the theologian Juwaynī. He was known in his youth for his extreme asceticism but later turned to "service of the poor". He was criticised for his lavish entertainments at which music and dancing were allowed, but his skill at "discernment" (*firāsa*) of the secret thoughts of others, including those of rulers, saved him from prosecution. (*EI*², I.145–7; Meier, *Abū Saʿīd ibn abī'l-Khayr*.)

ABŪ SULAYMĀN AL-DĀRĀNĪ, ʿAbd al-Raḥmān (d. 205 [820/1] or 215 [830/1]). Well-known to the Sufis for his piety and renunciation, he was responsible for characteristic maxims such as "The heart is ruined when fear departs from it even for one moment," and "The sign of perdition is the drying-up of tears." (Qushayrī, 108–10; Sulamī, 68–73; Hujwīrī, 112–3; Abū Nuʿaym, IX.254–80.)

ABŪ TURĀB AL-NAKHSHABĪ, ʿAskar b. al-Ḥusayn (d. 245 [859]). An ascetic Ṣufi of Kufan origins known for his scrupulosity and his learning, he was an associate of Ḥātim al-Aṣamm, among other masters of the time. (Sulamī, 136–40; Abū Nuʿaym, X.39–43, 185–87; Qushayrī, 97–8; Meier, *Abū Saʿīd*, 296–7.)

ABŪ ʿUBAYDA [or: ʿUTBAH] AL-KHAWWĀṢ is correctly known as ʿAbbād b. ʿAbbād al-Khawwāṣ al-Ramlī al-Ursufī (fl. 2d. [8th c.]). Of Persian descent, he ranks amongst the great scholars and Sufis of Syria. Sufyān al-Thawrī addressed an epistle on religious guidance and salvation to him. His extreme asceticism is said to have compromised his accuracy as a transmitter. (ʿAṣqalānī, V.87; Mizzī, XIV.134–6; Gramlich, 786.)

ABŪ YAZĪD AL-BISṬĀMĪ (d. 261 or 264 [874 or 877/8]). An early and very influential Sufi of great visionary gifts; though he wrote nothing, some 500 of his sayings, often of a provocative nature, have been preserved, including the notorious exclamation, "Glory be to me! How great is my state (*sha'nī*)!" His own master was of Indian origin and the influence of Hinduism has been detected in his doctrines, especially that of "self-annihilation" (*fanā'*). An ascetic as well, he said that he had been "the blacksmith of my own self" (*ḥaddād nafsī*). (*EI*², I.162–3; Sulamī, 60–67; *Lumaʿ*, 380–93; Abū Nuʿaym, X.33–42; Qushayrī, 16–17; R. C. Zaehner, *Hindu and Muslim Mysticism*, 93–134.)

AḤMAD IBN ABĪ AL-ḤAWĀRĪ, Abū al-Ḥasan (d. 230 or 246 [844–5 or 860–1]). An ascetic Sufi, of Damascene origin, and an associate of Abū Sulaymān al-Dārānī, he taught that "the sign of love of God is obedience to God," and that man could love God only if first inspired by God's love of him. (Sulamī, 88–92; Abū Nuʿaym, X.5–28; Qushayrī, 95.)

AḤMAD IBN ḤANBAL (d. 241 [855]). The great *ḥadīth* scholar, jurist, and theologian, responsible for the compilation of the *Musnad*, one of the canonical collections of Sacred Traditions, and the authority from whom the Ḥanbalī school of law takes its name. (*EI*², I.272–7.)

Appendix

AL-ʿALĀʾ or ABŪ AL-ʿALĀʾ, Yazīd Ibn ʿAbd Allāh Ibn al-Shikhkhīr al-ʿĀmirī al-Baṣrī, (d. 111 [729–30]). A senior Follower, he took reports from Abū Hurayra, ʿĀʾisha and other prominent Companions. (Mizzī, xxxii.175–7; ʿAṣqalānī, xi.296–7; Juynboll, 444.)

ʿALĪ IBN ABĪ ṬĀLIB (d. 40 (660)]. The cousin and son-in-law of the Prophet who married his daughter Fāṭima. The Prophet's standard-bearer on expeditions, he became the model of the Muslim knight for later generations. He lived a life of austerity and piety. Upon the death of ʿUthmān (35/656) he accepted, with some reluctance, the office of Caliph, which he held for five years disturbed by several rebellions, including that of Muʿāwiya, the governor of Syria. He was assassinated at Kūfa by Ibn Muljam, a member of the extreme Khārijite sect, which repudiated him for having agreed to negotiate with Muʿāwiyah. (*EI²*, i.381–6.)

ʿALĪ IBN AL-MUWAFFAQ, Abū al-Ḥasan al-ʿĀbid, al-Baghdādī (d. 265 [878–9]). An influential early Sufi ascetic, he is said to have made the pilgrimage more than fifty times. (Abū Nuʿaym, x.265–66; *Lumaʿ*, xxix, 290.)

ʿAMR IBN AL-ḤĀRITH al-Rāfiqī. Unidentified

ANAS IBN MĀLIK, ibn al-Naḍr (d. 91–3 (709/10–711/12]). A celebrated Companion of the Prophet, he had been presented to the Prophet at an early age by his mother in fulfilment of a vow. After the Prophet's death he participated in the wars of conquest. One hundred and twenty eight Sacred Traditions on his authority are to be found in the collections of Bukhārī and Muslim. (*EI²*, i.482; Juynboll, 131–4.)

BISHR AL-ḤĀFĪ, Abū Naṣr Bishr ibn al-Ḥārith (d. 226 or 227 [840 or 841/2]). A great ascetic Sufi, who lived by begging and came close to starvation on occasion, he was known as "Bishr the Barefoot". There are various anecdotes to account for this practice which Bishr seems to have based on Q. lxxi.19: "And God made the earth your carpet." A strong advocate of *tawakkul* ("trust in God"), he stressed action as the surest way to knowledge and influenced Ghazālī decisively in both respects. His guiding principle was, "first to know, then to act, then really to know." He enjoyed the respect of both Aḥmad ibn Ḥanbal and the caliph Maʾmūn. (*EI²*, i.1244–6; Sulamī, 33–40; ʿAṭṭār, i.106–114; Abū Nuʿaym, viii.336–60.)

AL-BUWAYṬĪ, Abū Yaʿqūb Yūsuf b. Yaḥyā al-Qurashī (d. 231 [846]). An Egyptian jurist, called "chief jurist" by Dhahabī and one of the best students of Shāfiʿī (who called him his "tongue", i.e., his spokesman). He was imprisoned during the Miḥna over the issue of "the createdness of the Qurʾān" which he refused to accept and died in prison. (Mizzī, XXXII.472–6; ʿAsqalānī, XI.374–5; Dhahabī, *Siyar aʿlām al-nubalā*, XII.58–61; Nawawī, *al-Majmūʿ*, I.158–9).

DHŪ AL-NŪN al-Miṣrī, Thawbān (d. 245 [859/60]). Born in Upper Egypt, he travelled to Mecca and Damascus, and became a leading exponent of Sufism. It was said that he was the first to give a systematic explanation of the *aḥwāl* ("states") and *maqāmāt* ("stations") encountered on the spiritual path. A number of miracles are attributed to him, as well as some fine poetry. (*EI²*, II.242; Sulamī, 23–32; Qushayrī, I.67–70; Hujwīrī, 100–3; Massignon, *Essai*, 206–13.)

FATḤ AL-MAWṢILĪ, Abū Naṣr b. Saʿīd (d. 220 [835]). A Sufi and well-known ascetic who was associated with Bishr al-Ḥāfī in Baghdad. (Abū Nuʿaym, VIII.292–4; Jāmī, *Nafaḥāt al-uns*, 47–8.)

FUḌAYL ibn ʿIyāḍ (d. 187 [803/4]). A brigand who repented and became a pioneer of early Sufism. He studied *ḥadīth* under Sufyān al-Thawrī and Abū Ḥanīfa, and became well-known for his sermons on the worthlessness of the world, which he likened to 'a madhouse, the people in which are lunatics wearing the shackles of desire and sin.' (*EI²*, II.936; *GAS*, I.636; Hujwīrī, 97–100; Sulamī, 7–12.)

GHULĀM AL-KHALĪL, Aḥmad ibn Muḥammad ibn Ghālib al-Bāhilī (d. 275 [888]). An ascetic Sufi and traditionist from Basra, sometimes described as a Ḥanbalī (but see van Ess below), he was active in Baghdad and instrumental in laying charges against Nūrī and other proponents of divine love. (*EI²*, IV.1083b; *GAS*, I.511; Massignon, *Passion*, III.118; van Ess, *Theologie u. Gesellschaft*, IV.283–4; Knysh, *Islamic Mysticism*, 61.)

HARIM IBN ḤAYYĀN al-ʿAbdī (d. after 26 [646–7]). An early pietist of Basra, considered a forerunner of Ḥasan al-Baṣrī. (EI², I.73b; Abū Nuʿaym, II.116–19; Juynboll, 283, n.1.)

AL-ḤASAN AL-BAṢRĪ (d. 110 [728/9]). The son of a Persian captive who was later manumitted, al-Ḥasan became one of the best known personalities among the second generation of Muslims; his influence on both Sufism and Islamic theology was huge. He served in the Muslim armies in eastern Iran and later worked as a tax official. After he moved to Basra, his sanctity and eloquence as a preacher attracted great numbers to his circle. He was also a judge and an authority on *ḥadīth*. His tomb at Basra remains an important centre for devout visits. (*EI²*, III.247–8; Hujwīrī, 86–7; Abū Nuʿaym, II.131–61; ʿAṭṭār, 19–26; van Ess, *Theologie u. Gesellschaft*, II.41–51.)

ḤĀTIM AL-ṬĀʾĪ ibn ʿAbd Allāh ibn Saʿd (6th century A.D.). Pre-Islamic poet renowned for his great generosity and hospitality; even after his death, according to legend, he would rise from his tomb to entertain guests. (*EI*², III.274–5.)

ḤUDHAYFA ibn al-Yamān al-ʿAbasī (d. 36 [656/7]). One of the earliest converts to Islam, he became governor of Ctesiphon under ʿUmar. He is particularly revered by Sufis. He related a considerable number of *ḥadīth*s, especially those relating to eschatology; reportedly he said that, "the Prophet told me all that would occur from the present until the Day of Judgement." (Abū Nuʿaym, I.249–59; Massignon, *Essai*, 159–61; Juynboll, 84–6.)

IBN ʿABBĀS, ʿAbd Allāh (d. 68 [687/8]). A cousin and close companion of the Prophet respected for his piety and commonly acknowledged as the greatest scholar of the first generation of Muslims, a narrator of *ḥadīth* and the founder of the science of Qur'ānic exegesis. He fought alongside ʿAlī at Ṣiffīn, and died at al-Ṭā'if, where the site of his grave is still visited. (*EI*², I.40–1; Nawawī, *Tahdhīb*, 351–4; Abū Nuʿaym, I.314–29; *Mashāhīr*, 9; *Iṣāba*, II.322–6.)

IBN AL-KARANBĪ, Abū Jaʿfar, al-Baghdādī (fl. 3d/9th c.). A well-known Sufi ascetic of Baghdad, famed for his eccentricities; he was the teacher of Junayd. (Abdel-Kader, *The Life, Personality, and Writings of al-Junayd*, 26–28; Sarrāj, *Lumaʿ*, 198; Ibn al-Jawzī, *Talbīs Iblīs*, 191; Meier, *Abū Saʿīd*, 284.)

IBN MASʿŪD, ʿAbd Allāh (d. 32 [652 or 3]). A favourite Companion of the Prophet, personally entrusted to carry Muḥammad's sandals, he was of Bedouin origin. The first to engage in public reading of the Qur'ān, he was present at the battles of both Badr and Uḥud and, later, at Yarmūk, and was also active in the founding of Kūfa. A respected traditionist, and source of traditions, he clashed with the Caliph ʿUthmān in the last years of his life. (*EI*² III.873–5; Abū Nuʿaym, I.122–35; Juynboll, 7–8; Daylamī, 17, 211, 224, 284, 285.)

IBN AL-MUBĀRAK, ʿAbd Allāh ibn Wāḍiḥ al-Ḥanẓalī (d. 181 [797–8]). An influential saint and scholar of the Law. Originally from Merv in Central Asia, he travelled to study with Mālik ibn Anas in Medina and Awzāʿī in Syria before he died in combat against the Byzantines. (*GAL* SI.256; Abū Nuʿaym, VIII. 137–63; ʿAṭṭār, 124–8.)

IBN ʿUMAR, ʿAbd Allāh (d. 73 [693/4]). A Companion of the Prophet who at the age of fourteen asked to be permitted to fight at Uḥud, which permission was denied. Possessed of high moral qualities, he commanded universal deference and respect. Although it is said that he was offered the caliphate on three separate occasions, he kept himself aloof from politics and occupied himself instead with study and instruction. (*EI*² I.53–4; *Iṣāba*, II.338–41; Abū Nuʿaym, I.292–314.)

IBRĀHĪM IBN ADHAM (d. 161 [777/8]). A famed Sufi of Khorasanian origin, often portrayed as "a prince of Balkh" (though he later moved to Syria), he was famed for his asceticism. Tales of his sudden conversion to Sufism—though probably apocryphal—are cited throughout the hagiographical literature. (*EI*^{2}, i.985–6; Sulamī, 13–22; ʿAṭṭār, i.85–106; Abū Nuʿaym, vii.367–95 and viii.3–58.)

ʿIMRĀN IBN AL-ḤUSAYN b. ʿUbayd, Abū Nujayd al-Khuzāʿī (d. 52 [672]). A Companion of the Prophet, credited with many important traditions. (Juynboll, 241.)

JAʿFAR IBN SULAYMĀN al-Ḍabuʿī (d. 178 [794–5]). A celebrated early traditionist with apparent Shīʿite tendencies. (Ṭabarī, *History*, xix.82.)

AL-JUNAYD, Abū al-Qāsim ibn Muḥammad (d. 298 [910/11]). The best known of the Sufis of Baghdad. A nephew and disciple of Sarī al-Saqaṭī, he vowed that he would not teach during the latter's lifetime out of deference to his preceptor; however he received a vision of the Prophet, who told him that "God shall make your words the salvation of a multitude of mankind;" he then began to teach. His gatherings "were attended by jurists and philosophers (attracted by his precise reasoning), theologians (drawn by his orthodoxy) and Sufis (for his discoursing upon the Truth)." In addition, he was an authority on theology and law, in which he followed the school of Abū Thawr. (*EI*^{2}, ii.600; *GAS*, i.647–50; Sulamī, 141–50; A. H. Abdel-Kader, *The Life, Personality and Writings of al-Junayd*; van Ess, *Theologie u. Gesellschaft*, iv.278–88.)

KAʿB al-Akhbār, ibn Mātiʿ al-Ḥimyarī (d. 32 [652/3] or 34 [654/5]). A rabbi from the Yemen who converted to Islam during the caliphate of ʿUmar. (*EI*^{2}, iv.316–7; *Mashāhīr*, 118.)

KHĀLID IBN AL-WALĪD (d. 21 [642]). A famed commander in the early conquests, he originally opposed the Prophet and fought against him at Uḥud, but later converted; he was known as "the Sword of God" (*sayf Allāh*). (*EI*^{2}, iv.928.)

MAʿRŪF AL-KARKHĪ, Ibn Fīrūz (d. 200–1 [815/6–816/7]). One of the major early Sufis. His parents are said to have been Christians. He had a strong influence on Sarī al-Saqaṭī; he is also reported to have instructed Ibn Ḥanbal in *ḥadīth*. His grave, restored in 1312 AH, is an important focus of the religious life of Baghdad, and many miraculous cures are said to be worked there. (*EI*^{2}, vi.613–14; Hujwīrī, 113–5; Sulamī, 74–9; Qushayrī, i.74–8.)

MASRŪQ ibn al-Ajdaʿ (d. 63 [682/3]). Chiefly resident in Kūfa, he was a respected traditionist and 'Follower' who taught Ibrāhīm al-Nakhaʿī. He is said to have fought on the side of ʿAlī against the Khārijites. (*Mashāhīr*, 101; *Kāshif*, iii.120.)

MAYMŪN IBN MIHRĀN al-Jazarī (d. *c* 117 [735/6]). An ascetic of Raqqa on the upper Euphrates, he was a pupil of Ḥasan al-Baṣrī and a traditionist who became secretary to the caliph ʿUmar ibn ʿAbd al-ʿAzīz. (*Mashāhīr*, 117; *Bidāya*, IX.314; Abū Nuʿaym, IV.82–97.)

MUḤAMMAD IBN ʿABD ALLĀH b. al-Mubārak al-Qurashī al-Mukharrimī, al-Baghdādī (d. 254 [868]). A strong traditionist and a teacher of Bukhārī, Abū Dāwūd, and Nasāʾī, he was acclaimed by the latter as the greatest scholar he had met in Iraq. (Mizzī, XXV.534–38; ʿAṣqalānī, IX.236–7.)

MUḤAMMAD IBN WĀSIʿ. Unidentified

MUṢʿAB IBN ʿUMAYR b. Hishām al-Dārī (d. 3 [625]). An early Companion of the Prophet, he came from a rich family but renounced a life of luxury when he converted to Islam; for this he is often held up as an exemplar of piety in later accounts. He fought at Badr and later at Uḥud, where he was killed. (*EI*^{2}, VII.649; Abū Nuʿaym, I.105–6.)

MUṬARRIF IBN ʿABD ALLĀH IBN AL-SHIKHKHĪR al-ʿĀmirī (d. *c* 87 [806/7]). An ascetic and traditionist of Basra; the brother of Yazīd b. ʿAbd Allāh ibn al-Shikhkhīr. Many miracles and prayers are attributed to him. (*Mashāhīr*, 88; Abū Nuʿaym, II.183–95; Sarrāj, *Lumaʿ*, 65; *Kāshif*, III.132.)

MUṬARRIF IBN ABĪ BAKR AL-HUDHALĪ (no dates). An early ascetic of Basra. (Zabīdī, X.373; Massignon, *Essai*, 164.)

AL-NŪRĪ, Abū al-Ḥusayn (d. 295 [907]). An early proponent of the love of God and a central figure in the Sufism of his time. He was famed for his love of ruins where he found solitude with God. (*EI*^{2} VIII.139; *GAS* I.650; Sulamī, 151–8; Abū Nuʿaym, X.212–17; Daylamī, 68; Massignon, *Passion*, I.121.)

QATĀDA ibn Diʿāma al-Baṣrī (d. 117 [735/6]). Although blind from birth, he became an authority on the exegesis of the Qurʾān. He was an associate of Ḥasan al-Baṣrī, and sometimes accused of Muʿtazilite sympathies. (*GAS*, I.31–2; *Fihrist*, 34; *Mashāhīr*, 96; Massignon, *Essai*, 200; Juynboll, 439–49; van Ess, *The Flowering of Muslim Theology*, 173.)

RĀBIʿA AL-ʿADAWĪYA, bint Ismāʿīl (d. 185 [801/2]). The most famous woman Sufi. It is said that she was stolen as a child and sold into slavery, but was released on account of her piety. She lived for a time in the desert, where she was fed miraculously by God. She later moved to Basra, where she taught Sufyān al-Thawrī and Shaqīq al-Balkhī, emphasising the importance of divine love, of which she was one of the earliest and most passionate advocates. She left a number of memorable prayers. (*EI*^{2}, VIII.354–6; M. Smith, *Rābiʿa the Mystic and her Fellow-Saints in Islam*.)

SAʿD IBN ABĪ WAQQĀṢ, al-Murrī (d. 50 [670/1] or 55 [674/5]). One of the ten Companions assured of Heaven by the Prophet, he distinguished himself particularly as a brilliant politician and soldier. To him goes the credit for the defeat of the Persians at al-Qādisīya (16/637), one of history's most decisive battles, and the subsequent founding of Kūfa as a military base. He remained governor of that city until the year 20 (640/1) when he was recalled to Medina following allegations, not credited by the Caliph, of misrule. ʿUmar later made him one of six men who were to choose the new caliph. (*EI*², VIII.696–7.)

SAHL AL-TUSTARĪ, Abū Muḥammad ibn ʿAbd Allāh (d. 283 [896]). A Sufi originating from Khuzistan, he placed great emphasis on the practice of *dhikr*. His prayer of preference was "God, my witness" (*Allāhu shāhidī*). He was for a time the teacher of Ḥallāj. He was also important in the development of exegesis, elaborating a four-fold approach (literal, allegorical, moral, and anagogical) to the sacred text, and his *Tafsīr* is extant. (*EI*², VIII.840–41; Sarrāj, *Lumaʿ*, 66, 74, 83, 89; Sulamī, 199–205; Qushayrī, 80–82; G. Böwering, *The Mystical Vision of Existence in Classical Islam*.)

SAʿĪD IBN AL-MUSAYYIB al-Makhzūmī (d. 93–4 [711/2–712/3]). A major genealogist and legal expert of Medina, held by some to have been the most erudite of the second Muslim generation. He refused to marry his devout and learned daughter to the caliph al-Walīd ibn ʿAbd al-Malik, for which he was flogged. (Abū Nuʿaym, II.161–76; Hujwīrī, 83; *Mashāhīr*, 63.)

SAʿĪD IBN YAḤYĀ. Unidentified

AL-SARĪ AL-SAQAṬĪ, ibn al-Mughallis (d. *c* 251 [865/6]). The maternal uncle of Junayd, and one of the first to present Sufism in a systematised fashion. According to Hujwīrī, his conversion to Sufism was instigated by the Baghdad saint Ḥabīb al-Rāʿī, who, upon being given a crust of bread by Sarī, said, "May God reward you!" "From that time on," Saqaṭī later remarked, "my worldly affairs never prospered again." He was perhaps the most influential disciple of Maʿrūf al-Karkhī. (*EI*², IV.171; Sulamī, 41–8; Qushayrī, 64–7.)

AL-SHĀFIʿĪ, Muḥammad ibn Idrīs al-Qurashī (d. 204 [820]). The founder of the Shāfiʿite school of Islamic law. Although born in Gaza, he was brought up with a Bedouin tribe, which gave him a good grounding in poetry and the Arabic language. He later studied *fiqh* with Sufyān ibn ʿUyayna and Mālik ibn Anas, developing a legal theory that stood halfway between literalism and personal opinion. He travelled extensively to Iraq and Egypt, where he died; his tomb is today one of the centres of Cairene religious life. (*EI*², IX.181–85; *GAS*, I.484–90.)

SHAQĪQ AL-BALKHĪ, al-Azdī (d. 194 [809/10]). One of the founders of the Khorasanian school of Sufism, he was the disciple of the ascetic Ibrāhīm ibn Adham. He was known for his discourses on the nearness of the Resurrection and the importance of trust (*tawakkul*) in God. He was also a noted scholar of the *sharīʿa*. (Qushayrī, I.96–9; Abū Nuʿaym, VIII.58–73; Sulamī, 54–9; Hujwīrī, 111–2.)

AL-SHIBLĪ, ibn Jaḥdar (d. 334 [945/6]). Formerly a chamberlain at the Caliph's palace, he converted to Sufism and became a follower of Junayd, whose teachings he later communicated to Naṣrābādhī. Well-known for his acts of asceticism and renunciation—as well as for his extravagant words and deeds—he is said to have put salt in his eyes to stay awake for his nocturnal devotions. He was also an authority on the Mālikite school of law. His tomb at Baghdad is still venerated. (*EI²*, IV.360–1; Qushayrī, I.182–3; Sulamī, 340–55; Hujwīrī, 155–6.)

SUFYĀN AL-THAWRĪ, Abū ʿAbd Allāh ibn Saʿīd (d. 161 [777/8]). A scholar and well-known saint of Kūfa, of whom a great number of anecdotes is recorded. He was one of the 'Eight Ascetics', who included (usual list) ʿĀmir ibn ʿAbd Qays, Abū Muslim al-Khawlānī, Uways al-Qaranī, al-Rabīʿ ibn Khuthaym, al-Aswad ibn Yazīd, Masrūq, and al-Ḥasan al-Baṣrī. It is said that he was offered high office under the Umayyads but consistently declined. (*EI²*, IX.770–72; *Fihrist*, 225; Abū Nuʿaym, VI.356–93, VII.3–144; Juynboll, 628–43.)

SUMNŪN AL-MUḤIBB, Sumnūn ibn ʿAbd Allāh Abū al-Ḥasan al-Khawāṣṣ (d. 300 [913]). Though widely known as "Sumnūn the Lover", he preferred to call himself "Sumnūn the Liar" (*Sumnūn al-kadhdhāb*). An ecstatic proponent of love of God, who was celebrated for "discoursing on love (*maḥabba*) most eloquently," he was a leading Sufi master in the Iraq of his day. His name is sometimes vocalized as "Samnūn." (Sulamī, 186–92.)

SUWAYD IBN AL-MATHʿABA al-Tamīmī al-Riyāḥī al-Rāwī (d. 1st c. [7th c.]). A prominent Syrian student of ʿAbd Allāh ibn Masʿūd, he was especially noted for his patience in affliction and exemplary expressions of gratitude to God. (Ibn Saʿd, *Ṭabaqāt al-kubrā*, VI.160; Ibn Abī Ḥātim, *Kitāb al-jarḥ waʾl-taʿdīl*, IV.235.)

ʿUMAR IBN ʿABD AL-ʿAZĪZ ibn Marwān (*regn.* 99–101 [717–20]). Sometimes called 'the fifth rightly-guided Caliph' for his piety, this Umayyad caliph was concerned to implement the *sharīʿa* in a number of neglected areas, such as the equal treatment of converts; he also ended the public cursing of ʿAlī from the pulpits. A large body of sermons and anecdotes connected with him soon found its way into religious literature. (*EI²*. X.821–22.)

ʿUMAR IBN AL-KHAṬṬĀB (*regn.* 13–23/634–44). Though originally opposed to the Prophet and his mission, ʿUmar eventually became one of his strongest defenders. After the Ḥijra, the Prophet married ʿUmar's daughter Ḥafṣa. He succeeded Abū Bakr as the second of the Rāshidūn caliphs. During the ten years of his caliphate, he oversaw the extension of the Conquests and the establishment of garrison towns, such as Basra, Kufa and Fustat. He was murdered under obscure circumstances by a Persian slave. (*EI*², x.818)

ʿURWA IBN ZUBAYR, ibn al-ʿAwwām al-Qurashī al-Asadī al-Madanī, Abū ʿAbd Allāh (d. 93 or 94 [711 or 712]). Among the most eminent early traditionists, and considered one of the "Seven Jurists of Medina," his transmissions of *ḥadīth* are attested throughout the canonical collections. (*EI*², x.910–13; Juynboll, 644–5.)

WAHĪB IBN AL-WARD, ʿAbd al-Wahhāb, al-Makkī (d. 153 [770]). An important early traditionist. (Abū Nuʿaym, viii.119–37.)

YAḤYĀ IBN MUʿĀDH al-Rāzī (d. 258 [871/2]). A Sufi active in Central Asia, and one of the first to teach Sufism in mosques, he left a number of books and sayings. Despite the emphasis he placed on *rajā'*: the hope for Paradise and for God's forgiveness, he was renowned for his perseverance in worship and his great scrupulousness in matters of religion. (*GAS*, i.644; Abū Nuʿaym, x.51–70; Sulamī, 98–104; *Fihrist*, 184; Hujwīrī, 122–3; Massignon, *Essai*, 268–72.)

YŪSUF IBN ASBĀṬ al-Shaybānī (d. 196 [811/2]). Dominated by the fear of God and of the Judgement, he influenced Bishr al-Ḥāfī. He also related a number of *ḥadīths* from Thawrī. (Abū Nuʿaym, viii.237–53; Zabīdī, x.343.)

ZAYD IBN ASLAM al-ʿAdawī al-Ṭūsī (d. 136 [753/4]). A respected traditionist and jurist who is said to have taught Mālik ibn Anas. A number of sayings on *rajā'*, hope for God's forgiveness, are ascribed to him. (*Mashāhīr*, 80; Abū Nuʿaym, iii.221–9; *Ghāya*, i.296; Juynboll, 689–90.)

BIBLIOGRAPHY

Abdel Haleem, M. A. S. *The Qur'an: A New Translation*, Oxford: Oxford University Press, 2004.

Abdel-Kader, A. H. *The Life, Personality and Writings of al-Junayd*. London, 1962. [Gibb Memorial Series, new series, XXII].

Abrahamov, Binyamin. *Divine Love in Islamic Mysticism: The Teachings of al-Ghazālī and al-Dabbāgh*. London: Routledge, 2003.

Abū Dāūd. *Al-Sunan*. Cairo, 1369–70/1950–1.

Anawati, G.-C. and Gardet, Louis. *Mystique Musulmane*. Paris: Vrin, 1976.

Anonymous, *Mukāshafāt al-qulūb*. Cairo, 1371/1952.

Arberry, A. J. *The Doctrine of the Sufis*. 2d ed. Cambridge, 1977.

———(tr.). *The Ring of the Dove: a Treatise on the Art and Practice of Arab Love*. London, 1953. [=Ibn Ḥazm, *Ṭawq al-ḥamāma*].

Aristotle. *The Nicomachean Ethics*. Tr. H. Rackham. Cambridge, MA: Harvard University Press, 1968. [The Loeb Library]

ʿAsqalānī, Ibn Ḥajar, al-. *Fatḥ al-bārī bi-sharḥ al-Bukhārī*. s.l. 1959–63.

———*Al-Iṣāba fī tamyīz al-Ṣaḥāba*. Cairo, 1358–9.

———*Tahdhīb al-tahdhīb*, ed. Muṣṭafā ʿAdb al-Qādir ʿAṭā'. 12 vols. Beirut: Dār al-Kutub al-ʿIlmiyyah (1st ed., 1994).

ʿAṭṭār, Farīd al-Dīn. *Tadhkirat al-awliyā'*. Ed. R.A. Nicholson. 2 vols. London: Luzac, 1905; rpt. Tehran, n.d.

Austin, R. W. J. (tr.). *The Bezels of Wisdom*. Ramsey, N.J.: Paulist Press, 1980. [=Ibn al-ʿArabī, *Fuṣūṣ al-ḥikam*].

ʿAzīzī, ʿAlī b. Aḥmad. *Al-Sirāj al-munīr*. Cairo, 1377/1957.

Baqlī, Rūzbihān. *Sharḥ shaṭḥīyāt*. Ed. Henry Corbin. Tehran, 1966.

Bousquet, G.-H. *Ih'ya ʿOuloûm ed-Dîn ou Vivification des sciences de la foi: analyse et index*. Paris: Maisonneuve, 1955.

Bouyges, Maurice. *Essai de chronologie des oeuvres de Al-Ghazali (Algazel)*. Ed. Michel Allard. Beirut: Imprimérie Catholique, 1959. [Recherches publiées sous la direction de L'Institut de Lettres Orientales de Beyrouth, XIV]

Böwering, Gerhardt. *The Mystical Vision of Existence in Classical Islam: the Qur'ānic Hermeneutics of the Ṣūfī Sahl al-Tustarī (d. 283/896)*. Berlin, 1980.

Brockelmann, C. *Geschichte der arabischen Litteratur*. 2nd. ed. Leiden, 1943–1949; *Supplement*, Leiden, 1937–1942.

Buchman, David (tr.). *The Niche of Lights: Mishkāt al-anwār: a parallel English-Arabic text*. Provo: Brigham Young University Press, 1998.

Bukhārī, Muḥamma b. Ismāʿīl. *Al-Ṣaḥīḥ*. 4 vols. Cairo, 1312.

———*Kitāb al-tārīkh al-kabīr*. Beirut: Dār al-Fikr, no date, although the publisher's note is dated 1986.

Burrell, David B. (tr.). *Faith in Divine Unity and Trust in Divine Providence*. Louisville, KY: Fons Vitae, 2001. [=Book xxxv of the *Iḥyā'*].

Burrell, David B. & Daher, Nazih (trs.). *The Ninety-Nine Beautiful Names of God*. Cambridge: The Islamic Texts Society, 1992. [=Ghazālī, *al-Maqṣad al-asnā*].

Chittick, William C. *The Self-Disclosure of God: Principles of Ibn al-ʿArabī's Cosmology*. Albany: SUNY Press, 1998.

Daftary, Farhad. *Ismaili Literature: a Bibliography of Sources and Studies*. London; New York: I. B. Tauris, in association with The Institute of Ismaili Studies, 2004.

Dārimī, Abū Muḥammad ʿAbd Allāh, al-. *Al-Sunan*. 2 vols. Medina, 1386/1966.

Dawood, N. J. (tr.). *The Koran, with a parallel Arabic Text*. London: Penguin, 1993.

Daylamī, Abū 'l-Ḥasan ʿAlī b. Muḥammad. *A Treatise on Mystical Love*. Trans. Joseph Norment Bell and Hassan Mahmood Abdul Latif Al Shafie. Edinburgh: Edinburgh University Press, 2005.

———*Kitāb ʿaṭf al-alif al-ma'lūf ʿalā l-lām al-maʿṭūf. Livre de l'inclinaison de l'alif uni sur le lām incliné*. Ed. J. C. Vadet. Cairo, 1962.

Dhahabī, Muḥammad b. Aḥmad, al-. *Al-Kāshif fī maʿrifa man la-hu riwāya fī al-kutub al-sitta*. Beirut, 1403/1983.

———*Mīzān al-iʿtidāl fī naqd al-rijāl*. 3 vols. Cairo, 1382/1963.

———*Siyar aʿlām al-nubalā'*, ed. Shuʿayb al-Arnā'ūṭ. 25 vols. Beirut: Mu'assasat al-Risālah, 1998.

Diwald, Susanne. *Arabische Philosophie und Wissenschaft in der Enzyklopädie: Kitāb Ihwān aṣ-ṣafā' (III): Die Lehre von Seele und Intellekt*. Wiesbaden: Otto Harrassowitz, 1975.

Dozy, Reinhardt. *Supplément aux dictionnaires arabes*. 2 vols. Leiden: Brill, 1881; rpt. Beirut, 1968.

Eklund, Ragnar. *Life between Death and Resurrection according to Islam*. Uppsala, 1941.

El-Bizri, Nader (ed.). *The Ikhwān al-Ṣafā' and their Rasā'il: an Introduction*. Oxford: Oxford University Press, in association with The Institute of Ismaili Studies, 2008. ["Epistles of the Brethren of Purity," 1]

The Encyclopaedia of Islam. 2d edition. 12 vols. Brill: Leiden, 1960–2004.

Ess, Josef van. *Anfänge muslimischer Theologie: Zwei antiqadaritische Traktate aus dem ersten Jahrhundert der Hiğra*. Beirut, 1977 [Beiruter Texte und Studien, 14].

———*Die Erkenntnislehre des ʿAḍudaddīn al-Īcī: Übersetzung und Kommentar des ersten Buches seiner Mawāqif*. Wiesbaden: Franz Steiner, 1966. [Akademie der Wissenschaften und der Literatur: Veröffentlichungen der orientalischen Kommission, XXII.]

———*The Flowering of Muslim Theology*. Tr. Jane Marie Todd. Cambridge, MA: Harvard University Press, 2006.

———*Die Gedankenwelt des Ḥārit al-Muḥāsibī*. Bonn, 1961 [Bonner orientalistische Studien, N.S., 12].

———*Theologie und Gesellschaft im 2. und 3. Jahrhundert Hidschra: eine Geschichte des religiösen Denkens im frühen Islam*. 6 vols. Berlin; New York: Walter de Gruyter, 1991–97.

Fārābī, Abū Naṣr, al-. *al-Farabi on the Perfect State: Abū Naṣr al-Fārābī's Mabādi' ārā' ahl al-madīna al-fāḍila*. Ed./tr. Richard Walzer. Oxford, 1985.

Frank, Richard M. *Creation and the Cosmic System: Al-Ghazālī and Avicenna*. Heidelberg: Carl Winter, 1992. [Abhandlungen der Heidelberger Akademie der Wissenschaften, Philosophisch-historische Klasse, 1].

Frankfurt, Harry G. *The Reasons of Love*. Princeton: Princeton University Press, 2004.

Gardet, Louis. *La pensée religieuse d'Avicenne*. Paris: Vrin, 1951.

Gardet, Louis and M.-M. Anawati. *Introduction à la théologie musulmane: essai de théologie comparée*. Paris: Vrin, 1948.

Ghazālī, Muḥammad Abū Ḥāmid, al-. *Iḥyā' ʿulūm al-dīn*. 4 vols. Cairo, 1334/1916; and 5 vols. Beirut: 1417/1996.

———*Iljām al-ʿawāmm ʿan ʿilm al-kalām*. On the margin of: ʿAbd al-Karīm al-Jīlī, *al-Insān al-kāmil*. Cairo, 1328/1949.

———*Al-Imlā' fī mushkilāt al-Iḥyā'*. On the margin of: *Iḥyā' ʿulūm al-dīn*, Beirut, 1417/1996.

———*Al-Iqtiṣād fi'l-iʿtiqād*. Ed. İbrahim Çubukçu and Hüseyin Atay. Ankara, 1962. [Ankara Üniversitesi Ilâhıyat Fakültesi Yayınları, 34].

———*K. al-arbaʿīn fī uṣūl al-dīn*. Cairo, 1344.

———*Makātīb-i fārsī*. Ed. ʿAbbās Iqbāl. Tehran, 1333.

———*Al-Maqṣad al-asnā fī asmā' Allāh al-ḥusnā*. Ed. F. Shehadi. Beirut, 1971.

———*Mishkāt al-anwār*. Beirut, 1407/1987.

———*Al-Munqidh min al-ḍalāl*. Ed./tr. F. Jabre. Beirut, 1959.

———*Al-Qusṭās al-mustaqīm*. Beirut, 1959.

———*Tahāfut al-falāsifa: The Incoherence of the Philosophers*. Ed/tr. Michael Marmura. Provo: Brigham Young Univ. Press, 1997.

[pseudo-Ghazālī]. *Al-Ḥikma fī makhlūqāt Allāh*. Aleppo; Cairo, 1352/1934.
Ghazālī, Aḥmad, al-. *Savāniḥ*. Ed. Naṣr Allāh Pūrjavādī. Tehran: Intishārāt-i Bunyād-i Farhang-i Īrān, 1359.
———*Sawāniḥ: Inspirations from the World of Pure Spirits*. Tr. Nasrollah Pourjavady. London: Routledge & Kegan Paul, 1986.
Giffen, Lois. *The Theory of Profane Love among the Arabs: the Development of the Genre*. New York: New York University Press, 1971.
Goldziher, Ignaz. *Gesammelte Schriften*. Ed. J. DeSomogyi. 6 vols. Hildesheim: Olms, 1967–73.
———"Die Gottesliebe in der islamischen Theologie," *Der Islam* IX (1919), 144–158.
———*Muslim Studies* (*Muhammedanische Studien*). Ed. S.M. Stern. Tr. C.R. Barber & S.M. Stern. 2 vols. London, 1971.
Gramlich, Richard. *Muḥammad al-Ġazzālīs Lehre von den Stufen zur Gottesliebe: Die Bücher 31–36 seines Hauptwerkes eingeleitet, übersetzt und kommentiert*. Wiesbaden: Franz Steiner Verlag, 1984. [Freiburger Islamstudien, X].
Griffel, Frank. "Al-Ghazālī or Al-Ghazzālī? On a lively debate among Ayyūbid and Mamlūk Historians in Damascus," in: Anna Akasoy & Wim Raven (eds.), *Islamic Thought in the Middle Ages: Studies in Text, Transmission and Translation, in Honour of Hans Daiber*. Leiden; Boston: Brill, 2008. Pp. 101–111.
Grunebaum, G. E. von. "*Risāla fī'l-ʿishq* and Courtly Love," *Journal of Near Eastern Studies*, 11:4 (1952), pp. 233–238.
Ḥāfiẓ, Shams al-Dīn. *Dīvān*. Ed. M. Qazvīnī & Q. Ghanī. Tehran, n.d.
Ḥallāj, Ḥusayn ibn Manṣūr, al-. *Dīwān*. Ed. L. Massignon. Paris, 1955; and Kāmil Muṣṭafā al-Shaybī. Baghdad, 1974.
Heer, Nicholas & Kenneth L. Honerkamp (trs.). *Three Early Sufi Texts*. Louisville: Fons Vitae, 2003.
Hourani, George F. "A Revised Chronology of Ghazālī's Writings," *JAOS* 104:2 (April–June 1984), 289–302.
Hujwīrī, ʿAlī b. ʿUthmān, al-. *Kashf al-maḥjūb: the Oldest Persian Treatise on Sufism*. Tr. R. A. Nicholson. London, 1911; rpt. 1976.
Ibn ʿAbd al-Barr. *Istīʿāb fī maʿrifat al-asḥāb*, ed. ʿĀdil Aḥmad ʿAbd al-Mawjūd and ʿAlī Muḥammad. 4 vols. Beirut: Dār al-Kutub al-ʿIlmiyyah, 1995.
Ibn Abī Ḥātim. *al-Jarḥ wa'l-taʿdīl*. 10 vols. Beirut: Dār al-Kutub al-ʿIlmiyyah (photocopy of Hyderabad edition.
Ibn al-ʿArabī, Muḥyi al-Dīn. *Fuṣūṣ al-ḥikam*. Ed. A. ʿAfīfī. Cairo, 1309.
———*Al-Futūḥāt al-makkīya*. Ed. ʿUthmān Yaḥyā. 14 vols. Cairo, 1972–92.
Ibn Bājja. *Tadbīr al-mutawaḥḥid*. Ed. M. Asín-Palacios. Madrid, 1946.
Ibn al-Dabbāgh, ʿAbd al-Raḥmān. *Mashāriq anwār al-qulūb wa-mafātiḥ asrār al-ghuyūb*. Ed. H. Ritter. Beirut, 1959.

Ibn Ḥanbal, Aḥmad. *Al-Musnad*. Ed. Ḥalabī (Cairo, 1313); ed. Aḥmad Muḥammad Shākir (Cairo, 1368/1949).

Ibn Ḥazm. *Rasā'il*. Ed. Iḥsān ʿAbbās. 4 vols. Beirut, 1980–83.

Ibn Ḥibbān, Muḥammad, al-Bustī. *Mashāhir ʿulamā' al-amṣār*. Ed. M. Fleischhammer. Cairo, 1959.

Ibn al-Jawzī, Abū al-Faraj. *Talbīs Iblīs*. Beirut, n.d.

Ibn al-Jazarī, Shams al-Dīn Muḥammad. *Ghāyat al-nihāya fī ṭabaqāt al-qurrā'*. Ed. G. Bergsträsser and O. Pretzl. Cairo, 1352/1933.

Ibn Kathīr, Ismāʿīl b. ʿUmar. *Al-Bidāya wa-al-nihāya*. Cairo, 1351/1932.

Ibn Māja, Abū ʿAbd Allāh. *Al-Sunan*. Cairo, 1952–3.

Ibn Manẓūr. *Lisān al-ʿarab*. 20 vols. Būlāq, 1308; rpt. Cairo, n.d.

Ibn al-Nadīm. *Fihrist*. Tehran, n.d.

Ibn Saʿd, Muḥammad. *Al-Ṭabaqāt al-kubrā*. 9 vols. Beirut: Dār Ṣādir, n.d.

Ibn Sīnā. *The Metaphysics of* The Healing: *al-Shifā': Ilāhīyāt. A Parallel English-Arabic Text*, trans. Michael Marmura. Provo: Brigham Young University Press, 2005.

———*Rasā'il*. Qum: Intishārāt-i Bīdār, [1400].

Ikhwān al-Ṣafā'. *The Case of the Animals versus Man Before the King of the Jinn: An Arabic Critical Edition and English Translation of Epistle 22*. Ed./tr. Lenn E. Goodman and Richard McGregor. Oxford: Oxford University Press in association with The Institute of Ismaili Studies, 2009. [Epistles of the Brethren of Purity].

———*Rasā'il*. 5 vols. Beirut, 1957.

ʿIrāqī, Zayn al-Dīn, al-. *Al-Mughnī ʿan ḥaml al-asfār fī'l-asfār fī takhrīj mā fī'l-Iḥyā' min al-akhbār*. [On margin of *Iḥyā'*, Cairo, 1358/1939, ed.]

Iṣfahānī, Abū Nuʿaym, al-. *Ḥilyat al-awliyā' wa-ṭabaqāt al-aṣfiyā'*. 11 vols. Beirut: Dār al-Fikr, 1996.

Jāḥiẓ. *Kitāb al-ḥayawān*. Ed. M. Hārūn. 8 vols. Cairo, 1938–43.

Jāmī, ʿAbd al-Raḥmān b. Aḥmad. *Nafaḥāt al-uns min ḥaḍarāt al-quds*. Ed. Mahdī Tawḥīdpūr. Tehran, 1336/1957.

Juynboll, G. H. A. *Encyclopedia of Canonical Ḥadīth*. Leiden; Boston: Brill, 2007.

Kalabādhī, Abū Bakr Muḥammad, al-. *Al-Taʿarruf li-madhhab al-taṣawwuf*. Ed. A. J. Arberry. Cairo, 1934.

Kassis, Hanna E. *A Concordance of the Qur'an*. Berkeley: University of California, 1983.

Keeler, Annabel. *Sufi Hermeneutics: The Qur'an Commentary of Rashīd al-Dīn Maybudī*. London: Oxford University Press in association with The Institute of Ismaili Studies, 2006.

Kennedy, Hugh. *An Historical Atlas of Islam/Atlas historique de l'Islam*. 2d rev. ed. Leiden; Boston; Köln, 2002.

Knysh, Alexander. *Islamic Mysticism: a Short History*. Leiden: Brill, 2000.

Landolt, Hermann. "Ghazali and 'Religionswissenschaft'" in *Recherches en spiritualité iranienne: recueil d'articles*. Tehran: Institut Français de Recherche en Iran, 2005. Pp. 25–81.

Lane, William Edward. *An Arabic-English Lexicon*. 8 vols. London: 1863–85; rpt. Lahore, 1978.

Lazarus-Yafeh, H. *Studies in al-Ghazzālī*. Jerusalem, 1975.

Littlejohn, H. T. *Al-Ghazālī on Patience and Thankfulness: Kitāb al-ṣabr wa'l-shukr*. Cambridge: Islamic Texts Society, 2011. [=Book xxxii of the *Iḥyā'*].

Lumbard, Joseph E. B. "From *Ḥubb* to *ʿIshq*: the Development of Love in Early Sufism," *Journal of Islamic Studies* 18:3 (2007), pp. 345–385.

Maimonides, Moses. *The Guide of the Perplexed*. Tr. Shlomo Pines. Chicago: University of Chicago Press, 1963.

Makkī, Abū Ṭālib, al-. *Qūt al-qulūb*. 4 vols. Cairo, 1351/1932.

Massignon, Louis. *Le Dîwân d'al-Hallâj*. New rev. ed. Paris, 1955.

———*Essai sur les origins du lexique technique de la mystique musulmane*. New rev. ed. Paris, 1954.

———*La passion de Husayn Ibn Mansûr Hallâj. Martyr mystique de l'Islam exécuté à Bagdad le 26 mars 922*. 2d ed. 4 vols. Paris: Gallimard, 1975.

———*The Passion of al-Hallāj: Mystic and Martyr of Islam*. Tr. Herbert Mason. 4 vols. Princeton: Princeton University Press, 1982.

McCarthy, Richard J. *Freedom and Fulfillment: an annotated translation of al-Ghazālī's* al-Munqidh min al-ḍalāl *and other relevant works*. Boston: Twayne, 1980.

Meier, Fritz. *Abū Saʿīd-i Abū l-Hayr (357–440/967–1049): Wirklichkeit und Legende*. Leiden; Tehran: Brill/Bibliothèque Pahlavi, 1976 [Acta Iranica, Textes et Mémoires, III/4].

Melchert, Christopher. *Ahmad Ibn Hanbal*. Oxford: Oneworld, 2006.

Miskawayhī, Abū ʿAlī Aḥmad. *Tahdhīb al-akhlāq. The Refinement of Character*. Ed. Constantine K. Zurayk. Beirut, 1966.

Mizzī, Yūsuf ibn ʿAbd al-Raḥmān Ḥāfiẓ, al. *Tahdhīb al-kamāl fī asmā' al-rijāl*, ed. Bashshār al-ʿAwwād. 35 vols. Beirut: Mu'assasat al-Risālah, 1994.

Mullā Ṣadrā (Ṣadr al-Dīn al-Shīrāzī). *Al-Ḥikma al-mutaʿālīya fī al-asfār al-ʿaqlīya al-arbaʿa*. 9 vols. Qum, 1378–83/1958–69.

Munāwī, ʿAbd al-Ra'ūf, al. *Fayḍ al-qadīr*. 6 vols. Cairo, 1356–7/1938.

———*Al-Kawākib al-durrīya fī tarājim al-sāda al-ṣūfīya*. Cairo, 1357/1938.

Muslim, Ibn al-Ḥajjāj. *Al-Ṣaḥīḥ*. Beirut, 1972.

Nabhānī, Yūsuf, al-. *Al-Fatḥ al-kabīr fī ḍamm al-ziyāda ilā al-Jāmiʿ al-ṣaghīr*. Cairo, 1350.

Nakamura, Kojiro (tr.). *Al-Ghazālī on Invocations and Supplications: Kitāb al-adhkār wa'l-daʿawāt*. Cambridge: Islamic Texts Society, 2000. [=Book IX of the *Iḥyā'*].
Nasā'ī, Abū ʿAbd al-Raḥmān Aḥmad, al-. *Al-Sunan*. Cairo, 1383/1964.
Nawawī, Yaḥyā ibn Sharaf, al-. *Tahdhīb al-asmā' wa-al-lughāt*. Ed. F. Wüstenfeld. Göttingen, 1842–7.
———*Al-Majmūʿ*. 22 vols. Beirut: Dār al-Fikr, 1996.
Niẓām al-Mulk. *The Book of Government or Rules for Kings: The* Siyāsat-nāma *or* Siyar al-mulūk. Tr. Hubert Darke. London: Routledge & Kegan Paul, 1975.
Nwyia, Paul. *Exégèse coranique et langage mystique: nouvel essai sur le lexique technique des mystiques musulmans*. Beirut: Dar El-Machreq, 1970.
Ormsby, Eric. "Abū Ḥāmid al-Ghazālī vu par Massignon," in Eve Pieruniek and Yann Richard (eds.), *Louis Massignon et l'Iran*. Leuven; Paris: Peeters, 2000. Pp. 51–59.
———*Ghazali: The Revival of Islam*. Oxford: Oneworld, 2008.
———"The Poor Man's Prophecy: Al-Ghazālī on Dreams," in: Louise Marlow (ed.), *Dreaming across Boundaries: The Interpretation of Dreams in Islamic Lands*. Boston; Washington, D.C.: Ilex Foundation and Center for Hellenic Studies, Harvard University, 2008. Pp. 142–152.
———"Purgatory (Islamic)," in Joseph Strayer (ed.), *Dictionary of the Middle Ages*. New York, Scribner's, 1982–. Vol. x, 214–15.
———"The Taste of Truth: the Literary Structure of the *Munqidh min al-ḍalāl* of al-Ghazālī," in: *Islamic Studies presented to Charles J. Adams*, ed. Donald P. Little and Wael Hallaq (Leiden: Brill, 1991), pp. 129–48.
———*Theodicy in Islamic Thought: The Dispute over al-Ghazālī's 'Best of All Possible Worlds.'* Princeton: Princeton University Press, 1984.
Qārī, ʿAlī, al-. *Al-Asrār al-marfūʿa fī al-akhbār al-mawḍūʿa*. Beirut, 1391/1971.
———*Al-Maṣnūʿ fī maʿrifat al-ḥadīth al-mawḍūʿ*. 2d ed. Beirut, 1389/1969.
Al-Qur'ān al-Karīm. Cairo: Dār al-Kutub al-Miṣrīya, 1371/1952.
Qushayrī, Abū al-Qāsim, al-. *Al-Risāla al-Qushayrīya*. 2 vols. Cairo: 1966.
Rāzī, Abū Bakr M. b. Zakarīyā', al-. *Rasā'il falsafīya*. Ed. Paul Kraus. Cairo, 1939; rpt. Tehran, n.d.
Rāzī, Fakhr al-Dīn, al-. *Al-Tafsīr al-kabīr*. 32 vols. Tehran, n.d.
Reinhart, A. Kevin. *Before Revelation: The Boundaries of Muslim Moral Thought*. Albany: SUNY Press, 1995.
Ritter, Hellmut. "Arabische und persische Schriften über profane und mystische Liebe," [*Philologika* VII], *Der Islam* 21 (1933), 84–109.
———(tr.). *Das Elixier der Glückseligkeit*. Düsseldorf; Köln: Diederichs Verlag, 1959; rpt. of 1923 ed. [= al-Ghazālī, *Kīmīyā'-yi Saʿādat*]

———*Das Meer der Seele: Mensch, Welt und Gott in den Geschichten Des Farīduddīn ʿAṭṭār*. Leiden: Brill, 1955.
———*The Ocean of the Soul: Man, the World and God in the Stories of Farīd al-Dīn ʿAṭṭār*. Tr. John O'Kane. Brill: Leiden, 2003.
Sarrāj al-Ṭūsī, Abū Naṣr, al-. *The Kitāb al-lumaʿ fi'l-taṣawwuf*. Ed. R. A. Nicholson. 2d ed. London, 1963.
———*Maṣāriʿ al-ʿushshāq*. Beirut, 1378/1958.
Sezgin, Fuat. *Geschichte des arabischen Schrifttums*. Bd. I: *Qur'ānwissenschaften. Ḥadīth. Geschichte. Fiqh. Dogmatik. Mystik. Bis ca. 430H*. Leiden: Brill, 1967.
Shiblī, Abū Bakr, al-. *Dīwān*. Ed. Kāmil Muṣṭafā al-Shaybī. Baghdad, 1967.
Siauve, Marie Louise. *L'amour de Dieu chez Ġazālī: une philosophie de l'amour à Bagdad au début du XII siècle*. Paris: Vrin, 1986. [Etudes musulmanes, 28].
———(Tr.) *Livre de l'amour, du désir ardent, de l'intimité et du parfait contentement*. Paris: Vrin, 1986.
Smith, Margaret. *Rābiʿa the Mystic and her Fellow Saints in Islam*. Cambridge, 1928.
Subkī, Tāj al-Dīn, al-. *Ṭabaqāt al-Shāfiʿīya al-kubrā*. 6 vols. Cairo, 1324; 2d ed., Cairo, 1964.
Sulamī, Abū ʿAbd al-Raḥmān, al-. *Kitāb Ṭabaqāt al-Ṣūfiyya*. Ed. Johannes Pedersen. Leiden: Brill, 1960.
Ṭabarī, Abū Jaʿfar, al-. *The History of al-Ṭabarī*. 35 vols. Albany: SUNY, 1985–98.
Taftāzānī, Saʿd al-Dīn, al-. *Sharḥ al-Maqāṣid*. Istanbul, 1277.
Tirmidhī, Abū ʿAbd Allāh, al-. *Kitāb khatm al-awliyā'*. Ed. ʿUthmān Yaḥyā. Beirut, 1965.
Tirmidhī, Abū ʿĪsā Muḥammad, al-. *Al-Sunan*. Cairo, 1356/1937.
Wensinck, A. J. *Concordances et indices de la tradition musulmane*. 7 vols. Leiden: Brill, 1936–68.
———*The Muslim Creed: Its Genesis and Historical Development*. Cambridge: Cambridge University Press, 1932.
———*La pensée de Ghazzālī*. Paris: Adrien-Maisonneuve, 1940.
Westermarck, Edward. *Wit and Wisdom in Morocco*. London: Routledge & Sons, 1930.
Winter, T. J. (tr.) *Al-Ghazālī on Disciplining the Soul & Breaking the Two Desires. Kitāb riyāḍat al-nafs & Kitāb kasr al-shahwatayn*. Cambridge: Islamic Texts Society, 1995. [=Books XXII & XXIII of the *Iḥyā'*].
———(tr.) *Al-Ghazālī on the Remembrance of Death and the Afterlife. Kitāb dhikr al-mawt wa-mā baʿdahu*. Cambridge: Islamic Texts Society, 1989. [=Books XL of the *Iḥyā'*].
———(ed.) *The Cambridge Companion to Classical Islamic Theology*. Cambridge: Cambridge University Press, 2008.

Wörterbuch der klassischen arabischen Sprache. Ed. Manfred Ullmann. Wiesbaden: Harrassowitz, 1957–.

Wright, William. *A Grammar of the Arabic Language*. 2 vols. 3d ed. Cambridge: Cambridge University Press, 1951.

Zabīdī, M. Murtaḍā, al-. *Itḥāf al-sādat al-muttaqīn bi-sharḥ Iḥyā' ʿulūm al-dīn*. 10 vols. Cairo, 1311/1894.

Zaehner, R. C. *Hindu and Muslim Mysticism*. New York: Shocken, 1969.

Zamakhsharī, Abū Qāsim Maḥmūd, al-. *al-Kashshāf ʿan ḥaqā'iq al-tanzīl wa-ʿuyūn al-aqāwīl*. 4 vols. Cairo, 1972.

INDEX TO QUR'ĀNIC QUOTATIONS

Index to Qur'ānic Quotations

Index

112, 124–5, 127, 160, 177, 178; description of, 128–9; inner state of, 125–6; intimacy with God, 133–4, 135; longing, 88, 89–90, 193; rank of, 48–9; ultimate goal of, 53; utmost knowledge of, 36n
God: attribute of transcendence, xiii–xiv, 34–6, 39, 59; and beauty, xix, 29, 35, 83, 155, 165; Causer of causes, 172; God's custom, 14, 57, 144; God's ruse, 123, 138; the only true Agent, xxvii, xxxi, xxxii, 85; the only true beloved, xix; the real benefactor, 29–30; 'real' divine existence, xiv, 23, 25, 81, 82, 85; sanctity, 125, 144; a source of pleasure, xix, xxiv, 2; *takhṣīṣ al-irāda*, 126n; see also Divine Attributes; Divine Essence; Divine Names
God's self-manifestation (*tajallī*), 59, 83, 84
goodness, 26–8, 100, 130, 181; attribute of transcendence, 34; see also benevolence
grace (*luṭf*), 8, 102, 122, 159, 172, 182
gratitude, 27, 90, 95, 150, 152, 172–3
grief, 63, 116–17

ḥadīth, 5n, 37, 48–9, 91; contentment, 147, 148–50, 153, 187, 193; death, 109; *dhikr*, 192; faith, 70, 187, 188; *ḥadīth qudsī*, xxix; hatred, 167; Hell, 75; Hereafter, 58; intellect, 192; *Kitāb al-maḥabba wa'l-shawq wa'l-uns wa'l-riḍā*, xxiii; knowledge, 193; longing, 91, 192; love as affinity, xxix, 21, 38, 39; love of beauty, xxvii, 11, 17; love for God, 5–7, 112; love of God, 99–100, 104–105; love for the Prophet, 5–6; nearness to God, xxix, 39, 100, 121; prayer, 11–12; 140, 193; sin, 167, 168; supererogatory virtues, xxix
Ḥāfiẓ, Shams al-Dīn, xxi
ḥāl/aḥwāl (state of mystical consciousness), 125, 128, 133
al-Ḥallāj, al-Ḥusayn b. Manṣūr, xvii, xx, xxi, xxix, 53n, 127n, 128n; incarnationism, 39n
al-Ḥakīm al-Tirmidhī, xxiii
Harim b. Ḥayyān, 8, 191
al-Ḥasan al-Baṣrī, 7, 24, 139, 142
hatred, xxv–xxvi, 10, 11, 15, 29, 123; destruction and non-being, 13–14; detestation, 11, 167; hate in God, 167; of sinners, 166, 167, 170–1
Ḥātim al-Ṭā'ī, 21
hawā, see appetite
heart (*qalb*), 1, 65, 67–8, 184; eye of the heart, 30, 96, 97; *fu'ād*, xxiii; intellect, 43; knowledge of God, xxiii; levels, xxiii; longing, 93; love 67–8; *lubb*, xxiii; *al-nūr al-ilāhī*, 42; prayer, 12; purity, purification of, 52, 69–70, 102, 117, 182; seat of faith, xxiii; secret of the heart, 181; sight vs. insight, 12, 30; sixth sense, 12; *tawḥīd*, xxiii; wholly engaged in love, 109–10
heedlessness, 65, 123, 126
Hell, 75, 113, 149; fear of hell, 8, 37, 50, 51; *ḥadīth*, 75; punishment in, 75n

Index